厚德博學
經濟匡時

 大学思政系列

面向国际学生的经管类课程跨文化教育案例集

曾芬钰　徐莉莉 ◎ 主编

上海财经大学出版社

图书在版编目(CIP)数据

面向国际学生的经管类课程跨文化教育案例集/曾芬钰,徐莉莉主编.—上海:上海财经大学出版社,2024.5
(匡时·大学思政系列)
ISBN 978-7-5642-4316-6/F·4316

Ⅰ.①面… Ⅱ.①曾…②徐… Ⅲ.①高等学校-思想政治教育-教案(教育)-中国 Ⅳ.①G641

中国国家版本馆 CIP 数据核字(2024)第 027029 号

面向国际学生的经管类课程跨文化教育案例集

著 作 者:曾芬钰 徐莉莉 主编
丛书策划:王永长
责任编辑:顾丹凤
封面设计:贺加贝
出版发行:上海财经大学出版社有限公司
地　　址:上海市中山北一路 369 号(邮编 200083)
网　　址:http://www.sufep.com
经　　销:全国新华书店
印刷装订:上海颛辉印刷厂有限公司
开　　本:710mm×1000mm 1/16
印　　张:26(插页:2)
字　　数:287 千字
版　　次:2024 年 5 月第 1 版
印　　次:2024 年 5 月第 1 次印刷
定　　价:88.00 元

编委会名单

主 编
曾芬钰　徐莉莉

编委（按姓氏拼音顺序）
蔡依平　崔树银　刘　玲
王凌斐　杨迎春

序 言
Preface

随着我国教育对外开放的不断深入,全英文或双语教学步入内涵式、高质量发展阶段。为深化教学改革,全面提高教育教学质量,上海市教委从 2009 年起开展上海高校示范性全英语教学课程建设,鼓励教师在全英语教学过程中,积极选用国外优秀原版教材。然而,在实际实施过程中仍面临一定的困惑。一是国外原版教材作者所处国家的政治、经济和文化背景与我国不同,教材中选用的案例以欧美国家企业为主,很多情况未必适用于中国,理论教学与实际案例或多或少存在不匹配的情况。二是相比国内教材,进口原版教材费用昂贵,一般是国内同类教材的 10 倍左右。有的高校会选用国内出版社的引进版教材,而原版教材从引进到编撰,再到出版,几经周折后教材到达读者手里时,其案例的时效性与可读性又受到了极大的影响。

With the deepening of opening to the outside world in the education sector of China, teaching in English or bilingual teaching has stepped into a new stage featuring connotative and high-quality development. In order to advance the teaching reform and improve the quality of education and teaching in an all-round way, the Shanghai Municipal Education Commission has started to develop model courses taught in English among universities in Shanghai since 2009, encouraging teachers to actively choose excellent original foreign textbooks in teaching. However, there are still some problems in actual implementation. First, the political, economic and cultural backgrounds of the countries where authors of the original foreign textbooks come from are all different from those of China, and most of the cases selected in the textbooks involve European and American enterprises, which may not be true of China. Thus, mismatches exist between theoretical teaching and actual cases to some extent. Second, compared with domestic textbooks, the imported original textbooks are expensive, usually about 10 times the price of similar Chinese textbooks. Therefore, some colleges and universities prefer the textbooks introduced by domestic publishing houses, leading to greatly reduced timeliness and readability of the cases in the textbooks available to readers after the tortuous process from introduction to re-editing to publication.

与此同时，随着经济的高速发展，国际地位的显著提升，中国已经成为亚洲、非洲最大的留学目的国。据教育部统计，2020年来华国际学生规模已近50万人。这些来华国际学生普遍存在对我国国情及传统文化不了解、不适应的情况，导致教育管理的难度加大。教育部印发的《来华留学生高等教育质量规范（试行）》（教外〔2018〕50号）明确提出要加强来华国际学生对"中国的认识和理解，来华留学生应当熟悉中国历史、地理、社会、经济等中国国情和文化基本知识，了解中国

序 言

政治制度和外交政策,理解中国社会主流价值观和公共道德观念,形成良好的法治观念和道德意识"。

Meanwhile, with the rapid economic development and the remarkable improvement of international status, China has become the hottest destination for foreign students from Asia and Africa. According to the statistics of the Ministry of Education, the number of international students heading for China in 2020 reached nearly 500,000. These foreign students find it hard to understand and adapt to China's national conditions and traditional culture, which makes educational management even more challenging. The Higher Education Accreditation for International Students in China (Trial) (JIAOWAI〔2018〕No. 50) issued by the Ministry of Education explicitly points out that international students in China "are supposed to improve their understanding of China, get familiar with our basic national conditions and culture, such as history, geography, society and economy, in addition to understanding our political system and foreign policies as well as mainstream values and moral codes to develop a strong sense of rule of law and moral awareness".

在此背景下,我们组织长期从事全英语教学和双语教学的骨干教师团队共同编写了这本经管类课程跨文化教育中英双语案例集。以海纳百川、守正创新为教育理念,解读中国实践,解释中国奇迹;讲好中国故事,传承中华优秀传统文化;总结中国规律,让中国经济发展与经济理论走向世界,丰富具有对外输出功能的优质教学资源。

In this context, we have organized a team of excellent teachers who have been engaged in teaching in English and bilingual teaching for a long

面向国际学生的经管类课程跨文化教育案例集

time to jointly compile this bilingual collection of cross-cultural education cases for economics and management courses. We interpret China's practice and explain China's miracle by adhering to the educational principle of listening to all sides and maintaining correct political direction while encouraging innovation. We share China's stories via good communications and inherit fine traditional Chinese culture. We enable China's economic development and economic theories to go global by summarizing the law of China's development, and strive to create high-quality teaching resources which can be exported.

本案例集涵盖七个板块：宏观经济学、管理学原理、战略管理、市场营销、物流管理、财务管理、国际结算，皆为经济管理类学科的核心课程。所选案例大多以当代中国社会经济文化为背景，致力于解读中国经济发展、管理思想、企业实践、组织文化、企业家精神、社会责任、企业伦理道德等当代中国社会发展缩影。案例集采用中英文对照，既兼顾不同语言基础的读者对象，也可以作为语言学习爱好者的读物。本书还运用了现代多媒体技术，书中21个图文并茂的案例均配有英语录音，读者通过手机扫描二维码可以随时随地收听。

This collection consists of seven parts, including macroeconomics, principles of management, strategic management, marketing, logistics management, finance management and international settlement, all of which are core courses of economics and management. Most of the selected cases are based on the social, economic and cultural background of contemporary China. They focus on introducing the development of contemporary Chinese society, such as economic development, management thought, practices of enterprises, organizational culture, entrepreneurship, social responsibility and business ethics. The bilingual cases for readers at different levels of language competency can serve as reading materials for language learners. Utilizing modern multimedia technologies, 21 illustrated cases in this collection are provided with English audio clips, which are available to readers at anytime and anywhere by scanning the QR code with their mobile phones.

"应对共同挑战、迈向美好未来,既需要经济科技力量,也需要文化文明力量。""文明因多样而交流,因交流而互鉴,因互鉴而发展。"习近平总书记在多个重要场合提出要推进中外文明交流互鉴,强调"让文明交流互鉴成为增进各国人民友谊的桥梁、推动人类社会进步的动力、维护世界和平的纽带"。我们希望本书的出版能够将当代中国社会经济发展中正在发生、正在经历的各种真实的事件以案例的形式向国际社会传播,使来华国际学生从中领悟和感受中国传统文化、民族意识的精神资源和价值追求。同时,希望本案例集能够对我国全英语教学事业以及国际学生教育事业有所帮助,对经济管理专业课程跨文化教学能有所促进。

"Tackling common challenges and moving towards a better future are always driven by both economy and technologies as well as cultures and civilizations." "Civilizations can become more diversified and prosperous with mutual exchanges and learning." On several important occasions, General Secretary Xi Jinping proposed to promote mutual exchanges and learning between Chinese and foreign civilizations, stressing that "the mutual exchanges and learning of civilizations should serve as a bridge for the friendship among people of all countries, a driving force for the development of human community, and a bond for safeguarding world peace". We hope that the publication of this book will narrate all kinds of true events that are happening during the social and economic development of contemporary China to the international community in the form of cases, so that the international students can understand and experience the spiritual resources and value orientation of China's traditional culture and national consciousness. Besides, we hope this collection of cases can be helpful for teaching in English in China and the education of international students, while promoting the cross-cultural teaching of economics and management courses.

本案例集素材选自国内外权威媒体报道, 学术期刊文章, 硕士、博士论文, 在此向被引用的文献作者表示感谢。由于编者知识与能力有限, 文中难免有疏漏之处, 欢迎广大读者给我们提出宝贵意见和建议, 共同开辟经管类课程跨文化教育发展的新篇章。

The materials of this collection are from reports of authoritative media at home and abroad, articles of academic journals, and master and doctoral dissertations, for which we would like to express our sincere gratitude to all authors involved. Limited by the knowledge and capabilities of editors, omissions are unavoidable herein. We are looking forward to your valuable opinions and suggestions to jointly open a new chapter for the development of cross-cultural education with economics and management courses.

目　录
Contents

第一篇　宏观经济学
PART Ⅰ　MACROECONOMICS

案例 1.1　改革开放 40 年中国经济增长的国际比较(1978—2018)　3

Case 1.1　China's Economic Growth over the Past 40 Years of Reform and Opening up Compared to Foreign Countries(1978—2018)　3

案例 1.2　中国应对金融危机的一揽子计划　21

Case 1.2　China's Package Plan for Handling the Financial Crisis　21

案例 1.3　"中等收入陷阱"对于中国是不是一个伪命题?　44

Case 1.3　Is the "Middle-Income Trap" a False Proposition for China?　44

第二篇　管理学原理
PART Ⅱ　PRINCIPLES OF MANAGEMENT

案例 2.1　"一带一路"倡议推动构建人类命运共同体　71

Case 2.1 The "Belt and Road Initiative" (BRI) Promotes the Construction of a Community of Shared Future for Mankind　71

案例 2.2　国家电网:"碳达峰""碳中和"行动派的国企担当　92

Case 2.2 State Grid: A State-Owned Enterprise Undertaking the Responsibilities for Practicing "Peak Carbon Dioxide Emissions and Carbon Neutrality"　92

案例 2.3　文化的力量:百度人工智能革命透视　112

Case 2.3 The Power of Culture: Insights into Baidu's AI Revolution　112

第三篇　战略管理
PART Ⅲ　STRATEGIC MANAGEMENT

案例 3.1　华为的品牌扩展战略　133

Case 3.1 Brand Expansion Strategy of Huawei　133

案例 3.2　小米公司的颠覆性创新战略　151

Case 3.2 Disruptive Innovation Strategy of Xiaomi　151

案例 3.3　上海迪士尼乐园本土化营销策略　165

Case 3.3 Localization Marketing Strategy of Shanghai Disney Resort　165

第四篇　市场营销
PART Ⅳ　MARKETING

案例 4.1　"人民需要什么,五菱就造什么"——五菱汽车营销案例　183

Case 4.1 "Wuling Makes Whatever People Need"—Marketing Case of Wuling Motors　183

案例 4.2　做有温度的品牌:民宿鼻祖 Airbnb(爱彼迎)与中国民宿　199

Case 4.2 A Brand with Warmth: Airbnb, the Originator of B&B, and Chinese B&B　199

案例 4.3　2022 年上海疫情防控期间的团购与物流配送　218

Case 4.3　Group Purchase and its Logistics & Distribution During the COVID-19 in Shanghai in 2022　218

第五篇　物流管理
PART Ⅴ　LOGISTICS MANAGEMENT

案例 5.1　爱回收:小回收做成大生意　239

Case 5.1　Aihuishou:Small Recycling Business Makes Big Difference　239

案例 5.2　菜鸟绿色物流,打造中国绿色物流新样本　257

Case 5.2　Cainiao Green Logistics Sets a New Example of Green Logistics in China　257

案例 5.3　顺丰冷运一路领先,靠的是什么?　274

Case 5.3　What has SF Cold Chain Relied on to Lead All the Way?　274

第六篇　财务管理
PART Ⅵ　FINANCE MANAGEMENT

案例 6.1　瑞幸咖啡财务问题分析　305

Case 6.1　Analysis of Financial Fraud of Luckin Coffee　305

案例 6.2　中集车辆从收购整合 Vanguard 到全球运营　324

Case 6.2　CIMC Vehicles:From Acquisition and Integration of Vanguard to Global Operation　324

案例 6.3　小米智能家居财务战略　341

Case 6.3　Financial Strategy of Xiaomi Smart Home　341

第七篇　国际结算
PART Ⅶ　INTERNATIONAL SETTLEMENT

案例 7.1　人民币被越来越多国家作为国际结算货币　363

面向国际学生的经管类课程跨文化教育案例集

Case 7.1　RMB-A Key Currency for International Settlement by an Increasing Number of Countries　363

案例7.2　新冠疫情防控背景下出口信用保险护航外贸企业"走出去"　373

Case 7.2　Export Credit Insurance (ECI) Supports Foreign Trade Enterprises to "Go Global" During COVID-19　373

案例7.3　美英等国禁止俄罗斯使用SWIFT国际结算系统　381

Case 7.3　Western Countries Like the US and UK Prohibit Russia from Using the SWIFT System for International Settlement　381

附表1　案例涵盖的专业知识与跨文化教育元素概览　388

Exhibit Ⅰ　Overview of key concepts and cross-cultural education elements covered by the case　388

附表2　术语表　393

Exhibit Ⅱ　Glossary　393

第一篇　宏观经济学
PART Ⅰ　MACROECONOMICS

案例1.1 改革开放40年中国经济增长的国际比较(1978—2018)

Case 1.1 China's Economic Growth over the Past 40 Years of Reform and Opening up Compared to Foreign Countries(1978—2018)

教学目标

Teaching Objectives

自1978年中国经济改革开放起,中国经济增长保持了近10%的年均增长率,人们的生活发生了天翻地覆的变化。40年间,中国国内生产总值(GDP)从1978年的3 645亿元人民币迅速跃升为2018年的900 309亿元人民币。经济总量在世界经济中的位次稳步上升,2012年超过日本,成为世界第二大经济体。如果从购买力平价的角度核算,中国在2014年已经超过美国成为世界第一大经济体。2018年,中国经济增长对世界经济增长的贡献率为30%。中国经济的高速增长成了世界经济增长的奇迹,也重塑了世界经济增长的格局。本案

面向国际学生的经管类课程跨文化教育案例集

例通过对中国 40 年经济发展的介绍,向来华国际学生展现真实的中国,加深他们对中国经济的了解和对中国未来走向低波动、中高速增长新常态的理解,让他们能够更好地解读中国经济增长的故事,并客观、公正和科学地评价中国对世界经济的贡献。

Since the economic reform and opening up in 1978, China's economic growth has maintained an average annual growth rate of nearly 10%, which brings about tremendous changes for the life of Chinese people. Over the past 40 years, China's GDP has rocketed from 364.5 billion yuan in 1978 to 90.030 9 trillion yuan in 2018. With its global ranking steadily rising, China surpassed Japan to be the second largest economy in the world in 2012. In terms of purchasing power parity, China overtook the US and became the world's largest economy as early as in 2014. In 2018, China contributed up to 30% to the global economic growth. China's high-speed growth which has created a miracle across the world reshaped the pattern of global economic growth. By introducing China's economic development in the past 40 years, the case shows the real China to international students to deepen their understanding of our economy and the new normal featuring low fluctuation and medium-high growth in the future. In that way, they will further understand the story of China's economic growth and evaluate China's contribution to the global economy in an objective, just and scientific manner.

本案例涉及宏观经济学中最重要的概念,国内生产总值(GDP)、通货膨胀和经济增长以及相关的知识点。

This case mentions several most important concepts in macroeconom-

案例 1.1　改革开放 40 年中国经济增长的国际比较(1978—2018)

ics: Gross Domestic Product(GDP), inflation, economic growth, as well as related key points.

案例内容
Contents

自改革开放以来,中国人民的生活发生了天翻地覆的变化。20 世纪七八十年代,大家出门靠骑自行车、坐绿皮火车,现在则可以坐地铁、预约专车、乘坐高铁或者飞机。以前结婚四大件是自行车、缝纫机、手表和录音机,现在结婚四大件是房子、车子、彩礼和存款。中国人民的生活可谓是日新月异。美好的生活源于中国经济的高速发展。经济发展可以用 GDP 来衡量。相信大家一定听说过 GDP 或者国内生产总值。那么你是否真的明白它的含义？一个国家某一年的 GDP 超过另一个国家的 GDP 说明了什么？说明这个国家比另一个国家更富有了吗？其实并非如此。GDP 表明一个国家在一定时期所生产的所有最终产品和劳务的市场价值,表明一个国家在这一时期的生产能力,而非一个国家所拥有的财富。只有通过生产能力的不断提高,不断生产出更多的产品和劳务,不断地积累,才会拥有更多的财富。中国经济 40 年持续高速增长,同时也带动了世界经济的增长,重塑了世界的经济格局。那么中国是如何一步一步从一个封闭的农业国转变为全球最大的工业制造国,又如何从工业化迈入城市化的呢？

Since the reform and opening up, the life of Chinese people has undergone tremendous changes. In the 1970s and 1980s, people used to travel by bike and the green train. Now they take subway, high-speed train or plane, or use online car-hailing services instead. Bike, sewing machine, watch and tape recorder that were four must-have items for marriage have been replaced by house, car, bride price and deposits. All these signify the fast-changing life of Chinese people which is benefited from the rapid development of China's economy. Economic development can be measured by GDP. You must have heard of GDP or Gross Domestic Product. Then, do you really understand what it means? What does it mean when a country's GDP exceeds that of another country in a certain year? Does it mean that this country is more affluent than the other country? Actually, the answer is no. GDP indicates the market value of all final products and services produced by a country within a certain period. It refers to the production capacity of a country during that period rather than its wealth, which can only be built by continuously improving production capacity as well as products and services. China's sustained rapid economic growth for four decades has also promoted the growth of the world economy and reshaped the global economic landscape. So how did China change from a closed agricultural country to the largest manufacturer in the world foot by foot, and how did it shift from industrialization to urbanization?

一、改革开放 40 年中国经济的高速增长

Ⅰ. Rapid economic growth of China over the four decades of reform and opening up

中国经济 40 年增长的经验事实是持续高速增长,并通过高速增长带动了世界经济,重塑了世界经济格局。2018 年,中国国内生产总

案例 1.1 改革开放 40 年中国经济增长的国际比较(1978—2018)

值达到 90.03 万亿元人民币,相当于 13.61 万亿美元。从购买力平价的角度计算,中国国内生产总值在 2018 年增长了 1.4 万亿美元。中国对全球经济增长的贡献率达到 30%。

The fact that China saw high-speed economic growth over the past 40 years has contributed to the development of world economy and reshaped the global economic landscape. In 2018, China's Gross Domestic Product reached 90.03 trillion yuan, equivalent to 13.61 trillion US dollars. From the perspective of purchasing power parity, China's Gross Domestic Product increased by 1.4 trillion US dollars in 2018, contributing up to 30% to the global economic growth.

中国改革开放以来,经济增长保持了近 10% 的增速。1978—2002 年,前 25 年中国 GDP 平均增长率为 9.7%。其间经历了改革开放的探索期,1978—1984 年的"拨乱反正"和农村土地承包制实行期,1985—1988 年的乡镇企业带动期,1989—1991 年的经济调整期;1992 年邓小平南方谈话迎来了中国全面对外开放的新历史时期,1993 年十四届三中全会奠定了社会主义市场经济理论,随后中国经历了 1997 年亚洲金融危机的冲击,2001 年互联网泡沫破灭的冲击,又于 2001 年 12 月 11 日成为 WTO 成员。

Since the reform and opening up, China's economic growth has maintained a growth rate of nearly 10%. From 1978 to 2002, its average GDP growth rate was 9.7% in the first 25 years. During this period, China went through several exploration stages of reform and opening up, including the stage featuring "bringing order out of chaos" and rural land contract system implementation from 1978 to 1984, the stage when the development was driven by township enterprises from

1985 to 1988, and the stage of economic adjustment from 1989 to 1991. In 1992, Deng Xiaoping's remarks during his inspection tour to the south ushered in another historical period when China was fully open to the outside world. In 1993, the Third Plenary Session of the 14th CPC Central Committee laid the foundation for the theory of socialist market economy, which was tested by the impacts of the Asian financial crisis in 1997 and the bursting of the Internet bubble in 2001. On December 11, 2001, we witnessed China's successful entry into the WTO.

中国自 1978 年以来的前 25 年增长,奠定了中国改革开放从探索到成熟的基础,中国坚定而又自信地走向了具有中国特色的社会主义市场经济道路,改革开放的伟大成绩深入人心。2003 年中国经济开始从工业化、对外开放的新起点向着工业化和城市化快速转变,2011 年中国城市化率超过 50%,自此中国从农业人口占优的农业国转变为以城市人口占优的现代经济体。2012 年服务业超过工业,成为经济发展的新引擎,中国经济结构服务化进程开启,经济增长逐步从高速增长转向中高速增长,2003—2018 年仍保持 9% 的增长速度。40 年来,中国经济增长从各个阶段上看均为世界经济增长的领头羊。

The growth in the first 25 years since 1978 laid the foundation for China's reform and opening up to become mature from the exploration stage. China has firmly and confidently embarked on the road of socialist market economy with China characteristics, and made great achievements in reform and opening up that are deeply rooted in the hearts of Chinese people. In 2003, China began to shift rapidly from a new starting point of industrialization and opening to the out-

案例 1.1 改革开放 40 年中国经济增长的国际比较(1978—2018)

side world to all-round industrialization and urbanization. In 2011, the urbanization rate of China exceeded 50%. Since then, China has changed from an agricultural country with a dominant agricultural population to a modern economy based on urban population. In 2012, its service sector surpassed the industrial sector and became the new engine for economic development, which starts the shifting process towards a service-oriented economic structure in China. Since then, China's economic growth rate has gradually turned from high to medium high, maintaining at 9% from 2003 to 2018. For 40 years, China has taken the lead in terms of economic growth in the world at all stages.

二、中国经济的国际比较

Ⅱ. China's economic growth compared to other countries

通过国际比较发现,中国经济增速超过发达国家 1 倍以上,比同期一些东亚、东南亚国家,如韩国、新加坡、马来西亚、印度尼西亚、泰国和菲律宾等高出 30% 以上,见表 1—1。

Through comparison with other countries, it is found that China's economic growth rate is more than twice that of the developed countries, and over 30% higher than that of some East Asian and Southeast Asian countries such as South Korea, Singapore, Malaysia, Indonesia, Thailand and the Philippines in the same period, see the table 1—1.

表 1—1　　中国与其他国家 GDP 增长率和人均 GDP 增长率的比较

Table 1—1　GDP Growth Rates and Per Capita GDP Growth Rates of Different Countries

国家 Country	GDP 增长率 GDP Growth Rate		人均 GDP 增长率 Per capita GDP Growth Rate	
	1978—2002 年 1978—2002	2003—2016 年 2003—2016	1978—2002 年 1978—2002	2003—2016 年 2003—2016
中国 China	9.7%	9.59%	8.37%	9.01%
美国 US	3.17%	1.85%	2.08%	1.01%
英国 UK	2.58%	1.63%	2.36%	0.90%
德国 Germany	2.14%	1.25%	1.92%	1.24%
法国 France	2.33%	1.09%	1.83%	0.52%
日本 Japan	2.96%	0.86%	2.50%	0.89%
韩国 South Korea	7.89%	3.59%	6.82%	3.05%
新加坡 Singapore	7.25%	5.60%	4.76%	3.42%
马来西亚 Malaysia	6.48%	5.10%	3.80%	3.21%
泰国 Thailand	6.19%	3.89%	4.64%	3.36%
印度尼西亚 Indonesia	5.12%	5.49%	3.20%	4.12%
菲律宾 Philippines	2.78%	5.56%	0.25%	3.77%

数据来源：世界银行 WID 数据库。

Source：WID database of World Bank.

案例1.1 改革开放40年中国经济增长的国际比较(1978—2018)

表1-1反映了中国与世界几大经济体增长规模的比较,从总量看中国超过美国仍需时日,但中国经济增长的速率远高于美国,始终保持着世界经济总量前三的地位,而且具备超越美国的趋势。2008年全球金融危机后,中国经济总量超过日本并遥遥领先,成为名副其实的全球第二大经济体,而后来的赶超者印度与中国的差距较大,2015年后其增长速度超过中国,但印度当前仍属于中等偏低收入国家,而中国正努力迈向高收入国家的行列。

The table 1-1 compares the growth scale between China with other major economies in the world. It will take some time for China to surpass the US in terms of the GDP. However, China boasts a much higher economic growth rate and has always been among top three largest economies in the world, with a great potential to surpass the United States. After the global financial crisis in 2008, China's GDP surpassed Japan and became the second largest economy in the world, when there was a huge gap between India and China. As a subsequent contender, India has outpaced China in growth rate after 2015. However, it is still a middle-low income country, while China is on the way to be a high-income country.

三、中国崛起重塑世界经济新格局

Ⅲ. The rise of China reshaped the landscape of the world economy

从世界经济格局看,自新中国成立到1978年,中国GDP占全球GDP的比重始终在5%以内,而人口占比却在20%左右,人均GDP不到全世界平均值的1/4,而出口占世界出口的比重更是不到1%,属于

面向国际学生的经管类课程跨文化教育案例集

贫困的、封闭的发展中人口大国。自 1978 年改革开放起,中国经济增长保持了近 10%的增长率。2000 年中国名义 GDP 超过意大利,2005 年超过法国,2006 年超过英国,2007 年超过德国。2010 年,中国 GDP 超过日本,成为仅次于美国的世界第二大经济体。但是,如果从购买力平价的角度核算,中国早在 1999 年就超越日本成为世界第二大经济体,而且在 2014 年已经超过美国成为第一大经济体。2016 年,中国人口占全球人口的比重下降到 18.8%,占世界经济的比重从 4.9%提升到了 14.8%,与之相应,中国出口占全球出口份额的 13.2%,人均 GDP 接近世界平均水平,如表 1—2 所示。

For the global economic landscape, from 1949 to 1978, China, a nation with around 20% of the world's population, had a GDP less than 5% of the global total and, a per capita GDP less than 1/4 of the global average, yet merely less than 1% of the world's exports. Thus, China was back then a poor and closed developing country. Since the reform and opening up in 1978, China's economy has maintained a growth rate of nearly 10%, with its nominal GDP surpassing Italy, France, Britain and Germany in 2000, 2005, 2006 and 2007 respectively. In 2010, China's GDP surpassed that of Japan, making it the second largest economy in the world, only after the US. However, in terms of purchasing power parity, China overtook Japan to become the second largest economy in the world as early as 1999, and then the US in 2014, making it the largest economy. In 2016, the proportion of China's population against the global total dropped to 18.8%, while its contribution of GDP to the world economy increased from 4.9% to 14.8%. Meanwhile, China exported 13.2% of the global total, with

12

案例 1.1 改革开放 40 年中国经济增长的国际比较(1978—2018)

its per capita GDP close to the global average, as shown in the table 1-2.

表 1-2 中国经济表现统计

Table 1-2   Statistics of China's Economic Performance

指标变量 Indicator Variables	1952 年 1952	1978 年 1978	2016 年 2016
中国经济占全球比例 Proportion of GDP against the global total	4.6%	4.9%	14.8%
中国人口占全球比例 Proportion of population against the global total	22.5%	22.3%	18.8%
人均 GDP 相对于世界平均水平 Proportion of per capita GDP against the global average	23.8%	22.1%	88.3%
中国出口世界占比 Proportion of exports against the global total	1.0%	0.8%	13.2%

数据来源:Maddison(2000) and WDI database。

Source:Maddison(2000) and WDI database.

以中国为首的新兴市场国家的快速增长已经重塑了世界格局。2008 年全球金融危机后,新兴市场经济体在全球 GDP 中的份额超过了发达经济体,在 GDP 新增量中,中国贡献超过了 30%,金砖国家贡献了 60%,全球经济呈现出新的增长格局。

The rapid growth of emerging market economies led by China has reshaped the global landscape. After the global financial crisis in 2008, the share of emerging market economies in global GDP has surpassed that of developed economies. For the total GDP increment, the BRICS countries have contributed 60%, including more than 30% from China. In this context, a new growth pattern is built in the world economy.

四、中国经济从高波动、高增长向低波动、中高速增长的成熟经济转变

Ⅳ. China's economy has shifted from one featuring high fluctuation and high growth to a mature one characterized by low fluctuation and medium-high growth

中国经济改革开放前 25 年基本情况是高速增长伴随高波动,经济增长起伏大,而且通货膨胀是 1997 年以前最主要的调控目标,1985 年通货膨胀率为 9.3%,1988 年为 18.8%,1989 年为 18%,1993 年为 14.7%,1994 年为 24%,1995 年为 17.1%,1997 年进入平稳状态,而后 1999 年到 2001 年进入通货紧缩,价格起伏很大(如图 1—1 所示)。后 15 年中仅有两年价格突破 5%,而且没有出现通货紧缩。用波动方差(各年的数值与均值差的平方)衡量,前 20 年物价波动比后 20 年波动大 10 倍。从增长波动看,前 20 年经济增长波幅较大,1984 年经济增长超过 15%,1989 年、1990 年回落到 4%左右,经济大起大落,并伴随着通货膨胀。从增长的波动方差来看,前 20 年比后 20 年增长波动大 2.55 倍。后 20 年经济增长出现了明显的波幅收敛趋向。2012 年后经济增长明显低于原有的 8%的调控均值轨迹,增长速度从 7.8%持续下滑。中共十九大报告中首次提出,中国经济已由"高速增长阶段"转向"高质量发展阶段",这意味着政府对增速回落的容忍度在不断提高。中国经济从 8%~10%的高速增长区间回落到 6%~8%的中高速增长区间。

In the first 25 years of China's economic reform and opening up, the rapid growth was basically accompanied by high fluctuations. Moreover, inflation was the major target for regulation before 1997 as the

案例 1.1 改革开放 40 年中国经济增长的国际比较(1978—2018)

inflation rate was 9.3% in 1985, 18.8% in 1988, 18% in 1989, 14.7% in 1993, 24% in 1994, and 17.1% in 1995, respectively. The economy maintained stable in 1997, and then faced deflation from 1999 to 2001, with the prices of commodities fluctuating sharply(as shown in the Figure 1−1). Of the last 15 years, only two years experienced an inflation rate exceeding 5%, without deflation. Measured by the variance of fluctuation (the square of the differences between the numerical value and the average value each year), the price fluctuation in the first 20 years is ten times greater than that in the following 20 years. According to the fluctuation of growth, the economic growth fluctuated greatly in the first 20 years. In 1984, the economic growth rate exceeded 15%, while in 1989 and 1990, it fell back to about 4%. This great change was accompanied by inflation. The fluctuation variance of growth indicates that the fluctuation of growth in the first 20 years is 2.55 times larger than that in the following 20 years, during which period the economic growth showed an obvious converging trend. After 2012, the economic growth rate that kept declining from 7.8% was significantly lower than the original average trajectory of 8%. The report of the 19th CPC National Congress put forward for the first time that China's economy has stepped from the "high-rate growth stage" to the "high-quality development stage". This shows a greater tolerance of the government towards the slowdown in growth rate, i.e., from the high growth range of 8%～10% to the medium-high growth range of 6%～8%.

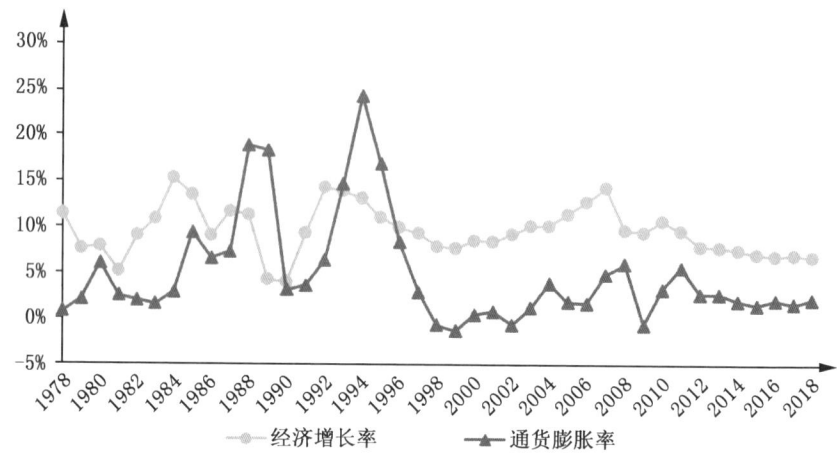

数据来源：中国统计年鉴。

Source：China Statistical Yearbook.

图 1—1　1978—2018 年中国经济增长率与通货膨胀率

Figure 1—1　Economic growth rates and inflation rates of China from 1978 to 2018

中国经济稳定性的加强直接体现在三个方面：一是市场体系的建立，微观主体理性选择和自我风险约束加强；二是成熟的宏观管理体系得以建立，宏观管理的经验加强，更能驾驭复杂的经济局面；三是改革进入深化阶段，体制改革对经济冲击程度下降。如 1988 年的价格闯关，1998 年后的国企改革，都加大了对经济体系的震动，而现有的改革秉承了"渐进式"改革的思路，越来越成熟，而且逐步进入法制的轨道，因此改革冲击相对较小。中国经济成熟度的不断提高降低了波动幅度，但开放程度越来越高，外部冲击的影响会加大，这是中国未来发展需要特别关注和防范的风险。

The increased China's economic stability is directly reflected in three aspects. First, the establishment of the market system has led to

案例 1.1　改革开放 40 年中国经济增长的国际比较(1978—2018)

more rational choices and greater self-risk constraints for micro-entities. Second, the establishment of a mature macro-management system has enriched the macro-management experience, contributing to better control of the complex economic situation. Third, the reform begins to be deepened, and the impacts of institutional reform on economy have declined. For instance, the price control removal in 1988 and the reform of state-owned enterprises after 1998 both aggravated the shock against the economic system. In contrast, the existing reforms, adhering to the concept of "gradual" pace, have become more and more mature under the rule of law, thus producing relatively weak impacts. The increasingly mature economy of China has reduced the fluctuations. Nevertheless, greater openness will unavoidably bring more impacts from the outside, which is a risk factor China needs to pay special attention to and guard against for future development.

点评

Comments

1978—2018 年中国改革开放 40 年来经济高速增长,成为世界经济增长的奇迹,既改善了中国居民的生活质量,也重塑了世界经济增长的格局。40 年间,中国成功地从一个封闭的农业国转变为全球最大的工业制造国,又从工业化迈入城市化。最近几年中国经济增长放缓。习近平总书记在 2014 年 5 月用经济增长"新常态"来描述接下来中国经济的发展状态。经济增长新常态的特点:一是增长速度由高速向中高速转换；二是产业结构由中低端向中高端转换；三是增长动力由要素投资驱动向创新驱动转换。在新常态下，中国未来的经济发展将会更有耐心，更注重公共利益和可持续发展。短期急速增长将会让位于长期利益。经济新常态将会带来长期稳定的繁荣，是实现中国梦的必经之路。

Over 40 years since the reform and opening up in China from 1978 to 2018, the rapid economic growth was a miracle, as it not only improved the quality of life of Chinese people, but also reshaped the landscape of world economic growth. During that period, China has successfully transformed from a closed agricultural country to the largest industrial manufacturer in the world, and also from industrialization to urbanization. Its economic growth has slowed down in recent years. In May, 2014, General Secretary Xi Jinping adopted the "new normal" of economic growth to describe the economic development of China in the future. The characteristics of such new normal are as follows: first, the economic growth has decreased from a high rate to a medium-high rate; second, the industrial structure has shifted from low-end to high-end; third, the driving force for growth has changed from factor investment to innovation. Under the new normal, China will be more patient to future economic development, and will pay more attention to public welfare and sustainable development. Short-term rapid growth will give way to long-term interests. This will bring long-term stability and prosperity as the only way to realize the Chinese Dream.

案例 1.1 改革开放 40 年中国经济增长的国际比较(1978—2018)

讨论题
Discussions

(1)什么是国内生产总值？

What is the Gross Domestic Product (GDP)?

(2)在复杂的外部环境和不断增加的下行风险下，2018年中国经济增长率达到了自1990年以来的最低。这是否意味着中国经济不能再保持持续的高速增长？请解释你的观点。

Facing the complex external environment and increasing downside risks, the economic growth rate of China in 2018 reached a record low since 1990. Does it mean that China's economy can no longer maintain high-speed growth? Please explain.

(3)试用经济增长理论解释中国的高速增长以及未来中国经济增长的动力。

Try to explain the rapid growth of China and the driving force of its economic growth in the future using the theory of economic growth.

资料来源

张平,楠玉. 改革开放 40 年中国经济增长与结构变革[J]. 中国经济学人,2018(1):22—57.

中国的历史 GDP 数据[DB/OL]. [2023－03－03]. https://en.wikipedia.org/wiki/Historical_GDP_of_China.

班娟娟,金辉,李思宇. 改革开放创 40 年经济增长奇迹[EB/OL]. [2023－03－03]. http://dz.jjckb.cn/www/pages/webpage2009/html/2018－05/02/content_43029.htm.

陈晓东,邓斯月. 改革开放40年中国经济增长与产业结构变迁[J]. 现代经济探讨,2019(2):11-18.

References

Zhang Ping, Nan Yu. China's economic growth and structure changes over the 40 years of reform and opening up[J]. China Economist,2018 (1):22-57.

Historical GDP of China[DB/OL]. [2023-03-03]. https://en.wikipedia.org/wiki/Historical_GDP_of_China.

Ban Juanjuan,Jin Hui,Li Siyu. 40 years of economic growth miracle created by reform and opening up[EB/OL]. [2023-03-03]. http://dz.jjckb.cn/www/pages/webpage2009/html/2018-05/02/content_43029.htm.

Chen Xiaodong,Deng Siyue. China's economic growth and industrial structure changes over the 40 years of reform and opening up[J]. Modern? Economic Research,2019 (2):11-18.

案例1.2 中国应对金融危机的一揽子计划
Case 1.2 China's Package Plan for Handling the Financial Crisis

教学目标
Teaching Objectives

2008年源于美国的金融危机迅速席卷全球。中国经济也遭受了严重冲击,经济社会发展形势极其严峻。经济增速从一季度的10.6%滑落到三季度的9%。外贸进出口增速放缓,珠三角、长三角地区部分企业出现倒闭裁员、农民工返乡等现象。面对金融危机的冲击,中国政府在2008年11月陆续出台了一系列扩大内需、促进经济平稳较快增长的措施,形成了应对国际金融危机、促进经济平稳较快增长的一揽子计划。与其他国家相比,这一揽子计划取得了显著成效。2009年,全球经济增速只有0.8%,而中国实现了8.7%的增长。中国对世界经济增长的贡献率由2008年的20%猛增到2009年的50%,成为名副其实的世界经济引擎。本案例回顾了中国应对国际金融危机一揽子计划的内容,所取得的成效和基本经验。

In 2008, the financial crisis originated in the US quickly swept over the world. China also suffered huge impacts, leading to an extremely severe economic and social development situation. The economic growth rate dropped from 10.6% in Q1 to 9% in Q3. The growth of import and export trade slowed down, and some enterprises in the Pearl River Delta and Yangtze River Delta even closed down and laid off employees so that migrant workers had to return home. In the face of the impacts of the financial crisis, in November 2008, the Chinese government successively introduced a series of measures and developed a package plan to expand domestic demand and promote steady and rapid economic growth. Compared with other countries, the package plan achieved remarkable results. In 2009, the global economic growth rate was only 0.8%, much lower than that of China: 8.7%. China's contribution rate to the world economic growth soared from 20% in 2008 to 50% in 2009, becoming a veritable engine driving the world economy. This case reviews the content, achievements and basic experience of the package plan launched by China to deal with the international financial crisis.

本案例涉及宏观经济学中在萧条经济背景下政府刺激经济增长的措施和方法，主要基于凯恩斯的需求管理理论和IS-LM模型的应用。

This case involves the measures and methods taken by the government to stimulate economic growth under the background of economic depression, which are mainly based on Keynes's demand management theory and the application of IS-LM model, as stated in the macroeconomics.

案例 1.2　中国应对金融危机的一揽子计划

案例内容
Contents

百年一遇的国际金融危机,犹如世界经济上空的沉沉黑云,滚滚翻卷,不断蔓延。这场金融危机是 20 世纪 30 年代经济大萧条以来最严重的一次经济危机。为应对危机,世界各国先后出台了一系列稳定金融、刺激经济的政策。已融入全球化的中国自然不能独善其身,那么中国政府如何应对国际金融危机对中国经济的冲击?"4 万亿"的一揽子计划成效如何?从这次危机中,我们又得到了哪些启示呢?

The once-in-a-century international financial crisis was like a dark cloud hanging over the world economy, rolling and spreading. It was the most serious economic crisis since the Great Depression in the 1930s. In response to the crisis, countries around the world successively introduced a series of policies to stabilize finance and stimulate the economy. China, which had been integrated into globalization, was unable to detach itself from the interconnected world. So how did the Chinese government deal with the impacts of the international financial crisis on China's economy? How effective was the "4-trillion-yuan" stimulus package plan? What lessons did we learn from this crisis?

一、迅速出台扩大内需、促进经济增长的十项措施

Ⅰ. Quickly introduce ten measures to expand domestic demand and promote economic growth

在经济全球化日益加深的今天,任何一个国家的经济都难以独善其身。在2008年国际金融危机的冲击下,中国在长三角、珠三角曾经如雪片般不断飞来的订单,陡然零落下来;曾经满负荷转动的生产线,突然停止了运转。中国面临着改革开放以来前所未有的困难。面对危机,时任国务院总理温家宝在2008年11月5日主持召开国务院常务会议,会议确定实行积极的财政政策和适度宽松的货币政策,并进一步推出扩大内需、促进经济增长的十项措施(如图1-2所示),提出在两年内投入4万亿元刺激经济增长。

Today, with the deepening of economic globalization, it is difficult for any country's economy to stay detached. Under the impacts of the international financial crisis in 2008, the great number of orders gained by the Yangtze River Delta and the Pearl River Delta regions of China declined sharply, and the production lines, which used to operate at full capacity, stopped running. China was faced with unprecedented difficulties since the reform and opening up. In response to this crisis, Wen Jiabao, then Prime Minister of the State Council, presided over a State Council executive meeting on November 5, 2008. In the meeting, decisions were made to enforce a proactive fiscal policy and a moderately loose monetary policy, and further introduce ten measures to expand domestic demand and promote economic growth (as shown in Figure 1-2), proposing to invest 4 trillion yuan to stimulate eco-

案例1.2 中国应对金融危机的一揽子计划

nomic growth within two years.

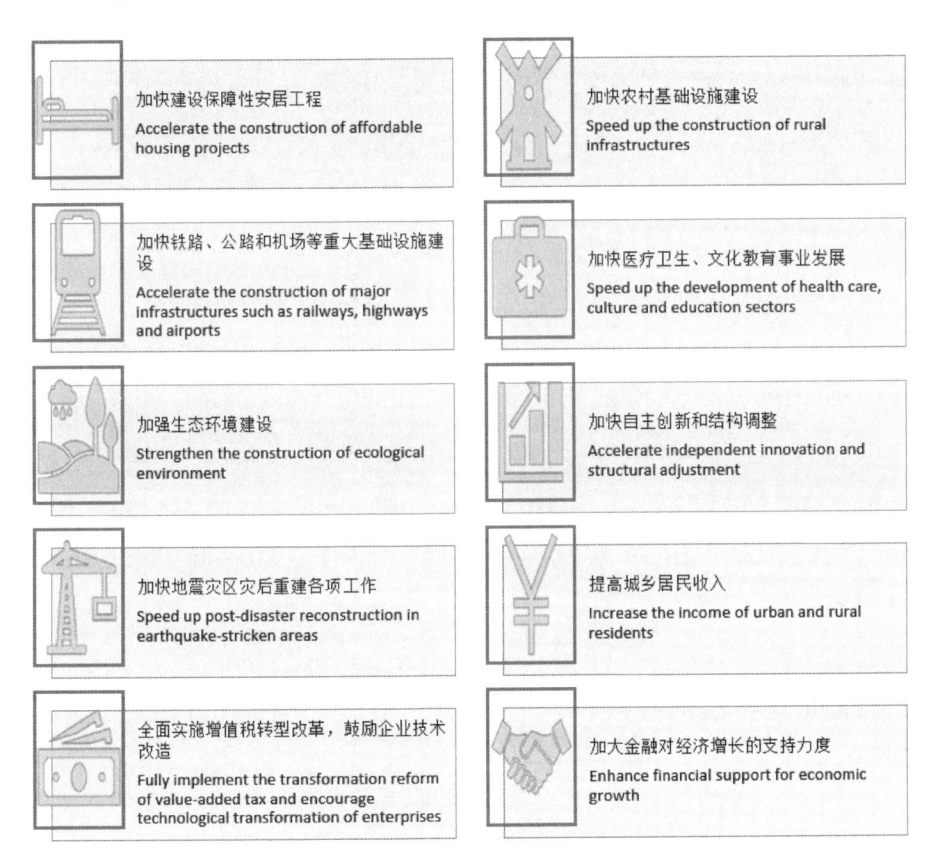

加快建设保障性安居工程 Accelerate the construction of affordable housing projects	加快农村基础设施建设 Speed up the construction of rural infrastructures
加快铁路、公路和机场等重大基础设施建设 Accelerate the construction of major infrastructures such as railways, highways and airports	加快医疗卫生、文化教育事业发展 Speed up the development of health care, culture and education sectors
加强生态环境建设 Strengthen the construction of ecological environment	加快自主创新和结构调整 Accelerate independent innovation and structural adjustment
加快地震灾区灾后重建各项工作 Speed up post-disaster reconstruction in earthquake-stricken areas	提高城乡居民收入 Increase the income of urban and rural residents
全面实施增值税转型改革，鼓励企业技术改造 Fully implement the transformation reform of value-added tax and encourage technological transformation of enterprises	加大金融对经济增长的支持力度 Enhance financial support for economic growth

图1－2 扩大内需、促进经济增长的10项措施

Figure 1－2 Ten measures for expanding domestic demand and promoting economic growth

在这个被简称为"4万亿"的经济刺激计划中，扩大基础设施建设成为理所当然的龙头，一轮基础设施建设的热潮迅速掀起。

In this "4 trillion yuan" economic stimulus package, expanding construction infrastructures took the lead as a matter of course, then a wave of infrastructure construction quickly swept over China.

松塘村,一个地处广东省韶关市翁源县江尾镇的小村落,却能清晰地感受到基础设施建设的热潮。村外的工地上机车穿梭,工人在挖沙砌石,焊接钢管,一条硕大的钢铁巨龙在这里向前延伸。进入6月,"西气东输二线工程"广东段主要工点已经全线开工。这条横贯大半个中国的能源大动脉穿戈壁沙漠,过黄土高原,越黄河,渡长江,南到珠江三角洲,干线支线总长8 704千米。

Songtang Village, located in Jiangwei Town, Wengyuan County, Shaoguan City in Guangdong Province, clearly felt the upsurge of infrastructure construction. Outside the village, trucks were running to and from the construction site, workers were digging sand, laying stones and welding steel pipes, like a huge steel dragon crawling forward from here. In June, the main construction sites in Guangdong section of the "Second West-East Gas Pipeline Project" had started. This energy artery, which traverses over half of China, runs through the Gobi Desert, the Loess Plateau, the Yellow River and the Yangtze River, and reaches the Pearl River Delta in the south, with a total length of 8,704 km.

东西"气龙"横贯,南北"钢龙"腾纵。这条"钢龙"就是2008年动工,世界上一次建成线路最长、标准最高的高速铁路——京沪高铁,项目总投资2 209.4亿元。

In addition to the "dragon of gas" that traverses from west to east, there is a "dragon of steel", the Beijing-Shanghai High-speed Railway that started construction in 2008, which runs from north to south. With a total investment of 220.94 billion yuan, it has the longest railway line and meets the highest standard in the world.

案例 1.2 中国应对金融危机的一揽子计划

基础设施建设有力地带动了上下游产业,为"保增长"增强了底气。来自京沪高铁办公室的统计显示,整条线路每天消耗水泥 4 万吨,沙石料 20 万立方米,钢材 1 万吨。综合计算设备、建材和人工投入,每天投资总额达到了 1.9 亿元。据调查,按照 2009 年铁路完成工程投资 6 000 亿元安排,根据定额水平测算,该工程可以创造 600 万个就业岗位,消费钢材 2 000 万吨、水泥 1.2 亿吨,直接带来全国 GDP 增幅提高 1.5%的拉动效应。

Infrastructure construction effectively promoted the upstream and downstream industries and enhanced China's confidence in "ensuring growth". Statistics from the Beijing-Shanghai High-speed Railway Office showed that the entire project consumed 40,000 tons of cement, 200,000 cubic meters of sand and gravel, and 10,000 tons of steel every day. The daily investment in equipment, building materials and labor input reached 190 million yuan. According to the survey, considering the arrangement of 600 billion yuan investment in railway projects completed in 2009 and based on the quota level, 6 million jobs would be created, and 20 million tons of steel and 120 million tons of cement would be consumed, which could directly contribute to 1.5% increase in China's GDP.

"西气东输"工程对经济的拉动作用同样显著。中石油昆仑天然气利用公司副总经理杜绍周告诉记者,据测算,三年建设期内,"西气东输"二线工程全线将需要 500 万吨 X80 级钢材,同时城市管网配套工程还将需要大量使用铸造管等。整个项目预计拉动直接投资超过 3 000 亿元,并且能大大促进冶金、机械等行业产品升级。

The "West-East Gas Pipeline Project" also played a significant role in stimulating the economy. Du Shaozhou, Deputy General Manager of Petro China Kunlun Natural Gas Utilization Co. , Ltd. , told the reporter that it was estimated that during the three-year construction period, the entire "Second West-East Gas Pipeline Project" would need 5 million tons of X80 grade steel, and meanwhile a large number of cast pipes would be consumed in the supporting projects of urban pipe networks. The whole project was expected to attract more than 300 billion yuan of direct investment, and could greatly promote the upgrade of products in metallurgy, machinery, etc.

这是一场与时间赛跑的"战役"。危急时刻，党中央、国务院见事早，出手快，出拳重，措施准，工作实。从扩大内需、促进经济增长的十项措施，到其后出台的一系列保增长、扩内需、调结构的政策，形成了系统完整的促进经济平稳较快增长的一揽子计划。

It was a "battle" against time. In times of crisis, the CPC Central Committee and the State Council predicted early, responded swiftly, imposed strict control, took accurate measures and implemented them decisively. From the ten measures to expand domestic demand and promote economic growth to a series of policies for ensuring growth, expanding domestic demand and adjusting the economic structure, a systematic and complete package plan for promoting steady and rapid economic growth was developed.

二、扩内需、稳外需成为政策的着力点

II. Polices focus on expanding domestic demand and stabilizing external demand

在拉动经济增长的"三驾马车"中,外需萎缩造成出口持续低迷,全面扩大国内需求成为政策的着力点。2009年中央财政预算安排250亿元补贴资金,支持家电、汽车、摩托车下乡。

Among the "three engines" driving economic growth, export remains sluggish due to the shrinking external demand, and thus expanding domestic demand in an all-round way has become the focus of policies. In 2009, the central budget allocated 25 billion yuan of subsidies to support home appliances, cars and motorcycles going to the countryside.

家电下乡自2009年2月起向全国推开。在实施过程中,补贴手续不断简化,补贴品种相继增加。微波炉、电磁炉、洗衣机、摩托车、电脑、热水器、空调等琳琅满目的家电商品走进千百万农民的生活。家电下乡产品产销两旺,带动了上游原材料行业劳动就业的增长,进一步促进了用电和其他消费的增长。

The home appliances had been supported going to the countryside around China since February 2009. In the process of implementing this policy, the subsidy procedures were simplified and the types of subsidies were increased one after another. Various household appliances like microwave ovens, induction cookers, washing machines, motorcycles, computers, water heaters and air conditioners entered the lives of millions of farmers. Both production and sales of home appliances going to the countryside were booming, which pushed the growth of upstream industries of raw materials and labor employment, and further promoted the consumption growth of electricity and other products.

之后中国政府又推出新的促进消费政策：鼓励汽车、家电"以旧换新"。为此，中央财政安排补贴资金70亿元。"下乡"政策填补了农村消费的空白，而"以旧换新"则是为城镇消费锦上添花。

Later, a new consumption promotion policy was introduced by the Chinese government, encouraging "trade-in" for cars and home appliances. For this purpose, the central government allocated 7 billion yuan as subsidies. The policy of "going to the countryside" fills the gap in rural consumption, while "trade-in" is the icing on the cake for urban consumption.

为促进汽车消费，中国政府出台了小排量车购置税减半的政策，加上汽车下乡、旧车换购补贴等鼓励政策，极大地提振了车市复苏的信心，并迅速显效。在国外汽车市场一片萧条的大背景下，中国车市不仅率先回暖，月销量更是屡创新高，连续5个月超越美国成为全球第一大市场。

In order to promote automobile consumption, the Chinese government introduced a policy of halving the purchase tax on small-displacement automobiles, and other incentive policies, such as subsidies for cars going to the countryside and exchanging used cars, which greatly boosted the confidence in the recovery of the automobile market and achieved quick results. When the foreign automobile market was still in a recession, China's automobile market has turned around and achieved record monthly sales repeatedly, surpassing the US to become the world's largest market for five consecutive months.

在扩大内需的同时,努力保住外部需求也是政府一直努力的方向。从 2008 年开始到 2009 年年底,中国相继出台了一系列支持外贸稳定增长的政策措施,连续 7 次上调出口退税率。出口退税率的上调提高了中国出口产品的国际竞争力,保证了对外贸易的持续增长。

While expanding domestic demand, the government was also working hard to maintain external demand. From 2008 to the end of 2009, China successively introduced a series of policies and measures to support the steady growth of foreign trade, and raised the export rebate rate seven times in a row, which improved the international competitiveness of China's export products and ensured the sustained growth of its foreign trade.

三、推进自主创新,推动节能减排和产业结构转型和升级

Ⅲ. Promote independent innovation and push forward energy conservation and emission reduction as well as transformation and upgrade of industrial structure

应对国际金融危机同样是深化改革的契机。伴随着应对国际金融危机一揽子计划的实施,一些重点领域和关键环节的改革取得新进展。航空、电信等行业实现重组,成品油价格和燃油税费改革、增值税转型改革先后实施,新的企业所得税法全面实施,国有金融企业股份制改革稳步推进。

Coping with the international financial crisis was also taken as an opportunity to deepen reform. With the implementation of the package plan to respond to the international financial crisis, new progress was made in the reform of some key areas and links. For example, aviation, telecommunications and other industries were reorganized; the reforms of refined oil prices, fuel taxes and fees, and value-added tax transformation were implemented successively; the newly enacted law of enterprise income tax was fully enforced; and the shareholding system reform of state-owned financial enterprises was steadily promoted.

外部经济的冲击,使结构不尽合理、产能过剩、缺乏核心技术等制约我国经济发展的诸多矛盾和问题更为凸显。推进产业结构调整和优化升级,成为一揽子计划中的关键内容之一。在4万亿元的投资计划中,投向自主创新和结构调整的资金约为3 700亿元。

The impacts from external economy made many conflicts and problems that once restricted China's economic development more prominent, such as unreasonable structure, overcapacity, and lack of core technologies. Promoting the adjustment, optimization and upgrading of industrial structure was one of the key points of the package plan. Of the 4 trillion yuan investment plan, about 370 billion yuan was invested in independent innovation and structural adjustment.

10项重点产业调整和振兴规划让相关产业的企业在国际金融危机的阴霾中看到了振兴的希望。受益于产业调整和振兴规划以及扩大投资促进消费的政策,大部分工业行业和工业产品的增速开始回升。

The adjustment and revitalization plans for ten key industries enabled enterprises in related industries to see the hope of revitalization amid the gloom of international financial crisis. Thanks to the industrial adjustment, revitalization plan and the policy of expanding investment and promoting consumption, the growth rates of most industrial sectors and industrial products began to pick up.

"历史发展的经验表明,每一次大的经济危机常常伴随着一场新的科技革命,而每一次新的科技革命又会成为新一轮经济增长和繁荣的重要引擎。"国务院常务会议先后部署:两年中央和地方财政集中投入1 000亿元,加快一批能够支撑经济增长的重大科技专项实施。高档数控机床与基础制造装备、大型飞机、新一代宽带无线移动通信网、核心电子器件等11个重大科技专项得到国家的大力支持。随着这些重大科技项目的积极推进,科技支撑经济发展的力量变得愈加强大。

"The experience of development in the past shows that every major economic crisis is often accompanied by a new scientific and technological revolution, which then will become an important engine for a new round of economic growth and prosperity." The executive meeting of the State Council successively made arrangements that the central government and local governments would invest 100 billion yuan in two years to accelerate the implementation of a number of major scientific and technological projects that can support economic growth. Eleven major scientific and technological projects, including high-grade CNC machine tools and basic manufacturing equipment, large aircraft, the new-generation broadband wireless mobile communication network and core electronic devices, received strong support from the state. With the active advancement of these major scientific and technological projects, the science and technology is playing a greater role in supporting economic development.

大力度地增加公共投资,扩内需、保增长,并不意味着可以"泥沙俱下",推动节能减排、能源结构调整和产业结构转型升级同样被摆在了显著的重要位置。在 4 万亿元的投资计划中,投向节能减排和生态工程的资金约为 2 100 亿元。

Vigorously increasing public investment, expanding domestic demand and ensuring growth do not mean that we can "mingle the good with the bad". Equal attention was also paid to promoting energy conservation and emission reduction, energy structure adjustment, and industrial structure transformation and upgrading. Of the 4 trillion yuan investment plan, about 210 billion yuan was invested in energy conservation, emission reduction and ecological projects.

2009 年政府推出的"节能产品惠民工程",更是被评价为拉动消费与节能减排的"双赢"工程。这一工程以财政补贴方式对空调、冰箱等 10 类高效节能产品以及高效照明产品、节能与新能源汽车进行推广应用。专家估算,每年将拉动消费需求数千亿元,节电 750 亿千瓦时,减排 7 500 万吨二氧化碳。

In 2009, the "Project of Benefiting the People with Energy-saving Products" introduced by the government was evaluated as a "win-win" project to stimulate consumption, save energy and reduce emissions. In this project, 10 types of high-efficiency energy-saving products such as air conditioners and refrigerators, as well as high-efficiency lighting products, energy-saving and new energy vehicles were promoted and applied by issuing financial subsidies. Experts estimated that it would boost consumer demand by hundreds of billions of yuan each year, save electricity by 75 billion kWh, and reduce carbon dioxide emissions by 75 million tons.

四、进一步完善社会保障体系
Ⅳ. Further improve the social security system

国际金融危机对人民群众的影响是实实在在的,就业压力凸显,部分群众的生活压力增大。同时各级财政收入有所减少,财政进一步吃紧。双重压力之下,保民生任务艰巨。但经济发展的最终目的是让老百姓生活得更好,经济困难也要着力完善社会保障体系,让老百姓学有所教、劳有所得、病有所医、老有所养、住有所居。危机下,一系列保障民生的政策以前所未有的密度和力度相继出台,给老百姓带来了真真切切的实惠。

The international financial crisis imposed huge impacts on the people, leading to prominent employment pressure and increased living pressure to a certain extent. Meanwhile, the fiscal revenue at all levels decreased and the government budget was severely strained. Under the double pressure, it was quite arduous to protect people's livelihood. However, the ultimate goal of economic development is to improve the living standard of the people. In spite of the economic difficulties, efforts should be made to improve the social security system, so that people could receive education, get paid for their work, have access to medical care when they are ill, enjoy care when they are old, and possess a shelter to live. Under the crisis, a series of policies to protect people's livelihood were introduced one after another with unprecedented density and intensity, bringing real benefits to the people.

2009年中央财政预算安排就业资金420亿元,同比增长66.7%。作为受到冲击最大的群体,大学生和农民工自然成为关注的重点。

In 2009, the central budget allocated 42 billion yuan for employment, up 66.7% year-on-year. As the groups suffered most, college students and migrant workers were undoubtedly the focus.

为促进高校毕业生顺利就业,中国从供求两方面出台了一系列鼓励和帮扶政策,鼓励和支持各类企业和科研单位招用、聘用高校毕业生,引导和鼓励毕业生到基层就业、自主创业。

In order to promote the smooth employment of college graduates, China issued a series of encouragement and support policies from both supply and demand sides to encourage and support various enterprises and scientific research units to recruit and employ college graduates, and guide and encourage graduates to find jobs at the grassroots level or start their own businesses.

为了农民工的顺利就业,中国各级政府加大了对农民工培训和再就业的投入,多渠道转移农村劳动力就业,扶持农民工就近就地就业和返乡创业。

For the smooth employment of migrant workers, governments at all levels in China increased investment in their training and re-employment, transferred rural labor force for employment through various channels, and supported migrant workers to find jobs nearby or start their own businesses in hometown.

此次国际金融危机使农民和城市低收入群体的生活受到更大的挑战。强化社保体系、提高社保水平,给他们的生活带来了更大的希望。2009年1月1日起,调整企业退休人员基本养老金的政策已经兑现到企业退休人员;关闭破产国有企业退休人员也将全部被纳入城镇职工医疗保障体系。此外,包括农民工工伤、医疗、养老在内的保障体

案例1.2 中国应对金融危机的一揽子计划

系也逐步健全,养老保险和转移接续制度正在逐步确立。在全国10%的县(市、区)开展新型农村社会养老保险试点的工作也已启动。

The international financial crisis posed great challenges to the lives of farmers and urban low-income groups. Strengthening the social security system and improving the level of social security brought greater hope to them. Since January 1, 2009, the policy of adjusting the basic pension for enterprise retirees was implemented. Retirees from closed and bankrupt state-owned enterprises would also be fully included in the medical security system for urban workers. In addition, the security system including work-related injuries, health care and endowment insurance for migrant workers was gradually improved, and the endowment insurance transfer and renewal system was being established. The pilot work of new endowment insurance for rural residents was also launched in 10% of the counties (cities and districts) across the country.

2009年中央财政安排用于"三农"方面的支持资金达7 161.4亿元,同比增长20.2%。中央继续提高粮食最低收购价格,增加对农民的补贴,仅农资综合直补、良种补贴、农机具补贴等就达到1 230.8亿元。

In 2009, the central government allocated 716.14 billion yuan to support agriculture, rural areas and rural residents, up 20.2% year-on-year. The minimum purchase price of grains and subsidies for farmers continued to rise. The investment in general direct subsidies for agricultural materials, subsidies for improved varieties, and subsidies for agricultural machinery and tools reached 123.08 billion yuan.

医疗、教育、住房作为老百姓最为关心的民生问题,也是老百姓心头的三件大事。

Health care, education and housing, as people's most concerned livelihood issues, are also the uppermost in Chinese people's minds.

医改于2009年正式启动,全体城乡居民都将被纳入基本医疗保障体系。教育中长期规划正在加快制定,国家对教育的投入大幅度增加。保障性住房建设提速,2009年中央财政安排保障性安居工程投入增加到493亿元,增长1.7倍。3年内,约750万户城市低收入家庭、240万户林区垦区等棚户区居民的住房困难得以提前解决。

The medical reform was officially launched in 2009, and all urban and rural residents were included in the basic medical security system. The development of medium and long-term planning for education was pushed forward, and the government's investment in education increased substantially. The construction of affordable housing was accelerated. In 2009, the investment in the affordable housing projects arranged by the central government increased to 49.3 billion yuan, an increase of 1.7 times. Within three years, the housing difficulties facing about 7.5 million urban low-income families and 2.4 million shanty town residents in forest reclamation areas were solved in advance.

空前的举措,艰苦的努力,收获的是中国经济在全球经济一片低迷中仍然保持良好发展势头。经过近两年的努力,中国经济运行出现积极变化,总体形势企稳向好:投资增速持续加快,消费稳定较快增长,国内需求对经济增长的拉动作用逐步增强;农业生产形势良好,夏粮再获丰收;工业增速稳中趋升,结构调整和节能减排取得新进展,区域协调发展呈现新态势;金融市场运行平稳,市场预期继续向好,社会

案例 1.2　中国应对金融危机的一揽子计划

信心进一步提升;城镇新增就业继续增加;灾后重建加快推进。

Unprecedented measures and hard work yielded a good momentum of economic development despite the global economic downturn. After nearly two years of efforts, China's economic operation underwent positive changes, and the overall situation showed an increasingly steady trend. For example, the growth rate of investment continued to accelerate, the consumption grew steadily and rapidly, and the domestic demand pulls economic growth more effectively. The situation of agricultural production was good, with another harvest of the summer grain crops. The industrial growth rate rose steadily, with new progress made in structural adjustment, energy conservation and emission reduction, and a new trend in regional coordinated development. The financial market was running smoothly, with continuously improving market expectation and further enhanced public confidence. There were more new jobs available in cities and towns, and post-disaster reconstruction was accelerated.

点评

Comments

为了应对国际金融危机的冲击,中国政府实施积极的财政政策和适度宽松的货币政策,迅速出台并不断充实完善应对危机、促进发展的一揽子计划。从之后三年中国经济的发展来看,在 4 万亿元投资计划的刺激下,中国经济取得了很好的成绩。不仅保持了较高的经济增长,而且在结构调整、节能减排、提升就业、社会保障等各个方面都取得了新进展,为未来经济的发展打下了良好基础。到2010年,中国经济基本从金融危机的萧条阴影中走了出来,GDP达到39.8万亿元,比上年增长10.3%,全社会固定资产投资27.8万亿元,比上年增长了23.8%,两年新增4万亿元投资计划圆满完成。全年国家财政收入8.3万亿元,增长21.3%,财政赤字比预算减少500亿元。从本案例可以看出,财政政策的实施不仅是针对"消费、投资和出口三驾马车",而且要配合货币政策和产业政策。单独的财政政策有可能对民间投资产生"挤出效应",挤占民间投资的资金来源和民间资本的投资空间。但是从实际效果看,这次4万亿元投资计划并没有对民间投资产生"挤出效应"。一是适度宽松的货币政策为各方面投资主体的资金来源提供了有力保障,实际利率基本平稳,并没有增加民间投资的成本;二是一揽子计划迅速拉动了市场需求,稳定了各方面信心,为民间投资的持续发展创造了条件。总之,在这次危机中,中国政府的一揽子计划化"危"为"机",使得中国经济逆流而上,为其经济理论的发展提供了更多的可能。

In order to cope with the impacts of the international financial crisis, the Chinese government implemented a proactive fiscal policy and a moderately loose monetary policy. It also quickly introduced and constantly enriched and improved a package plan to cope with the crisis and promote development. It can be seen from the economic development of China in the next three years that China's economy achieved great results, stimulated by the 4 trillion yuan investment plan. In addition to maintaining a high economic growth rate, China made new progress in structural adjustment, energy conservation and emission reduction, employment promotion, social security and other

案例 1.2　中国应对金融危机的一揽子计划

aspects, laying a good foundation for future economic development. By 2010, China's economy had basically got out of the depression shadow of the financial crisis, as its GDP reached 39.8 trillion, up 10.3% year-on-year, and the investment in fixed assets nationwide had been 27.8 trillion, up 23.8% over the previous year. The plan to increase investment by 4 trillion yuan within two years was successfully completed. Throughout the year, the national fiscal revenue was 8.3 trillion yuan, increasing 21.3%, and the fiscal deficit was 50 billion yuan less than the budget. This case indicates that the implementation of fiscal policy should not only aim at the "three engines of consumption, investment and export", but also work with the monetary policy and the industrial policy. The fiscal policy alone may have a "crowding-out effect" on private investment as it will occupy the sources of funds for private investment and the investment space of private capital. As a matter of fact, the 4 trillion yuan investment plan didn't produce any "crowding-out effect" on private investment for the following two reasons. First, the moderately loose monetary policy provided a strong guarantee for the sources of funds for all investors, and the real interest rate remained basically stable without increasing the cost of private investment. Second, the package plan quickly stimulated market demand, consolidated confidence in all aspects, and created conditions for the sustainable development of private investment. In a word, during this crisis, the Chinese government utilizes the package plan to turn "crisis" into "opportunity", making China's economy move forward despite obstacles and providing more possibilities for the development of economic theory.

讨论题

Discussions

(1)在应对金融危机的一揽子计划中,中国政府所使用的政策工具有哪些?

What were the policy instruments adopted by the Chinese government in the package plan to deal with the financial crisis?

(2)什么是"挤出效应"? 4万亿元的投资计划有挤占民间投资吗? 请简要说明。

What is the "crowding-out effect"? Did the 4 trillion yuan investment plan crowd out private investment? Please explain briefly.

(3)宽松的货币政策是否引起了高通货膨胀? 请查阅相关数据,说明你的答案。

Did the loose monetary policy give rise to high inflation? Please refer to the relevant data and give your answer.

资料来源

刘铮,韩洁,杜宇,等. 来自一线的调研报告——一揽子经济刺激实施一周年[EB/OL]. [2023-04-21]. http://www.gov.cn/jrzg/2009-11/04/content_1456552.htm.

国务院常务会议部署扩大内需促进经济增长的措施[EB/OL]. [2023-04-21]. http://www.gov.cn/ldhd/2008-11/09/content_1143689.htm.

车玉明,周英峰,韩洁,等. 新华社:我国应对金融危机一揽子计划初见成效[EB/OL]. [2023-04-22]. http://finance.sina.com.cn/g/20090524/14296265698.shtml.

李斌,赵超,贾楠. 果断决策、从容应对——中国应对金融危机启示录[EB/OL]. [2023-04-22]. http://www.gov.cn/jrzg/2010-02/21/content_1538059.htm.

案例 1.2 中国应对金融危机的一揽子计划

刘磊,彭俊,沈寅,等.惊涛拍岸自岿然——中国应对金融危机促进经济增长[EB/OL].[2023－04－22].http://www.gov.cn/jrzg/2009－07/02/content_1354967.htm.

宋振远,韩冰,储国强.应对金融危机一周年"一揽子计划"回眸与展望[EB/OL].[2023－04－22].http://www.gov.cn/jrzg/2009－11/05/content_1456910.htm.

References

Liu Zheng, Han Jie, Du Yu, et al. Front-line research report-the first anniversary of implementing the economic stimulus package[EB/OL].[2023－04－21].http://www.gov.cn/jrzg/2009－11/04/content_1456552.htm.

The executive meeting of the State Council deploys measures to expand domestic demand and promote economic growth[EB/OL].[2023－04－21].http://www.gov.cn/ldhd/2008－11/09/content_1143689.htm.

Che Yuming, Zhou Yingfeng, Han Jie, et al. Xinhua News Agency: our package plan for dealing with the financial crisis has achieved initial success[EB/OL].[2023－04－22].http://finance.sina.com.cn/g/20090524/14296265698.shtml.

Li Bin, Zhao Chao, Jia Nan. Take decisive measures and give calm response-enlightenment of China's response to the financial crisis[EB/OL].[2023－04－22].http://www.gov.cn/jrzg/2010－02/21/content_1538059.htm.

Liu Lei, Peng Jun, Shen Yin, et al. Keep calm despite the terrifying waves-China promotes economic growth while responding to the financial crisis and[EB/OL].[2023－04－22].http://www.gov.cn/jrzg/2009－07/02/content_1354967.htm.

Song Zhenyuan, Han Bing, Chu Guoqiang. Review and outlook of the "package plan" at the first anniversary of responding to the financial crisis[EB/OL].[2023－04－22].http://www.gov.cn/jrzg/2009－11/05/content_1456910.htm.

案例1.3 "中等收入陷阱"对于中国是不是一个伪命题?
Case 1.3　Is the "Middle-Income Trap" a False Proposition for China?

教学目标
Teaching Objectives

2007年世界银行在题为《东亚复兴:有关经济增长的看法》的长篇报告中,首次提到"中等收入陷阱"(Middle-Income Trap)。自此,该概念被广泛讨论。其中,有关中国是否会掉进"中等收入陷阱"的话题引起国内外的特别关注。每当中国经济增长遇到困难时,一些国际评论员就开始预测中国快要掉进"中等收入陷阱"了。那么,什么是"中等收入陷阱"? 真的存在"中等收入陷阱"吗? 中国会跨过"中等收入陷阱"成功迈入高收入国家的行列吗? 本案例详细讨论了"中等收入陷阱"的由来,并结合相关历史数据和中国的实际情况,对中国是否会掉入"中等收入陷阱"展开讨论。

案例1.3 "中等收入陷阱"对于中国是不是一个伪命题?

In 2007, the World Bank mentioned the "Middle-Income Trap" for the first time in a long report entitled An East Asian Renaissance: Ideas for Economic Growth. This concept has been widely discussed since then. Among them, the topic of whether China will fall into the "Middle-Income Trap" has attracted special attention at home and abroad. Whenever China's economic growth encounters difficulties, some international critics always predicts that China will soon fall into the "Middle-Income Trap". So, what is the "Middle-Income Trap"? Is there really a "Middle-Income Trap"? Will China skip the "Middle-Income Trap" and successfully enter the ranks of high-income countries? This case discusses the origin of the "Middle-Income Trap" in detail, and discusses whether China will fall into the "Middle-Income Trap" by combining relevant historical data and the actual situation in China.

本案例适用于宏观经济学中经济增长理论的学习,主要目的是帮助学生理解经济增长规律以及中国经济增长的特点和未来发展趋势。

This case is applicable to the study of the economic growth theory in the Macroeconomics. It aims to help students understand the law of economic growth, the characteristics and future development trend of China's economic growth.

案例内容
Contents

过去10年里,国际上一种新的提法——"中等收入陷阱"——引起了经济学者、新闻媒体、政府官员、国际组织甚至普通民众的关注,成为流行概念。百度指数和谷歌趋势显示,对这个提法的关注度从2007年起不断攀升,直到2015年后才有所回落。如果搜索两个主要英文学术论文库(Web of Science,EBSCOhost)和一个主要中文学术论文库(中国知网),就会发现,至今有关"中等收入陷阱"的研究仍是方兴未艾。

Over the past 10 years, a new term "Middle-Income Trap" has attracted wide attention of economists, news media, government officials, international organizations and even ordinary people across the world, making it a popular concept. Baidu Index or Google Trends shows that the attention to this term had been rising since 2007, and it did not fall back until after 2015. If we search two major English academic theses and dissertations databases (Web of Science and EBSCOhost) and one major Chinese academic theses and dissertations database (CNKI), we will find that the research on the "Middle-Income Trap" is still in the ascendant.

2011年中国人均收入为5 577美元,已经进入中高收入国家。2016年中国政府表示,中国经济发展进入新常态,未来将呈"L形走势"。那么中国会不会遇到"中等收入陷阱"并落入其中呢?厉以宁认为,只要应对得当,改革措施及时到位,中国完全可以跨越"中等收入陷阱"。2001年诺贝尔经济学奖获得者迈克尔·斯宾塞在"2014金家岭财富论坛"上称,中国正致力于促进经济结构调整,促进市场机制发挥作用,因此不会陷入"中等收入陷阱"。但是,也有部分经济学家表示,中国已经掉入"中等收入陷阱"。那么,什么是"中等收入陷阱"?纵观世界经济,是否真的存在"中等收入陷阱"?中国如何才能成功从案例1.3 "中等收入陷阱"对于中国是不是一个伪命题？

中等收入国家进入高收入国家的行列呢？

In 2011, China's per capita income reached 5,577 US dollars, making it one of the middle and high income countries. In 2016, the Chinese Government stated that China's economic development has entered a new normal, and people will see an "L-shaped trend" in the future. So, will China encounter the "Middle-Income Trap" and fall into it? Li Yining believes that as long as the response is proper and the reform measures are put in place in a timely manner, China can skip the "Middle-Income Trap". Michael Spence, winner of the Nobel Prize in Economics in 2001, said at the "Jinjialing Fortune Forum 2014" that China is committed to promoting economic restructuring and pushing the market mechanism to play its role, so it will not fall into the "Middle-Income Trap". However, some economists argue that China has fallen into the "Middle-Income Trap". So, what is the "Middle-Income Trap"? Is there really a "Middle-Income Trap" in the world economy? How can China successfully enter the ranks of high-income countries from middle-income countries?

一、什么是"中等收入陷阱"？

Ⅰ. What is the "Middle-Income Trap"?

所谓的"中等收入陷阱"是指当一个国家的人均收入达到中等水平后，由于不能顺利实现经济发展方式的转变，导致经济增长动力不足，最终出现经济停滞的一种状态。当今世界，绝大多数国家是发展中国家，存在所谓的"中等收入陷阱"问题。像巴西、阿根廷、墨西哥、智利、马来西亚等，在20世纪70年代均进入了中等收入国家行列，但直到 2007 年,这些国家仍然挣扎在人均 GDP3 000 美元至 5 000 美元的发展阶段,并且见不到增长的动力和希望。

The so-called "Middle-Income Trap" refers to a state of economic stagnation where a country's per capita income reaches a medium level, and its failure to realize the smooth transformation between two economic development modes results in insufficient economic growth momentum. In today's world, as most countries are developing countries, there is the so-called "Middle-Income Trap" problem. Countries like Brazil, Argentina, Mexico, Chile and Malaysia all entered the ranks of middle-income countries in 1970s, but until 2007, they were still struggling in the development stage with a per capita GDP of 3,000~5,000 US dollars, with no impetus and hope for growth.

"中等收入陷阱"这个概念是世界银行在 2007 年发布的《东亚复兴:关于经济增长的观点》中提出的。按照世界银行的标准,人均国民总收入(GNI)在 975 美元以下为低收入国家,在 976 美元到 3 855 美元为中等偏下收入国家,在 3 856 美元到 11 905 美元为中高收入国家,超过 11 905 美元为高收入国家。2018 年的最新收入分组标准为:人均国民总收入低于 995 美元为低收入国家,在 996 美元至 3 895 美元为中等偏下收入国家,在 3 896 美元至 12 055 美元为中等偏上收入国家,高于 12 055 美元为高收入国家(如表 1—3 所示)。2018 年世界银行所统计的 218 个经济体中,高收入国家 81 个,中等偏上收入国家 56 个,中等偏下收入国家 47 个,低收入国家 34 个。如果一个国家在进入中等收入之后,经过一段时间的增长,未能进入高收入国家行列,就会掉入"中等收入陷阱"。

The concept of "Middle-Income Trap" was put forward by the

案例 1.3 "中等收入陷阱"对于中国是不是一个伪命题?

World Bank in the An East Asian Renaissance: Ideas for Economic Growth published in 2007. According to the criteria of the World Bank, countries with a GNI per capita below 975 US dollars are low-income countries, those between 976 and 3,855 US dollars are lower-middle-income countries, those between 3,856 and 11,905 US dollars are upper-middle-income countries, and those above 11,905 US dollars are high-income countries. According to the latest criteria of income classifications in 2018, low-income countries have a per capita GNI below 995 US dollars, lower-middle-income countries between 996 and 3,895 US dollars, upper-middle-income countries between 3,896 and 12,055 US dollars, and high-income countries above 12,055 US dollars (as shown in Table 1-3). Among the 218 economies included by the World Bank in 2018, there were 81 high-income countries, 56 upper-middle-income countries, 47 lower-middle-income countries and 34 low-income countries. If a middle-income country fails to enter the ranks of high-income countries after a period of time, it will fall into the "Middle-Income Trap".

表 1—3　　　　　　　　　　国家收入分组标准

Table 1—3　　　　　**Criteria of National Income Classifications**

国家划分 Classifications	2007 年的标准 Criteria in 2017	2018 年的标准 Criteria in 2018
低收入国家 Low-income countries	975 美元以下 Below 975 US dollars	995 美元以下 Below 995 US dollars
中等偏下收入国家 Lower-middle-income countries	976 美元到 3 855 美元 976~3,855 US dollars	996 至 3 895 美元 996~3,895 US dollars

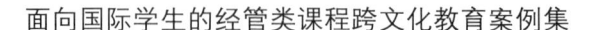

续表

国家划分 Classifications	2007年的标准 Criteria in 2017	2018年的标准 Criteria in 2018
中等偏上收入国家 Upper-middle-income countries	3 856美元到11 905美元 3,856~11,905 US dollars	3 896至12 055元 3,896~12,055 US dollars
高收入国家 High-income countries	高于11 905美元 Above 11,905 US dollars	高于12 055美元 Above 12,055 US dollars

二、真的存在"中等收入陷阱"吗？

Ⅱ. Is there really a "Middle-Income Trap"?

在经济发展研究领域，"陷阱"并不是一个新词，"马尔萨斯陷阱""纳尔逊低水平均衡陷阱""贫困陷阱"便是耳熟能详的例子。严格地讲，"陷阱"至少应该具备三个特征：(1)存在一种自发延续与自我加强机制；(2)处于持续的稳定状态；(3)难以突破。

"Trap" is not a new term in the field of research on economic development. "Malthusian Trap" "Nelson's Low-Level Equilibrium Trap" and "Poverty Trap" are all well-known examples. Strictly speaking, a "trap" should have at least three characteristics: (1) there is a spontaneous continuation and self-strengthening mechanism; (2) it is in a continuous and stable state; (3) it is difficult to break through.

如果说在经济发展过程中有过什么陷阱，那么低收入或贫困肯定是一种陷阱。人类历史已长达300万年，但直到大约200年前，经济增长极为缓慢，人均收入几乎没有多大变化，除极少数靠剥削、压迫他人为生的富人外，绝大多数人恐怕一直都生活在贫困状态。

If there is any trap in the process of economic development, low

案例1.3 "中等收入陷阱"对于中国是不是一个伪命题?

income or poverty is definitely one. Humans boast a history as long as 3 million years, but until about 200 years ago, the economic growth was extremely slow, with few changes in per capita income. Except for a few rich people who exploited and oppressed others for a living, most people were probably living in poverty.

18世纪下半叶爆发工业革命后,世界各地才出现"大分流",其标志是有些国家和地区经济增长开始加速。荷兰是1827年率先从"低收入"跨入"中低收入"门槛的经济体,也许是全球第一例。在随后半个世纪里,英国(1845年)、澳大利亚(1851年)、比利时(1854年)、新西兰(1860年)、美国(1860年)、瑞士(1868年)、乌拉圭(1870年)、丹麦(1872年)、法国(1874年)、德国(1874年)、奥地利(1876年)也相继进入"中低收入"俱乐部。低收入陷阱或贫困陷阱明显符合上述三个特征,因为人类花费了几百万年才摆脱它,的确是地地道道的陷阱。

After the industrial revolution broke out in the second half of the 18th century, there was a "great divergence" around the world, symbolized by the acceleration of economic growth in some countries and regions. In 1827, the Netherlands was the first economy to enter the threshold of "lower-middle income" from "low income", perhaps the first of its kind in the world. In the following 50 years, Britain (in 1845), Australia (in 1851), Belgium (in 1854), New Zealand (in 1860), the US (in 1860), Switzerland (in 1868), Uruguay (in 1870), Denmark (in 1872), France (in 1874), Germany (in 1874), and Austria (in 1876) also entered the "lower-middle income" club one after another. Obviously, the low income trap or poverty trap has the three characteristics mentioned above. It took millions of years for human beings to get out of it, so it is indeed a trap.

那么是否存在严格意义上的"中等收入陷阱"呢？如果我们回看西方发达国家曾经走过的路（但今天往往被人遗忘）会发现，这种陷阱似乎也是存在的。以荷兰为例，它于 1827 年跨入"中低收入"门槛，但直到 128 年后的 1955 年才进入"中高收入"群组。美国在"中低收入"阶段停留的时间短一些，不过也足足花费了 81 年（1860—1941 年）。

So is there a "Middle-Income Trap" in a strict sense? The traces of this trap can be found if we look back at the journey that western developed countries have taken, which is often forgotten today. For example, the Netherlands entered the threshold of "lower-middle income" in 1827, but it was not until 128 years later in 1955 that it was included into the group of "upper-middle income". Even the US, which stayed in the "lower-middle income" stage for a relatively shorter time, took 81 years (1860—1941).

对这些国家而言，从"中高收入"阶段进一步过渡到"高收入"阶段也十分艰难。美国花费了 21 年（1941—1962 年），加拿大花费了 19 年（1950—1969 年），澳大利亚花费了 20 年（1950—1970 年），新西兰花费了 23 年（1949—1972 年）。也就是说，西方发达国家都曾经落入"中等收入陷阱"（包括中等收入与中高收入两个阶段）长达百年之久，甚至更长。不过，这些国家历尽艰辛，最终还是跳出了陷阱，进入高收入阶段。

For these countries, it is also very difficult to further upgrade from the "upper-middle income" stage to the "high income" stage. It took the US 21 years (1941—1962), Canada 19 years (1950—1969), Australia 20 years (1950—1970), and New Zealand 23 years (1949—

案例1.3 "中等收入陷阱"对于中国是不是一个伪命题?

1972). In other words, western developed countries once fell into the "Middle-Income Trap" (including middle income and upper-middle income) for a hundred years or even longer, though they have managed to get out of the trap and entered the high-income stage after going through many hardships.

西方发达国家的经验未必具有普世价值。它们曾经一度落入"中等收入陷阱",是否意味着后发经济体也一定会重蹈覆辙?在一篇于2004年发表在《外交事务》的文章里,当时在美国任教的澳大利亚学者杰弗里·格瑞特提出一个论点:中等收入国家处于两面夹击的境地——技术上比不过富国,价格上拼不赢穷国。为了论证其观点,格瑞特按1980年人均GDP将世界各经济体分为高、中、低三组,然后计算各组在其后20年(1980—2000年)的人均收入增长情况。结果他发现:中等收入组的增长速度(不到20%)既慢于高收入经济体(约50%),也慢于低收入经济体(超过160%)。3年后,在题为《东亚复兴:有关经济增长的看法》的长篇报告中,世界银行的两位研究人员引用了格瑞特的文章,并首次使用了"中等收入陷阱"的提法。几年后,这个概念一下子火爆起来,不少人听到它便想当然地认为,高收入经济体已修成正果,低收入经济体的"起飞"相对容易,只有中等收入经济体很可能会落入增长陷阱,且很难跳出陷阱。

The experience of western developed countries may not be universally applicable. They once fell into the "Middle-Income Trap", does it mean that the latecomers will certainly make the same mistakes? In an article published in the Foreign Affairs in 2004, Jeffrey Greet, an Australian scholar who was teaching in the US at that time, put forward an argument that middle-income countries are stuck in a dilemma, as they are not able to compete with rich countries in technologies and poor countries in price. In order to prove this point, he classified the world economies into three groups according to the per capita GDP in 1980, and then calculated the per capita income growth of each group in the next 20 years (1980—2000). As a result, he found that the growth rate of middle-income group (less than 20%) is slower than that of high-income economies (about 50%) and low-income economies (over 160%). Three years later, in a long report entitled An East Asian Renaissance: Ideas for Economic Growth, two researchers from the World Bank quoted his article and used the term "Middle-Income Trap" for the first time. After a few more years, this concept suddenly went viral. When hearing this concept, people took it for granted that the high-income economies had achieved positive results, and the "take-off" was relatively easy for the low-income economies. And only the middle-income economies were likely to fall into the growth trap and it was difficult for them to jump out of it.

其实,格瑞特和世界银行报告的作者都不曾在严格意义上使用"陷阱"这个概念,前者根本没有提及这个词,后者在10年后发表的反思文章中解释:他们原本的意思只是说中等收入经济体可能落入增长停滞的陷阱,而不是说中等收入经济体一定会比低收入和高收入经济体更容易落入增长陷阱;这种陷阱存在于各种收入水平,从低收入到高收入。他们澄清,"中等收入陷阱"只是一种说法、一种预警,为的是激发有关中等收入经济体发展方式的讨论,但这个提法缺乏严谨的定义,也没有像样的数据支撑。

In fact, neither Jeffrey nor the authors of the World Bank report

案例 1.3 "中等收入陷阱"对于中国是不是一个伪命题？

adopted the concept of "trap" in a strict sense. The former did not mention it at all, and the latter explained in a reflective essay published 10 years later that what they originally intended to indicate that middle-income economies might fall into the trap of stagnant growth, but not that middle-income economies would definitely fall into the growth trap more easily than low-income and high-income economies. This trap can be found at all income levels, from low income to high income. They clarified that the "Middle-Income Trap" is just a statement and an early warning, aiming to trigger discussions on the development mode of middle-income economies. But this concept is not well defined and supported by adequate data.

中等收入经济体之所以在 21 世纪初引起研究者的高度关注，原因有二。一是与战后初期相比，世界经济的格局发生了巨大的变化。以 124 个有连续数据的经济体为例：1950 年时，其中 80 个是低收入经济体，41 个是中等收入经济体，高收入经济体只有 3 个；而到 2013 年时，低收入经济体的数量降至 37 个，高收入经济体增至 33 个，中等收入经济体的数量成为大头，达到 54 个，尤其是在亚洲，中等收入经济体的比例更高，涵盖了亚洲发展中国家 95% 以上的人口。二是现有经济理论存在一个巨大的空白。理解低收入经济体（大约 10 亿人口）的发展，有索洛增长模型；理解高收入经济体（大约 10 亿人口）的发展，有内生增长理论；但对理解中等收入经济体（大约有 50 亿人口）的发展，到目前为止并没有什么令人满意的理论或模式。因此，世界银行 2007 年报告的执笔者 10 年后说，"中等收入陷阱"与其说是中等收入经济体注定的命运，不如说是经济理论上"一个无知的陷阱"。

There are two reasons why middle-income economies have attracted great attention from researchers at the beginning of the 21st century. First, compared with the early postwar period, the pattern of the world economy has undergone tremendous changes. Taking 124 economies with continuous data as an example: in 1950, 80 of them were low-income economies, 41 middle-income economies, and only 3 high-income economies. By 2013, the number of low-income economies dropped to 37, the number of high-income economies increased to 33, and the number of middle-income economies became the largest, reaching 54. Especially in Asia, the proportion of middle-income economies was higher, covering more than 95% of the population in developing countries in Asia. Second, there is a huge gap in the existing economic theory. People could refer to Solow growth model to understand the development of low-income economies (with a population of about one billion), and the endogenous growth theory to understand the development of high-income economies (with a population of about one billion). But so far, there has been no satisfactory theory or model available to figure out the development of middle-income economies (with a population of about five billion). Therefore, the authors of the World Bank report in 2007 stated 10 years later that the "Middle-Income Trap" is more of an "ignorant trap" in terms of the economic theory than a doomed fate of middle-income economies.

如果"中等收入陷阱"的提出者都不曾在严格意义上使用"陷阱"的概念,严格意义上的陷阱是不是根本就不存在呢?格瑞特提供的证据事后被证明不足为凭。有研究者用更新的数据重新计算了各类经案例1.3 "中等收入陷阱"对于中国是不是一个伪命题？

济体在1980—2000年间的增长率，发现中等收入经济体与高收入经济体之间的差距并不像格瑞特描绘的那么大。如果采用与格瑞特不同的指标划分高、中、低三类经济体，这种差距则会完全消失。可见数据与尺度的选择可能严重影响研究的结论。更重要的是，即使沿用格瑞特的划分指标，无论是在1990—2010年间，还是在1995—2015年间，中等收入经济体的增长速度都比高收入经济体高。也就是说，从某个时段看，陷阱似有还无；换成别的时段，根本不存在什么增长陷阱。

If the initiators of the "Middle-Income Trap" have never adopted the concept of "trap" in a strict sense, does the trap actually not exist at all? The evidence provided by Jeffrey was proved to be insufficient afterwards. Some researchers recalculated the growth rates of various economies from 1980 to 2000 with updated data, and found out that the gap between middle-income economies and high-income economies was not as big as described by him. If we use different indicators from him to divide the high-income, middle-income and low-income economies, this gap will disappear completely. Thus, the choices of data and scales may seriously affect the conclusion of the study. More importantly, even if his classification indicators are adopted, the growth rates of middle-income economies are higher than those of high-income economies both from 1990 to 2010 and from 1995 to 2015. In other words, it seems that there is a trap in a certain period of time, but not at all during other periods.

在谈到这个问题时，很多人马上就会联想到那些落入"中等收入陷阱"的拉美国家，仿佛这几个国家的经历就是所有后发国家的宿命。拉丁美洲确有几个国家很早就进入中低收入阶段，如乌拉圭（1870

年)、阿根廷(1890年)、智利(1891年)、委内瑞拉(1925年)、墨西哥(1942年)、巴拿马(1945年)、哥伦比亚(1946年)、巴西(1958年)。到目前为止,只有乌拉圭和智利于2012年迈入高收入的门槛,阿根廷也曾短暂进入这个门槛,其余国家仍停留在中高收入群组。但是,正如前面谈到的西方发达国家在中等收入阶段(包括中低收入与中高收入阶段)普遍停留很长时间,但这并不妨碍它们最终进入高收入阵营。后发经济体的过渡期普遍比西方发达国家短,我们有什么理由认为现在那些后发国家一定会落入陷阱呢?更多的经济体(如大多数亚洲国家和一些非洲国家)虽然仍未过渡到下一阶段,但一直在砥砺前行。既然落入"中等收入陷阱"并非大概率事件,完全没必要谈虎色变,认为中等收入就是一道难以迈过的槛儿。

When talking about this issue, many will immediately think of those Latin American countries that fell into the "Middle-Income Trap", as if the experiences of these countries indicate the fate of all developing countries. It is true that several countries in Latin America entered the lower middle income stage a long time ago, such as Uruguay (in 1870), Argentina (in 1890), Chile (in 1891), Venezuela (in 1925), Mexico (in 1942), Panama (in 1945), Colombia (in 1946), and Brazil (in 1958). So far, only Uruguay and Chile entered the ranks of high income countries in 2012, and Argentina once made it for quite a short period of time, with the rest of the Latin American countries still staying in the upper middle income group. However, as previously mentioned, most western countries stayed in the middle-income stage (including lower-middle income and upper-middle income stages) for a long time, but this did not prevent them from entering the

案例1.3 "中等收入陷阱"对于中国是不是一个伪命题?

ranks of high-income countries at last. The transition period of latecomers is generally shorter than that of western countries. What reasons do we have to believe that those latecomers will definitely fall into the trap now? Although more economies (such as most Asian countries and some African countries) have not yet made it to the next stage, they have been forging ahead. Since falling into the "Middle-Income Trap" is not an event with high probability, there is absolutely no need to get frightened at the mere mentions of it, considering middle income as an insurmountable obstacle.

三、对于中国,"中等收入陷阱"是个伪命题吗?
III. Is the "Middle-Income Trap" a false proposition for China?

中国的崛起是一部当代世界的伟大史诗。在成立之初的1950年,新中国曾是世界上最贫穷的国家之一,不要说与周边的国家与地区比,就是与以贫穷落后著称的非洲国家比,也远远落在后面。当时,在有数据的25个非洲国家中,21个国家的人均GDP比中国高,且不是高出一点点,而是高出很多。例如,当时安哥拉的人均GDP是中国的10倍之多。改革开放前30年为改革开放后40年奠定了坚实的政治、社会、经济基础。不过,即便到1978年,中国的人均国民总收入仍然不足低收入国家平均水平的一半。

The rise of China is a great epic in the contemporary world. In 1950, one year after the People's Republic of China was founded, China was one of the poorest countries in the world, as it lagged far behind neighboring countries and regions and even African countries. At that time, among the 25 African countries with data, 21 have a per capita GDP much higher than that of China. For example, at that time, the per capita GDP of Angola was 10 times that of China. The first 30 years of reform and opening-up laid a solid political, social and economic foundation for the development of the next 40 years. However, even in 1978, China's GNI per capita was still less than half of the average level of low-income countries.

依据世界银行的数据,中国终于在1999年摆脱了困扰中国人几千年的贫困陷阱,从低收入迈入中低收入阶段。十几亿人摆脱贫困本是值得大书特书的历史性事件,但国际上总有一些人希望看到并预测中国会跌入"中等收入陷阱"。中国是否会陷入"中等收入陷阱"? 一方面,我们应该承认,从中等收入国家跃升为高收入国家是一个国家经济发展比较特殊的阶段,要比从低收入国家过渡到中等收入国家更加复杂,中国在这一阶段将面临方方面面的挑战。从这个意义上讲,"中等收入陷阱"这一概念对现阶段的中国发展具有警示意义。另一方面,我们也可以找到中国跨越"中等收入陷阱"的大量有利条件,我们完全有理由坚信,中国完全可以跨越"中等收入陷阱",完成从中等收入阶段向高收入阶段的跨越。

According to the data of the World Bank, China finally got rid of the poverty trap that has plagued Chinese people for thousands of years in 1999, and entered the lower-middle income stage from the low income stage. It is a historic event that more than one billion people are lifted out of poverty, but there are always some in the world who hope to see and predict that China will fall into the "Middle-Income Trap". Will China fall into the "Middle-Income Trap"? On the one hand, we should admit that the transition from a middle-income

案例 1.3 "中等收入陷阱"对于中国是不是一个伪命题?

country to a high-income country is a special stage for the economic development of any country, which is more complicated than the transition from a low-income country to a middle-income country. China will face challenges in all aspects at this stage. In this sense, the concept of "Middle-Income Trap" has a warning significance for the development of China at this stage. On the other hand, we can also find a lot of favorable conditions for China to skip the "Middle-Income Trap", and we have every reason to believe that China can smoothly make it and complete the leap from the middle income stage to the high income stage.

从 1999 年中国进入中低收入阶段后,时间已过了 20 多年。站在这个节点上,展望中国迈向高收入的前景,我们有十足的信心:未来的基本方向就是进入高收入阶段,在未来 10 年内中国将跨越"中等收入陷阱",成功进入高收入国家行列。中国人的这份自信绝不是虚幻缥缈的玄想,而是靠扎实的数据支撑的。按照世界银行的分类标准,中国在中低收入阶段仅停留了 12 年(1999—2011 年)便跨入了下一阶段——中高收入阶段。前面引述的另一份研究也表明,与其他任何有历史数据的经济体相比,中国从中低收入到中高收入的过渡期最短。在过去 100 多年的世界经济发展史中,从中低收入到中高收入的过渡期一般会比从中高收入到高收入的过渡期长:前一个过渡期的中位数是 55 年,后一个过渡期的中位数是 15 年。近年来,中国经济的增速虽然有所放缓,但依旧保持着中高速增长的态势。这让我们有充分的理由相信,中国完成从中高收入到高收入的过渡期不会超过 15 年。

More than 20 years have passed since China entered the lower-middle income stage in 1999. Standing on this node to forecast the prospects of China, we are fully confident that our fundamental direction for the future is to enter the high income stage, skipping the "Middle-Income Trap", and successfully enter the ranks of high-income countries in the next 10 years. Chinese people's confidence is by no means based on an illusory fantasy, but supported by solid data. According to the classification criteria of the World Bank, China only stayed in the lower-middle income stage for 12 years (1999—2011) and then entered the next stage: the upper-middle income stage. Another study quoted earlier also shows that compared with any other economy with historical data, China has the shortest transition period from the lower-middle income stage to the upper-middle income stage. In the history of world economic development over the past 100 years, the transition period from the lower-middle income stage to the upper-middle income stage is generally longer than that from the upper-middle income stage to the high income stage. The median of the previous transition period is 55 years, while that of the latter one only takes 15 years. In recent years, although the economic development of China has slowed down, it still maintains the trend of medium-high growth. This gives us every reason to believe that it will take less than 15 years for China to complete the transition from the upper-middle income stage to the high income stage.

  其实,中国的很多省份已经为这种成功跨越提供了范例。众所周知,中国31个省区市中有27个人口超过1 500万人,其中最大的3个省(广东、山东、河南)人口达到1亿人上下,放到世界范围,这些省区市的人口规模都相当于中型国家或大型国家。判断中国整体能不能

案例 1.3 "中等收入陷阱"对于中国是不是一个伪命题?

跨越中等收入阶段,可以先看看各个省区市的表现。截至 2015 年,中国已有 5 个省区市(江苏、浙江、上海、北京、天津)达到高收入水平,其中江苏、浙江人口规模超过韩国,上海人口规模超过中国台湾。与此同时,广东、山东、辽宁、福建、内蒙古等省区市的人均 GDP 也已经超过 10 000 美元,接近高收入的门槛。这两类省区市按常住人口计算合计为 5.078 亿人,占中国总人口(13.746 亿人)的比重为 36.9%,相当于欧盟的总人口(5.096 亿人),相当于美国总人口(3.214 亿人)的 1.58 倍。既然占中国人口 1/3 以上的地区已经成功跨越"中等收入陷阱",进入或接近高收入阶段,那么其他省区市跨越中等收入水平、迈向高收入阶段,是没有任何问题的。

As a matter of fact, a number of provinces in China have provided examples for this successful leap. As we all know, 27 of the 31 provinces, autonomous regions and municipalities in China have a population over 15 million, with the top three provinces (Guangdong, Shandong and Henan) having around 100 million. It means that the population of these provinces, autonomous regions and municipalities is equivalent to that of a medium-sized or large country. To judge whether China as a whole can leapfrog the middle-income stage, we can first look into the performance of different provinces, autonomous regions and municipalities. By 2015, five provinces, autonomous regions and municipalities (Jiangsu, Zhejiang, Shanghai, Beijing and Tianjin) in China had reached the high income level, among which the population of Jiangsu and Zhejiang surpassed that of South Korea, and the population of Shanghai was larger than that of Taiwan Province, China. Meanwhile, the per capita GDP of Guangdong, Shandong, Liaoning, Fujian, Inner Mongolia and other provinces, autonomous regions and municipalities also exceeded 10,000 US dollars, close to the threshold of the high income stage. These two types of provinces, autonomous regions and municipalities have a total population of 507.8 million, accounting for 36.9% of China's total population (1,374.6 million), equivalent to the total population of the European Union (509.6 million) and 1.58 times that of the US (321.4 million). Now that the regions with over one third of China's population have successfully skipped the "Middle-Income Trap" and entered or approached the high-income stage, other provinces, autonomous regions and municipalities will undoubtedly make it.

点评
Comments

从全球经济的表现来看,确实只有少数国家进入高收入国家行列,绝大多数国家的经济到了中高收入阶段之后便停滞不前。虽然那些进入高收入的国家在中等收入阶段也停留了很长时间,但并没有妨碍它们成为高收入国家。"中等收入陷阱"并不是不能跨越。另外,经济发展的历史表明没有任何一个国家的经济增长一直保持高速。随着经济规模、产业结构以及社会矛盾的变化,经济增长速度从高速到常态增长是正常的,经济增速慢下来并不代表进入"陷阱"。我们承认中等收入国家在经济发展上面临更多的问题和困难,所以"中等收入陷阱"对中国具有重要的警示意义。

Judging from the performance of the global economy, it is true

案例 1.3 "中等收入陷阱"对于中国是不是一个伪命题?

that only a few countries have entered the ranks of high-income countries, and most economies have stuck in stagnation after reaching the upper-middle income stage. Although those countries that have entered the high-income stage used to stay in the middle-income stage for a long time, it did not prevent them from becoming high-income countries. Therefore, the "Middle-Income Trap" is not insurmountable. In addition, the history of economic development shows that it is impossible for any country to always maintain rapid economic growth. With the changes of economic scale, industrial structure and social contradictions, it is not unusual for economic growth to shift from fast to normal, and the slowdown of economic growth does not mean entering a "trap". We admit that middle-income countries are faced with more problems and difficulties than others in economic development, so in this sense the "Middle-Income Trap" has important warning significance for China.

2020年中国人均GDP为10 836美元,与高收入国家12 696美元的标准比较接近。但是我们也要知道,人均收入是一个平均的概念,对于拥有14亿人口的中国来讲,人均收入并不代表所有人的收入都达到了某一水平。中国人民追求的不是人均收入的提高,而是共同富裕,是在收入提高的基础上,缩小贫富差距,人民群众普遍具有较高的幸福感、获得感、安全感,这才是中国人民追求的目标。

In 2020, China's per capita GDP was 10,836 US dollars, close to 12 696 US dollars, the level of high-income countries. However, we should also be aware that per capita income is a concept featuring average. For a country with a population of 1. 4 billion, the per capita income level does not mean that everyone's income level has reached the high-income level. What the people of China are pursuing is not the increase in per capita income but common prosperity, which means that the people generally have a strong sense of happiness, acquisition and security while increasing their income and bridging the gap between the rich and the poor. It is the very goal pursued by Chinese people.

讨论题
Discussions

(1)结合案例,浅谈中等收入国家发展慢于高收入国家和低收入国家的原因。

Please talk about the reasons why middle-income countries are developing slower than high-income countries and low-income countries based on the case.

(2)与其他东亚国家相比,你认为中国有可能跨越"中等收入陷阱"吗？为什么？

Compared with other East Asian countries, do you think it is possible for China to skip the "Middle-Income Trap"? Why?

(3)你认为,对于中等收入国家,促进经济进一步增长的关键因素是什么。

What do you think is the key factor for middle-income countries to achieve further economic growth?

案例1.3 "中等收入陷阱"对于中国是不是一个伪命题?

资料来源

"中等收入陷阱"对中国而言是不是一个伪命题?[EB/OL].[2023-04-22]. https://www.thepaper.cn/newsDetail_forward_7813047.

年巍. 中等收入陷阱[EB/OL].[2023-04-22]. http://views.ce.cn/view/ent/201204/11/t20120411_23232656.shtml.

中等收入陷阱是什么与中等收入陷阱的10大特征[EB/OL].[2023-04-22]. https://www.cnrencai.com/salarinfo/562203.html.

References

Is the "Middle-Income Trap" a false proposition for China?[EB/OL].[2023-04-22]. https://www.thepaper.cn/newsDetail_forward_7813047.

Nian Wei. Middle Income Trap[EB/OL].[2023-04-22]. http://views.ce.cn/view/ent/201204/11/t20120411_23232656.shtml.

What is the "Middle-Oncome Trap" and what are its ten characteristics[EB/OL].[2023-04-22]. https://www.cnrencai.com/salarinfo/562203.html.

第二篇　管理学原理
PART II　PRINCIPLES OF MANAGEMENT

案例 2.1 "一带一路"倡议推动构建人类命运共同体

Case 2.1　The "Belt and Road Initiative"(BRI) Promotes the Construction of a Community of Shared Future for Mankind

教学目标
Teaching Objectives

2013年中国习近平主席提出的"一带一路"是一条包括"丝绸之路经济带"和"21世纪海上丝绸之路"在内的合作倡议。其基本原则是平等互利,共同打造政治互信、经济融合、文化包容的利益共同体、命运共同体和责任共同体。同中方签署"一带一路"合作文件的伙伴国家已超过140个,"一带一路"成为当今世界范围最广、规模最大的国际合作平台。本节通过案例分析,提升学生对于全球化管理、人类命运共同体等概念和理念的认知,帮助学生理解国际、区域经济和社会合作的重要性,增强"同命运、共呼吸"使命担当意识,形成正确的全球协同发展理念,提升参与人类命运共同体构建的意识与能力。

The Belt and Road Initiative proposed by Chinese President Xi Jinping in 2013 is a cooperative initiative involving "the Silk Road Economic Belt" and "the 21st Century Maritime Silk Road". Adhering to the basic principle of equality and mutual benefit, it aims to jointly create a community featuring common interests, a shared future and shared responsibilities with political mutual trust, economic integration and cultural tolerance. More than 140 partner countries have signed the BRI cooperation documents with China, and the BRI has become the largest international cooperation platform covering the largest number of countries and regions in the world. Through case analysis, we can enhance students' understanding of ideas and concepts such as global management and a community of shared future for mankind, help them understand the importance of international and regional economic and social cooperation, enhance their sense of mission featuring "sharing a common fate", cultivate a correct concept of global coordinated development for them, and improve their awareness and capability to participate in the construction of a community of shared future for mankind.

案例涉及管理学原理中全球观、全球环境、区域性贸易联盟、全球环境中的管理等相关知识点。

The case involves the global view, global environment, regional trade alliance, management in a global environment and other related concepts in Principles of Management.

案例 2.1 "一带一路"倡议推动构建人类命运共同体

案例内容
Contents

萨希瓦尔电站是巴基斯坦装机容量最大的清洁型燃煤电站之一,由中国两家公司共同投资建设,项目包含两台 660 兆瓦超临界燃煤发电机组,均已建成投产,发电量 90 亿千瓦时(如图 2—1 所示)。

The Sahiwal Power Plant is one of the clean coal-fired power plants with the largest installed capacity in Pakistan. It was jointly invested and built by two Chinese companies. The project consists of two 660 MW supercritical coal-fired generating units, both of which have been completed and put into operation, with a power generation capacity of 9 billion kWh(as shown in Figure 2—1).

中方投资公司的一位负责人说,萨希瓦尔电站的建设,有效缓解了巴基斯坦电力短缺的状况,仅 1 号机组就填补了当地近 25% 的用电缺口,对巴基斯坦调整电力能源结构、降低发电成本等具有十分重要的意义。点亮万家灯火的同时,萨希瓦尔电站项目还一直坚持环保优先,烟气排放等指标均远优于当地标准,也优于世界银行相关环保标准。

A person in charge of the Chinese company invested in the project said that the construction of the Sahiwal Power Plant has effectively alleviated the power shortage in Pakistan. Unit 1 alone has dealt with nearly 25% of the local power shortage, which is of great significance to Pakistan's power restructuring and reduction of power generation costs. While lighting up thousands of households, the Sahiwal

Power Plant project has always been adhering to the priority of environmental protection. Its flue gas emission and other indicators are well above the local standards and the relevant environmental protection standards of the World Bank.

图片来源:https://ishare.ifeng.com/c/s/7ox2YZrSRge,2023-12-8。
Source:https://ishare.ifeng.com/c/s/7ox2YZrSRge,2023-12-8.

图 2-1 萨希瓦尔燃煤电站

Figure 2-1 Sahiwal Coal-fired Power Plant

能源、电力是巴基斯坦经济发展的迫切需要,近年来中巴能源合作成果斐然,这也为中巴在交通运输、港口建设、信息通信等领域深入合作奠定了基础,将进一步促进互联互通格局形成。中巴经济走廊起点在中国新疆喀什,终点在巴基斯坦瓜达尔港,全长3 000千米。这条走廊北接丝绸之路经济带,南连21世纪海上丝绸之路,是贯通南北丝路的关键枢纽,是一条包括能源工程、交通基础设施、产业合作、社会民生合作等在内的经济走廊,也是共建"一带一路"的标志性项目。

Energy and electricity are urgently needed in Pakistan's econom-

案例2.1 "一带一路"倡议推动构建人类命运共同体

ic development. In recent years, China-Pakistan energy cooperation has achieved remarkable results, which has laid the foundation for in-depth cooperation between China and Pakistan in the fields of transportation, port construction, information communication, and will further promote the formation of an interconnection pattern. The China-Pakistan Economic Corridor starts in Kashgar, Xinjiang, China and ends in Gwadar Port, Pakistan, with a total length of 3,000 km. It is connected to the Silk Road Economic Belt in the north and the 21st Century Maritime Silk Road in the south. It is a key hub connecting the Northern Silk Road and the Southern Silk Road, an economic corridor including energy projects, transportation infrastructures, industrial cooperation, social and people's livelihood cooperation, and also a landmark project for jointly building the "Belt and Road".

"一带一路"(The Belt and Road, B&R)是"丝绸之路经济带"和"21世纪海上丝绸之路"的简称,2013年9月和10月由中国国家主席习近平分别提出建设"新丝绸之路经济带"和"21世纪海上丝绸之路"的合作倡议。依靠中国与有关国家既有的双多边机制,借助既有的、行之有效的区域合作平台,"一带一路"旨在借用古代丝绸之路的历史符号,高举和平发展的旗帜,积极发展与沿线国家的经济合作伙伴关系,共同打造政治互信、经济融合、文化包容的利益共同体、命运共同体和责任共同体。该倡议包括"五大流通",即"政策沟通、设施联通、贸易畅通、资金融通、民心相通"。

The "Belt and Road" (abbreviated as B&R) is the abbreviation of Silk Road Economic Belt and 21st Century Maritime Silk Road. In September and October, 2013, Chinese President Xi Jinping put forward the cooperation initiative of building the Silk Road Economic Belt and 21st Century Maritime Silk Road respectively. Relying on the existing bilateral and multilateral mechanisms between China and relevant countries and the existing effective platforms for regional cooperation, the Belt and Road Initiative aims to follow the historical symbols of the ancient Silk Road, hold high the banner of peaceful development, and actively develop economic cooperation partnerships with countries along the Belt and Road to jointly build a community featuring common interests, a shared future and shared responsibilities with political mutual trust, economic integration and cultural tolerance. The Initiative adopts the "Five-Pronged Approach", namely "Policy Coordination, Connectivity of Infrastructure, Unimpeded Trade, Financial Integration and Closer People-to-People Ties".

以下为2021年6月23日,时任中国国务委员兼外长王毅在"一带一路"亚太区域国际合作高级别会议上的主旨发言:坚定信心,加强团结,携手建设更加紧密的"一带一路"伙伴关系。

The following is the keynote speech delivered by Wang Yi, then State Councilor and Foreign Minister of China, at the Asia and Pacific High-level Conference on Belt and Road Cooperation on June 23, 2021 about enhancing confidence, strengthening solidarity and working together to build a closer "Belt and Road" partnership.

各位同事,各位朋友:

Colleagues, Friends,

2013年习近平主席提出共建"一带一路"倡议以来,在各方共同参与和努力下,这一重要倡议展现出旺盛生机与活力,取得了积极成

案例 2.1 "一带一路"倡议推动构建人类命运共同体

果和进展。

In 2013, President Xi Jinping proposed the Belt and Road Initiative (BRI). Since then, with the participation and joint efforts of all parties, this important initiative has shown strong vigor and vitality, and yielded good results and progress.

8年来,"一带一路"从理念变为实践,得到国际社会积极响应和支持。迄今,同中方签署"一带一路"合作文件的伙伴国家已达到140个。"一带一路"真正成为当今世界范围最广、规模最大的国际合作平台。

Over the past eight years, the BRI has evolved from a concept into real actions, and received warm response and support from the international community. To date, up to 140 partner countries have signed documents on Belt and Road cooperation with China. The BRI has truly become the world's broadest-based and largest platform for international cooperation.

8年来,"一带一路"从蓝图变为现实,为世界各国带来巨大机遇和红利。中国与"一带一路"合作伙伴贸易额累计超过9.2万亿美元,中国企业在沿线国家直接投资累计超过1 300亿美元。世界银行报告认为,"一带一路"倡议全面实施将使全球贸易额和全球收入分别增长6.2%和2.9%,并有力促进全球经济的增速。

Over the past eight years, the BRI has evolved from vision into reality, and brought about enormous opportunities and benefits to countries around the world. Trade between China and BRI partners has exceeded 9.2 trillion US dollars. Direct investment by Chinese companies in countries along the Belt and Road has surpassed 130 billion US dollars. A World Bank report suggests that when fully implemented, the BRI could increase global trade by 6.2 percent and global real income by 2.9 percent, and give a significant boost to global growth.

尤其是去年以来，面对突如其来的新冠疫情，"一带一路"合作不但没有按下"暂停键"，反而逆风前行，展现出强大韧性和旺盛活力。

Notably last year, despite the sudden outbreak of COVID-19, the Belt and Road cooperation did not come to a halt. It braved the headwinds and continued to move forward, showing remarkable resilience and vitality.

我们携手构筑国际抗疫"防火墙"。中国与各方举行了100多场疫情防控经验交流会，截至6月中旬已向世界各国提供了2 900多亿只口罩、35亿多件防护服、45亿多份检测试剂，帮助很多国家建设病毒检测实验室。中国与多国广泛开展疫苗合作，已通过捐赠、出口等方式，向90多个国家提供了超过4亿剂疫苗和原液，其中大多数是"一带一路"合作伙伴。

Together, we have put up an international firewall of cooperation against COVID-19. China and BRI partners have held over 100 meetings to share experience on COVID prevention and control. By mid-June, China has provided more than 290 billion masks, 3.5 billion protective suits and 4.5 billion testing kits to the world, and helped many countries build testing labs. China is engaged in extensive vaccine cooperation with many countries, and has donated and exported more than 400 million doses of finished and bulk vaccines to more than 90 countries, most of which are BRI partners.

我们合力打造全球经济稳定器。先后举行数十场"一带一路"国

案例2.1 "一带一路"倡议推动构建人类命运共同体

际会议,交流发展经验、协调发展政策、推进务实合作。大多数"一带一路"合作项目继续推进,中巴经济走廊能源合作为巴基斯坦贡献了三分之一电力供应,斯里兰卡卡塔纳供水项目解决了当地45个村庄的饮水困难。据统计,去年,中国与"一带一路"合作伙伴货物贸易额达1.35万亿美元,创历史新高,为各国抗疫情、稳经济、保民生做出了积极贡献。

Together, we have provided a stabilizer for the world economy. We have held dozens of BRI international conferences to share development experience, coordinate development policies, and advance practical cooperation. We have kept most BRI projects going. Energy cooperation under the China-Pakistan Economic Corridor provides one-third of Pakistan's power supply. The Katana Water Supply Project in Sri Lanka has made safe drinking water available to 45 villages there. Statistics show that last year, trade in goods between China and BRI partners registered a record 1.35 trillion US dollars, making a significant contribution to the COVID response, economic stability and people's livelihood of relevant countries.

我们齐心搭建世界联通新桥梁。中国与22个伙伴国开展"丝路电商"合作,有力促进了疫情形势下的贸易畅通。连接亚欧大陆的中欧班列2020年全年开行数量和货物运量都创造了历史新高,今年第一季度,开行列数和发送货物标箱数又分别同比增长75%和84%,成为名副其实的"钢铁驼队",为助力各国抗疫发挥了重要作用。

Together, we have built new bridges for global connectivity. China has carried out Silk Road e-commerce cooperation with 22 partner countries. This has helped sustain international trade flows throughout the pandemic. In 2020, the China-Europe Railway Express, which runs through the Eurasian continent, hit new record numbers in both freight services and cargo volumes. In the first quarter of this year, the Express dispatched 75 percent more trains and delivered 84 percent more TEUs of goods than in the same period last year. Hailed as a "steel camel fleet", the Express has truly lived up to its name and played an important role in giving countries the support they need in fighting COVID.

各位同事,

Colleagues,

共建"一带一路"之所以取得如此迅速发展,收获如此丰硕成果,得益于各合作伙伴的团结合作,更重要的是,正如习近平主席在本次会议的书面致辞中所指出,共建"一带一路"坚持了共商共建共享原则,践行了开放绿色廉洁理念,致力于高标准、惠民生、可持续的合作目标。

The fast-growing and fruitful Belt and Road cooperation is a result of the solidarity and cooperation among BRI partners. More importantly, as President Xi Jinping pointed out in his written remarks to this Conference, Belt and Road cooperation is guided by the principle of extensive consultation, joint contribution and shared benefits. It practices the concept of open, green and clean development. And it is aimed at high-standard, people-centered and sustainable growth.

我们始终坚持平等协商。在共建"一带一路"大家庭中,无论经济体量大小,每位合作伙伴都是平等的。我们开展的每项合作,都不附带任何政治条件,都不从所谓"实力地位"强加于人,更不会对任何国家构成威胁。

案例 2.1 "一带一路"倡议推动构建人类命运共同体

We are always committed to equal consultation. All cooperation partners, regardless of economic size, are equal members of the BRI family. None of our cooperation programs are attached with political strings. We never impose our will on others from a so-called position of strength. Neither do we pose a threat to any country.

我们始终坚持互利共赢。共建"一带一路"倡议源于中国,但机遇和成果惠及各方,造福世界。我们通过政策沟通、设施联通、贸易畅通、资金融通和民心相通,推进经济大融合、发展大联动、成果大共享,让中国梦与世界各国梦想更好相连。

We are always committed to mutual benefit and win-win. The BRI came from China, but it creates opportunities and good results for all countries, and benefits the whole world. We have strengthened policy, infrastructure, trade, financial and people-to-people connectivity to pursue economic integration, achieve interconnected development, and deliver benefits to all. These efforts have brought closer the Chinese dream and the dreams of countries around the world.

我们始终坚持开放包容。"一带一路"是大家携手前进的阳光大道,没有小院高墙;容纳不同的制度和文明,没有意识形态偏见。对于国际上任何有利于加强互联互通、实现共同发展的合作倡议,我们都愿以开放态度,加强相互配合和相互促进。

We are always committed to openness and inclusiveness. The BRI is a public road open to all, and has no backyard or high walls. It is open to all kinds of systems and civilizations, and is not ideologically biased. We are open to all cooperation initiatives in the world that are conducive to closer connectivity and common development, and we are ready to work with them and help each other succeed.

我们始终坚持创新进取。面对疫情,我们打造"健康丝路";面对低碳转型,我们深耕"绿色丝路";面对数字化浪潮,我们搭建"数字丝路";面对发展鸿沟,我们建设"减贫之路"。"一带一路"始于经济合作,但不止于经济,正在日益成为完善全球治理的新平台。

We are always committed to innovation and progress. In the wake of COVID-19, we have launched the Silk Road of health. To achieve low-carbon transition, we are cultivating a green Silk Road. To harness the trend of digitalization, we are building a digital Silk Road. To address development gaps, we are working to build the BRI into a pathway to poverty alleviation. Belt and Road cooperation began in the economic sector, but it does not end there. It is becoming a new platform for better global governance.

各位同事,

Colleagues,

再过几天,中国共产党就将迎来百年华诞。在中国共产党领导下,中国人民即将全面建成小康社会,并乘势而上开启全面建设社会主义现代化国家新征程。在新的历史起点上,中国愿同各方携手努力,继续高质量共建"一带一路",打造更紧密的卫生合作伙伴关系、互联互通伙伴关系、绿色发展伙伴关系和开放包容伙伴关系,为各方提供更多机遇,分享更多红利。

In a few days, the Communist Party of China (CPC) will mark its centenary. Under the CPC leadership, the Chinese people will soon complete the building of a moderately prosperous society in all respects, and on that basis, embark on a new journey of fully building a

案例2.1 "一带一路"倡议推动构建人类命运共同体

modern socialist country. At a new historical starting point, China will work with all other parties to continue our high-quality Belt and Road cooperation and build closer partnerships for health cooperation, connectivity, green development, and openness and inclusiveness. These efforts will generate more opportunities and dividends to all.

第一,要继续深化疫苗国际合作。我们将共同发起"一带一路"疫苗合作伙伴关系倡议,促进疫苗在全球范围内公平分配,构筑全球防疫屏障。中方将积极落实习近平主席在全球健康峰会上宣布的重要举措,尽己所能向包括"一带一路"合作伙伴在内的国家提供更多亟需的疫苗等抗疫物资,支持本国疫苗企业向发展中国家转让技术、合作生产,支持新冠疫苗知识产权豁免,助力各国最终战胜疫情。

First, we need to continue to deepen international cooperation on vaccines. We will jointly launch the Initiative for Belt and Road Partnership on COVID-19 Vaccines Cooperation to promote fair international distribution of vaccines and build a global shield against the virus. China will actively implement the important measures announced by President Xi Jinping at the Global Health Summit. China will provide more vaccines and other urgently-needed medical supplies to BRI partners and other countries to the best of its ability, support its vaccine companies in transferring technologies to other developing countries and carrying out joint production with them, and support waiving intellectual property rights on COVID-19 vaccines, all in an effort to help all countries defeat COVID-19.

第二,要继续加强互联互通合作。我们将进一步对接各方基础设施发展规划,合作建设交通基础设施、经济走廊、经贸产业合作区。进一步发挥中欧班列作用,推动海上丝绸之路港航合作、空中丝绸之路建设。我们将抓住数字产业化和产业数字化发展潮流,加快建设数字丝绸之路,构建面向未来的智能化互联互通新格局。

Second, we need to continue to strengthen cooperation on connectivity. We will continue to synergize infrastructure development plans, and work together on transport infrastructure, economic corridors, and economic and trade and industrial cooperation zones. We will further harness the China-Europe Railway Express to promote port and shipping cooperation along the Maritime Silk Road and build a Silk Road in the Air. We will embrace the trend of digital transformation and development of digital industries by accelerating the building of the digital Silk Road, and make smart connectivity a new reality in the future.

第三,要继续推动绿色发展合作。我们将共同发起"一带一路"绿色发展伙伴关系倡议,为建设绿色丝绸之路提供新动力。同各方加强绿色基建、绿色能源、绿色金融等领域合作,高标准、高质量建设更多环境友好型项目。支持"一带一路"能源合作伙伴关系参与方进一步加强绿色能源合作,鼓励参与"一带一路"合作企业履行社会责任,践行环境、社会和治理(ESG)理念。

Third, we need to continue to promote cooperation on green development. We will jointly put forth the Initiative for Belt and Road Partnership on Green Development to inject new impetus into building the green Silk Road. We are ready to step up coopcration in such areas as grcen infrastructure, green energy and green finance, and develop more environment-friendly projects with a high standard and

案例 2.1 "一带一路"倡议推动构建人类命运共同体

high quality. We support parties to the Belt and Road Energy Partnership in enhancing cooperation on green energy. We encourage businesses involved in Belt and Road cooperation to fulfill their social responsibilities and improve their environmental, social and governance (ESG) performance.

第四,要继续推进区域及全球自由贸易。我们将推动区域全面经济伙伴关系协定(RCEP)早日生效,加快地区经济一体化进程,共同维护全球产业链和供应链的开放、安全和稳定。中国对外开放的大门将越开越大,愿与各方分享市场红利,实现国内循环与国际循环的相互促进,让"一带一路"合作伙伴的联系更加紧密、经济合作的空间更加宽广。

Fourth, we need to continue to advance free trade in our region and the world. China will work for the early entry-into-force of the Regional Comprehensive Economic Partnership (RCEP) and faster regional economic integration. China will work with all sides to keep global industrial and supply chains open, secure and stable. We will open our doors even wider to the world. And we are ready to share China's market dividends with all to make sure that domestic and international circulations will be mutually reinforcing. This will also enable closer ties and broader space for economic cooperation among BRI partners.

各位同事,

Colleagues,

亚太地区作为全球发展速度最快、潜力最大、合作最活跃的区域,拥有全球60%的人口和70%的GDP,为世界贡献了超过三分之二的

85

增长率,在全球抗疫和经济复苏进程中发挥着越来越重要的作用。亚太应当是发展合作的高地,而不是地缘政治的棋局,亚太稳定繁荣的大好局面值得地区国家共同珍惜。

The Asia-Pacific is the fastest-growing region with the greatest potential and most dynamic cooperation in the world. It is home to 60 percent of the world's population and 70 percent of its GDP. It has contributed over two-thirds of global growth, and is playing an increasingly important role in the global fight against COVID-19 and economic recovery. The Asia-Pacific region should be a pacesetter of development and cooperation, not a chessboard for geopolitics. The stability and prosperity of this region should be treasured by all regional countries.

亚洲和太平洋国家也是"一带一路"国际合作的先行者、贡献者、示范者。作为亚太地区一员,中方愿与亚太各国本着合作伙伴精神,推动"一带一路"高质量发展,为全球抗疫提供亚太方案,为全球互联互通注入亚太活力,为世界经济可持续复苏传递亚太信心,为构建亚太命运共同体和人类命运共同体做出更大贡献!谢谢!

Asian and Pacific countries are the pioneers, contributors and examples of Belt and Road international cooperation. As a member of the Asia-Pacific region, China is ready to work with Asia-Pacific countries in the spirit of partnership to promote high-quality Belt and Road development, provide Asia-Pacific solutions to the global fight against COVID-19, inject Asia-Pacific vitality into global connectivity, and transmit Asia-Pacific confidence to the sustainable recovery of the world economy, so as to make greater contributions to building a

案例 2.1 "一带一路"倡议推动构建人类命运共同体

community with a shared future in the Asia-Pacific region as well as a community with a shared future for mankind. Thank you!

共建"一带一路"顺应了人类追求美好未来的共同愿望。国际社会越来越认同共建"一带一路"倡议所主张的构建人类命运共同体的理念,构建人类命运共同体符合当代世界经济发展需要和人类文明进步的大方向。共建"一带一路"倡议正成为构建人类命运共同体的重要实践平台。

Jointly building the "Belt and Road" conforms to the common aspiration of mankind to pursue a better future. The idea of building a community with a shared future for mankind, as advocated by the BRI, is becoming increasingly popular in the international community, as it meets the needs of contemporary economic development of the world and the general development direction of human civilization. The BRI is becoming an important practical platform for building a community with a shared future for mankind.

点评
Comments

"一带一路"倡议为全球治理体系变革提供了中国方案。当今世界面临增长动能不足、治理体系滞后和发展失衡等挑战。共建"一带一路"体现开放包容、共同发展的鲜明导向,超越社会制度和文化差异,尊重文明多样性,坚持多元文化共存,强调不同经济发展水平国家的优势互补和互利共赢,着力改善发展条件、创造发展机会、增强发展动力、共享发展成果。

The BRI offers a Chinese solution for the reform of the global governance system. The world today is facing challenges such as insufficient growth momentum, lagging governance system and unbalanced development. Jointly building the "Belt and Road" shows the clear orientation of openness, tolerance and common development, goes beyond differences in social systems and cultures, respects the diversity of civilizations, adheres to the coexistence of diversified cultures, emphasizes complementing each other's advantages, mutual benefits and win-win results of countries at different economic development levels, and strives to improve development conditions, create development opportunities, enhance development momentum, and share development achievements.

"一带一路"倡议蕴含中华文化"协和万邦""和而不同"的世界观。人类只有一个地球,各国共处一个世界。为了应对人类共同面临的各种挑战,追求世界和平繁荣发展的美好未来,世界各国应风雨同舟,荣辱与共,构建持久和平、普遍安全、共同繁荣、开放包容、清洁美丽的世界。当代大学生应该在整体利益基础上思考问题,具备兼济天下、经世济民的大思想大格局。

The BRI contains the world view of "peace among all nations" and "harmony in diversity" in Chinese culture. As the Earth is the only home for mankind, where all countries should coexist. In order to meet the challenges faced by mankind and pursue a bright future featuring world peace, prosperity and development, all countries should stick together through thick and thin to build a world of lasting peace, universal security, common prosperity, openness, inclusive-

案例 2.1 "一带一路"倡议推动构建人类命运共同体

ness, cleanliness, and beauty. Contemporary college students should think about problems on the basis of overall interests, and boast a structure of thoughts of governing and benefiting the people to achieve common prosperity.

"一带一路"倡议体现"天下兴亡,匹夫有责"命运与共的责任意识。它融入了利益共生、情感共鸣、价值共识、责任共担、发展共赢等内涵。这不仅要求培养大学生具有公共意识、社会荣誉感,唤起大学生的社会责任感与使命担当,还致力于培养大学生具有世界胸襟情怀和参与全球治理的能力,进而推动人类命运共同体的构建。

The BRI embodies the sense of responsibility for a shared future when "everyone is responsible for the rise and fall of the world". It incorporates the connotations of interconnected interests, emotional resonance, common understanding of values, shared responsibility, and win-win development. Therefore, we should not only cultivate college students' sense of public awareness and social honor, and arouse their sense of social responsibility and mission, but also foster their ability to possess a global mindset and participate in global governance, thus promoting the construction of a community of shared future for mankind.

讨论题
Discussions

(1)区域性贸易联盟有哪些? 它们有何作用?

What are the regional trade associations? What roles do they play?

(2)什么是"一带一路"倡议？它对促进全球发展有何积极作用？

What is the Belt and Road Initiative? What positive roles does it play in promoting global development?

(3)如何评价中国政府在抗击新冠疫情方面的治理水平,以及对国际社会的贡献？

How to evaluate the governance level of Chinese government in fighting against COVID-19 and its contribution to the international community?

资料来源

孙少雄,顾煜.示范工程迈入新阶段[EB/OL].[2023-03-22].https://www.yidaiyilu.gov.cn/xwzx/hwxw/305933.htm.

王毅国务委员兼外长在"一带一路"亚太区域国际合作高级别会议上的主旨发言(双语全文)[EB/OL].[2023-03-22].https://language.chinadaily.com.cn/a/202106/24/WS60d3f762a31024ad0bacb3ed.html.

《共建"一带一路"倡议:进展、贡献与展望》(八语种)[R/OL].[2023-03-22].https://www.yidaiyilu.gov.cn/zchj/qwfb/86697.htm.

辛智广,辛熙恒.人类命运共同体理论融入高校思想政治教育的意义及路径[J].中国多媒体与网络教学学报,2020(04):50-51.

References

Sun Shaoxiong, Gu Yu. A demonstration project steps into a new stage[EB/OL]. [2023-03-22]. https://www.yidaiyilu.gov.cn/xwzx/hwxw/305933.htm.

Keynote speech made by Wang Yi, State Councilor and Foreign Minister, at the "Belt and Road" high-level conference on international cooperation in the Asia-Pacific region[EB/OL]. [2023-03-22]. https://language.chinadaily.com.cn/a/202106/24/WS60d3f762a31024ad0bacb3ed.html.

案例 2.1 "一带一路"倡议推动构建人类命运共同体

The "Belt and Road" Initiative:Progress,Contributions and Prospect(in eight languages)[R/OL].[2023—03—22]. https://www.yidaiyilu.gov.cn/zchj/qwfb/86697.htm.

Xin Zhiguang,Xin Xiheng. The significance and path of integrating the theory of a community with a shared future for mankind into the ideological and political education of colleges and universities[J]. China Journal of Multimedia & Network Teaching,2020(04):50—51.

案例 2.2 国家电网:"碳达峰""碳中和"行动派的国企担当
Case 2.2 State Grid: A State-Owned Enterprise Undertaking the Responsibilities for Practicing "Peak Carbon Dioxide Emissions and Carbon Neutrality"

教学目标
Teaching Objectives

2020年中国在联合国大会上提出了"2030年前达到碳峰值、2060年前实现碳中和"的目标。这表明中国将在推动高质量发展中促进经济社会发展全面绿色转型,为全球应对气候变化做出更大贡献的坚定决心。2021年3月1日,国家电网发布"碳达峰""碳中和"行动方案,提出了能源电力落实"碳达峰""碳中和"的实施路径。作为关系国家能源安全和国民经济命脉的特大型国有重点骨干企业积极作为勇于担当,自觉肩负起推动能源转型和绿色发展的历史使命,推动构建清

案例2.2 国家电网:"碳达峰""碳中和"行动派的国企担当

洁低碳、安全高效能源体系,推进"双碳"目标的实现。本节通过案例分析,帮助学生更好地理解企业社会责任的含义,并区别社会义务、社会应对和社会责任的不同层次,以及探讨国有企业在履行社会责任方面发挥的重要作用。

In 2020, China put forward the goal of "achieving peak carbon emissions by 2030 and carbon neutrality by 2060" at the UN General Assembly. This shows China's firm determination to promote a comprehensive green transformation of economic and social development and make greater contributions to the global response to climate change while promoting high-quality development. On March 1, 2021, State Grid released the action plan for "peak carbon dioxide emissions and carbon neutrality", and put forward their implementation roadmap in energy and power. As a super-large state-owned key enterprise related to national energy security and the lifeline of national economy, it actively takes responsibility, consciously shoulders the historical mission of promoting energy transformation and green development to facilitate the construction of a clean, low-carbon, safe and efficient energy system, and continuously contributes to the goals of "peak carbon dioxide emissions and carbon neutrality". Through case analysis, this section aims to help students better understand the meaning of corporate social responsibility, and differentiate between social obligation, social response and social responsibility, and explore the important role of state-owned enterprises in fulfilling social responsibility.

案例涉及管理学原理中企业社会责任、绿色管理、可持续发展、企业类型等相关知识点。

The case involves corporate social responsibility, green management, sustainable development, type of business, and other related concepts in Principles of Management.

案例内容
Contents

2020年9月22日，中国国家主席习近平在第七十五届联合国大会上宣布，中国力争2030年前二氧化碳排放达到峰值，努力争取2060年前实现"碳中和"目标，简称"双碳"目标。中国将在推动高质量发展中促进经济社会发展全面绿色转型，为全球应对气候变化做出更大贡献。国家对于"碳中和"目标明确而坚定，如何绘制"碳达峰""碳中和"行动路线成为务实行动派、先行者的使命，国家电网有限公司（简称"国家电网"）率先就这一问题给出答案。

On September 22, 2020, Chinese President Xi Jinping announced at the 75th UN General Assembly that China would strive to achieve peak carbon dioxide emissions by 2030 and carbon neutrality by 2060, hereinafter referred to as the "dual carbon" goals. China will push forward a comprehensive green transformation of economic and social development while promoting high-quality development, making greater contributions to the global response to climate change. China has a clear and firm goal of "carbon neutrality". The State Grid Corporation of China (hereinafter referred to as "State Grid") takes the lead in giving a solution on how to draw the action roadmap of "peak carbon

案例 2.2　国家电网:"碳达峰""碳中和"行动派的国企担当

dioxide emissions and carbon neutrality" and become a pragmatic activist and pioneer.

2021年3月1日,国家电网发布"碳达峰""碳中和"行动方案,提出了能源电力落实"碳达峰""碳中和"的实施路径,发挥电网"桥梁""纽带"作用,推动能源电力行业尽早以较低峰值达峰,当好"引领者";加强技术、机制和模式创新,引导绿色低碳生产生活方式,推动全社会尽快实现"碳中和",当好"推动者";系统梳理输配电各环节、生产办公全领域减排清单,深入挖掘减排潜力,实现企业碳排放率先达峰,当好"先行者"。

On March 1, 2021, State Grid issued the action plan for "peak carbon dioxide emissions and carbon neutrality", which proposed their implementation roadmap for energy and power, so as to play the roles of "bridge" and "link" of the power grid. As a good "leader", it will promote the energy and power sector to reach its peak at a lower level as soon as possible. As a good "promoter", it will strengthen innovation in technology, mechanism and mode, provide guidance on green and low-carbon production and lifestyle, and promote the entire society to achieve "carbon neutrality" as early as possible. As a good "pioneer", it will systematically sort out the list of emission reduction in all aspects of power transmission and distribution, production and office, and deeply tap the potential of emission reduction to realize the peak carbon emissions among enterprises in the industry.

业内人士分析,国家电网发布的"碳达峰""碳中和"行动方案之所以引人关注,是因为电网是衔接能源供给侧和需求侧的关键环节,国家电网"碳达峰""碳中和"行动方案解决了新能源供需难题,做好了能源供给侧和需求侧的有效衔接。

According to industry insiders, the action plan for "peak carbon dioxide emissions and carbon neutrality" issued by State Grid attracts people's attention as the power grid is a key link connecting the energy supply side and the demand side. It solves the problem of new energy supply and demand, and effectively connects the energy supply side and the demand side.

国家电网有限公司成立于2002年12月29日,以投资建设运营电网为核心业务,是关系国家能源安全和国民经济命脉的特大型国有重点骨干企业。20多年来,国家电网持续创造全球特大型电网安全纪录,建成多项特高压输电工程,成为世界上输电能力最强、新能源并网规模最大的电网之一,专利拥有量连续10年位列央企前列(如图2—2所示)。

The State Grid Corporation of China was established on December 29, 2002. Its core business is investing in constructing and operating the power grid. It is a super-large state-owned key enterprise related to the national energy security and the lifeline of the national economy. For more than 20 years, State Grid has been a safety record breaker for a global super-large power grid. With a number of extra-high voltage transmission projects built, it is one of the power grids with the strongest transmission capacity and the largest scale of new energy grid connection in the world. The number of its patents has been among the top central enterprises for 10 consecutive years (as shown in Figure 2—2).

案例2.2 国家电网:"碳达峰""碳中和"行动派的国企担当

图片来源:https://www.sohu.com/a/463470053_1206895341,2023—02—28。

Source:https://www.sohu.com/a/463470053_1206895341,2023—02—28.

**图 2—2　国网检修人员在世界最高电压等级
±1100 千伏吉泉线上实施直升机吊篮法带电作业**

Figure 2—2　Maintenance personnel of the State Grid carry out live work using the helicopter basket on the Jiquan line of ±1100 kV, the highest voltage level in the world

一、行动派:发布"碳达峰、碳中和"行动方案

Ⅰ. Activist:Release the action plan for "peak carbon dioxide emissions and carbon neutrality"

数据显示,截至2021年3月,中国国内的碳排放85.5%来源于能源活动,15.4%来源于工业过程,剩下一小部分来源于农业等。其中,在能源活动中,非化石能源碳排放比重达到15.3%。实现"碳中和"将深刻改变国内目前的能源结构、工业生产和消费方式。要实现低碳减排,能源行业的绿色转型是关键。关键性挑战包括:为实现低碳新能

源大规模并网,交流网架薄弱;新能源出力造成电力流变化频繁,电网运行和调度难度大;电、热、煤、油、汽等综合能源运行相对独立,协同规划与运行能力不足;等等。

According to relevant data, as of March 2021, 85.5% of China's domestic carbon emissions come from energy activities, 15.4% from industrial processes, and a small portion from agriculture. Among them, the proportion of non-fossil energy carbon emissions in energy activities reached 15.3%. Achieving "carbon neutrality" will profoundly change the current energy structure, industrial production and consumption patterns in China. The green transformation of the energy industry plays a vital role in achieving low carbon and emission reduction. The key challenges are as follows. First, the AC grid is weak for large-scale grid connection of low-carbon new energy. Second, the output of new energy causes frequent changes in power flow, which makes it difficult for the operation and dispatch of the power grid. Third, electricity, heat, coal, oil, steam and other energy sources are operated independently to some extent, and there is insufficient ability in collaborative planning and operation, and so forth.

所谓"碳达峰"指温室气体排放总量要在2030年前达到顶点,此后便要开始下降;"碳中和"指温室气体净排放为零,即通过植树造林和碳捕捉等方式抵消全部的温室气体排放。"碳达峰"是基础前提,要尽早实现能源消费,尤其是化石能源消费达峰;"碳中和"是最终目标,要加快清洁能源替代化石能源的步伐,通过碳捕捉、利用和封存技术,实现碳排放和碳吸收的平衡。

The so-called "peak carbon dioxide emissions" mean that the to-

案例 2.2　国家电网："碳达峰""碳中和"行动派的国企担当

tal amount of greenhouse gas emissions will reach its peak before 2030, and then decline. The "carbon neutrality" refers to that the net greenhouse gas emissions are zero, namely all greenhouse gas emissions are offset by afforestation and carbon capture. The "peak carbon dioxide emissions" are the fundamental premise, so it is necessary to realize the peak carbon dioxide emissions of energy consumption as soon as possible, especially fossil energy consumption. The "carbon neutrality" is the ultimate goal. We should accelerate the pace of replacing fossil energy with clean energy, and balance carbon emissions with carbon absorption through carbon capture, utilization and storage technologies.

国家电网发布的"碳达峰""碳中和"行动方案提出通过供给侧结构调整和需求侧响应"双侧"发力，解决"双高""双峰"问题，推动能源清洁低碳安全高效利用。实现"双碳"目标，关键在于推动能源清洁低碳安全高效利用，在能源供给侧构建多元化清洁能源供应体系，在能源消费侧全面推进电气化和节能提效。在能源供给侧，坚持和完善能源双控制度，合理控制能源消费总量，严格控制能耗强度，重点控制化石能源消费；在能源消费侧，大力推进终端用能电气化，将电气化纳入行业规划、城市发展规划和生态环保考核指标体系，提高各领域电气化普及率。

The action plan for "peak carbon dioxide emissions and carbon neutrality" issued by State Grid proposes to solve the problems of "a high proportion of renewable energy and a high proportion of power and electronic equipment" and "peak loads of power supply in summer and winter" by adjusting the supply side structure and responding to the demand side, so as to promote the clean, low-carbon, safe and efficient use of energy. To achieve the "dual carbon" goals, the solution lies in promoting clean, low-carbon, safe and efficient use of energy, building a diversified clean energy supply system on the energy supply side, and comprehensively promoting electrification, energy saving and efficiency improvement on the energy consumption side. On the energy supply side, it is proposed to adhere to and improve the dual control of energy, namely reasonably control the total energy consumption, and strictly control the intensity of energy consumption, focusing on fossil energy consumption. On the energy consumption side, it is proposed to improve the electrification penetration rate in various fields by vigorously promoting the electrification of energy for the users, and incorporating electrification into industry planning, urban development planning and eco-environmental assessment indicator system.

2021年4月的浙江湖州，春意正浓，长湖申航道两岸繁花似锦。这条开凿于西晋的古航道历经1 700多年沧桑后依旧繁忙，年货运量超亿吨。"如果长湖申堵航，上海的建筑材料就会涨价!"57岁的船民陆先生已在这条航道上忙碌了20年。船一靠岸，老陆熟练地用手机扫码、拉线，"浙湖州货2719"号便连接岸上充电桩，通了电。"跑了20年船，如今终于能在船上睡安稳觉了!"老陆说。狭窄的船舱一到夏天常常闷热难熬，有了岸电后，夜里开着空调睡觉，没了过去柴油发电机的轰鸣噪音和呛人油烟，让他感到格外幸福。"柴油发电一天要烧100多元钱，现在只要十几元!"让老陆津津乐道的岸电是电力系统电能替代的重要项目，而电能替代是实现"碳达峰""碳中和"目标的重要手

案例2.2 国家电网:"碳达峰""碳中和"行动派的国企担当

段。在湖州,这种岸电桩已设置381套,每年可减少燃油消耗136吨,减排二氧化碳428吨。

In Huzhou, Zhejiang Province in April 2021, while the spring was at its fullness, flowers were in full bloom on both banks of Changxing-Huzhou-Shanghai Channel. This ancient waterway dating back to the Western Jin Dynasty was still busy after 1,700 years of vicissitudes, with an annual freight volume of over 100 million tons. "If the channel is blocked, the prices of building materials in Shanghai will rise!" Mr. Lu, a 57-year-old boatman, has been busy on this channel for 20 years. As soon as the ship docked, Lu skillfully scanned the code with his mobile phone and pulled the wire. Then the "Zhehuzhouhuo No. 2719" was connected to the charging pile on the shore for charging. "After engaging in this business for 20 years, I can finally have a sound sleep onboard!" Lu said. The narrow cabin used to be hot and suffocating in summer. With onshore power, now he is able to sleep with the air conditioner on at night, free from the roaring noise and choking fumes of diesel generators in the past. These all make him particularly happy. "Diesel power generation costs more than 100 yuan a day, but now a dozen yuan is enough!" Onshore power, which Lu talked about great relish, is significant in power system for electric energy replacement, an important means to achieve the goals of "peak carbon dioxide emissions and carbon neutrality". In Huzhou, 381 such onshore charging piles have been installed, which can reduce fuel consumption by 136 tons and carbon dioxide emissions by 428 tons every year.

二、弯道超车：抢占世界制高点

II. Overtake around the corner: Seizing the commanding heights of the world

国家电网分析，很多发达经济体碳排放已经达峰，从"碳达峰"到"碳中和"有50~70年的过渡期，中国碳排放量占全球的30%左右，不仅总量超过美国、欧盟、日本的总和，而且从"碳达峰"到"碳中和"仅有30年时间；其次，欧美主要国家已完成工业化，经济增长与碳排放脱钩，中国尚处于工业化阶段，能源电力需求还将持续攀升，经济发展与碳排放仍存在强耦合关系。如何既保持经济持续稳定增长又实现减排，是一道高难度竞赛题。

According to the analysis of State Grid, the carbon emissions of many developed economies have reached the peak, and it takes 50~70 years from peak carbon dioxide emissions to carbon neutrality. China's carbon emissions account for about 30% of the global total, which exceeds the sum of the US, the European Union and Japan, meanwhile only 30 years is left for China's transition from peak carbon dioxide emissions to carbon neutrality. Moreover, major western economies have completed industrialization, whose economic growth has been decoupled from carbon emissions. However, China is still in the stage of industrialization, which means its demand for energy and electricity will continue to rise. There is still a strong coupling relationship between economic development and carbon emissions. So how to maintain sustained and stable economic growth while achieving emission reduction is a huge challenge facing China.

案例 2.2　国家电网:"碳达峰""碳中和"行动派的国企担当

2021年的《政府工作报告》明确提出,扎实做好"碳达峰""碳中和"各项工作,制定2030年前碳排放达峰行动方案。中央经济工作会议此前也对做好2021年"碳达峰""碳中和"工作做出明确部署,强调要加快调整优化产业结构、能源结构,推动煤炭消费尽早达峰,大力发展新能源,继续打好污染防治攻坚战,实现减污降碳协同效应。

The Government Work Report in 2021 clearly stated that we should steadily advance peak carbon dioxide emissions and carbon neutrality and develop an action plan for the peak carbon emissions before 2030. Earlier, the Central Economic Work Conference also made clear arrangements for peak carbon dioxide emissions and carbon neutrality in 2021, emphasizing that China will accelerate the adjustment and optimization of industrial structure and energy structure to promote the peak coal consumption as soon as possible, vigorously develop new energy, and continue to fight the tough battle of pollution prevention and control to realize the synergistic effect of pollution reduction and carbon reduction.

这对国家电网而言是一个巨大的挑战,也是一个巨大的机会。国家电网勾勒出了能源产业升级的路线图和时间表。包括把电网进一步向能源互联网提升,做好绿色能源并网工作;同时,在终端消费方面大力提升电气化方向,加大科技创新能力等。

This is a huge challenge and great opportunity for State Grid. State Grid has outlined the road map and timetable for upgrading the energy industry, including further upgrading the power grid to the Energy Internet and promoting green energy connection to the grid. Meanwhile, in terms of end-user consumption, we will vigorously push forward electrification and improve our ability in scientific and technological innovation.

国家电网发布的"碳达峰""碳中和"行动方案提出了具体应对方案。方案包括：推动电网向能源互联网升级，着力打造清洁能源优化配置平台；推动网源协调发展和调度交易机制优化，着力做好清洁能源并网消纳；推动全社会节能提效，着力提高终端消费电气化水平；推动公司节能减排加快实施，着力降低自身碳排放水平；推动能源电力技术创新，着力提升运行安全和效率水平；推动深化国际交流合作，着力集聚能源绿色转型最大合力。

The action plan for "peak carbon dioxide emissions and carbon neutrality" issued by State Grid provides specific solutions, including promoting the upgrading of power grid to Energy Internet, and making efforts to build a platform for optimal allocation of clean energy; advancing the coordinated development of grid and power sources and the optimization of dispatching and trading mechanism, and striving to achieve grid connection and consumption of clean energy; promoting the whole society to save energy and improve efficiency, and working hard to improve the electrification level of end-user consumption; pushing forward State Grid to accelerate the implementation of energy conservation and emission reduction, and striving to reduce its own carbon emissions; advancing technological innovation in energy and power, and making efforts to improve the level of operational safety and efficiency; promoting in-depth international exchanges and cooperation, and trying best to pool the greatest joint efforts for green transformation of energy.

案例2.2 国家电网:"碳达峰""碳中和"行动派的国企担当

三、尽责担当:推进实现"双碳"目标
Ⅲ. Fulfill responsibilities:Promoting the "dual carbon" goals

近年来,国家电网认真贯彻"四个革命、一个合作"能源安全新战略(即推动能源消费革命、能源供给革命、能源技术革命、能源体制革命,全方位加强能源国际合作),把推进能源转型作为根本任务,全面推动电网向能源互联网升级,有力支撑了绿色低碳发展。截至2020年年底,公司经营区清洁能源发电装机7.1亿千瓦、占比42%,其中新能源发电装机4.5亿千瓦、占比26%,比2015年提高14个百分点。

In recent years, State Grid has conscientiously implemented the new energy security strategy of "Four Revolutions and One Cooperation" (namely promoting energy consumption revolution, energy supply revolution, energy technology revolution and energy system revolution to strengthen all-round international cooperation). It takes promoting energy transformation as the fundamental task and comprehensively promotes the upgrading of power grid to Energy Internet, providing a strong support for green and low-carbon development. By the end of 2020, the installed capacity of clean energy power generation in its operating area reached up to 710 million kWh, accounting for 42%, including 450 million kWh for new energy power generation, which accounted for 26%, a 14% increase compared to that in 2015.

在能源生产环节,国家电网服务于新能源等清洁能源的大规模开发利用。近10年,中国风电、太阳能发电等新能源发电装机年均增长33.6%,发电量年均增长34.8%,均比全球平均水平高13个百分点以

105

上;2020年,中国煤电装机容量占总装机容量比重为49.1%,历史性降至50%以下。在能源消费环节,国家电网促进电能占终端能源消费比重不断提升。2000—2019年,全球电能占终端能源消费比重从15.4%增至19.6%;中国从10.9%增至26%,提高约15个百分点。

For energy production, State Grid offers services for the large-scale development and utilization of clean energy sources such as new energy. Over the past decade, the installed capacity of new energy power generation such as wind power and solar power generation in China has increased by 33.6% annually, and the generating capacity has grown by 34.8% annually, both of which are more than 13% higher than the global average. In 2020, the installed capacity of coal-fired power in China accounted for 49.1% of the total, below 50% for the first time in history. In terms of energy consumption, State Grid promotes a higher proportion of electric energy in end-use energy consumption. From 2000 to 2019, the proportion of electric energy in end-use energy consumption increased from 15.4% to 19.6% globally. In China, it increased from 10.9% to 26%, up about 15%.

作为全球最大的公用事业企业和国有能源骨干企业之一,国家电网的经营区域覆盖中国26个省(自治区、直辖市),供电范围占国土面积的88%,供电人口超过11亿。投资运营菲律宾、巴西、葡萄牙、澳大利亚、意大利、希腊、阿曼、智利和中国香港9个国家和地区的骨干能源网,连续16年获得国务院国资委业绩考核A级,连续8年获得标准普尔、穆迪、惠誉三大国际评级机构国家主权级信用评级。

As the world's largest enterprise engaging in public utilities and one of the state-Owned backbone energy enterprises, the operating ar-

案例2.2　国家电网:"碳达峰""碳中和"行动派的国企担当

ea of State Grid covers 26 provinces (autonomous regions and municipalities directly under the Central Government) in China, supplying power for 88% of the China's land area with a population of over 1.1 billion. It has invested in and is operating the backbone energy networks in 9 countries and regions, including the Philippines, Brazil, Portugal, Australia, Italy, Greece, Oman, Chile and China HongKong. It won the A-level in the performance appraisal of the State-Owned Assets Supervision and Administration Commission of the State Council for 16 consecutive years, and the sovereign credit ratings of three international rating agencies, including Standard & Poor's, Moody's and Fitch, for 8 years in a row.

气候变化关乎人民福祉和人类未来,应对气候变化需要雄心和决心。中国作为地球村的一员,正在以实际行动为全球应对气候变化做出应有贡献。

Climate change is related to people's well-being and the future of mankind, and it needs ambition and determination to deal with climate change. As a member of the global village, China is making its due contributions to the global response to climate change through practical actions.

点评
Comments

"双碳"目标的提出是中国主动承担应对全球气候变化责任的大国担当。1992年,中国成为最早签署《联合国气候变化框架公约》的缔约方之一。之后,中国不仅成立了国家气候变化对策协调机构,而且根据国家可持续发展战略的要求,采取了一系列与应对气候变化相关的政策措施,为减缓和适应气候变化做出了积极贡献。在应对气候变化问题上,中国坚持共同但有区别的责任原则、公平原则和各自能力原则。"双碳"目标是中国基于推动构建人类命运共同体的责任担当和实现可持续发展的内在要求而做出的重大战略决策,展示了中国为应对全球气候变化做出的新努力和新贡献,向全世界展示了应对气候变化的大国担当。

The "dual carbon" goals show that China, as a major power in the world, takes the initiative to hold responsibility for global climate change. In 1992, China became one of the first signatories to the United Nations Framework Convention on Climate Change. Since then, China has not only established a national coordinating body for climate change countermeasures, but also introduced a series of policies and measures related to climate change according to the requirements of the national sustainable development strategy, making positive contributions to mitigating and adapting to climate change. In dealing with climate change, China adheres to the principles of common but differentiated responsibilities, fairness and respective capabilities. The "dual carbon" goals are a significant strategic decision made by China based on the responsibility of promoting the construction of a community of shared future for mankind and the inherent requirement of realizing sustainable development. It shows China's new efforts and contributions and its sense of responsibility as a major power for addressing global climate change.

案例 2.2　国家电网:"碳达峰""碳中和"行动派的国企担当

从义务到响应到责任,国家电网有限公司成为履行企业社会责任的标杆。一家具有社会责任感的企业不仅需要承担法律义务,或应对流行的社会需求,还应竭尽所能致力于改善社会,因为这是应该去做的正确的事情。社会责任指一个组织在其法律和经济义务之外愿意做正确的事情并以有益于社会的方式行事的意向。国家电网是中国首家发布企业履行社会责任指南的企业。在"双碳"目标指引下,国家电网自觉肩负起推动能源转型和绿色发展的历史使命,推动构建清洁低碳、安全高效能源体系,成为践行企业社会责任的先锋。

From obligation to response to responsibility, the State Grid Corporation of China has become the benchmark for fulfilling corporate social responsibility. An enterprise with a sense of social responsibility should not only undertake legal obligations or respond to popular social needs, but also make every effort to improve the society as a whole. This is the right thing to do. Social responsibility refers to the intention of an organization to do the right thing and act in a way beneficial to society beyond its legal and economic obligations. State Grid is the first enterprise in China to issue a guide on corporate social responsibility. Under the guidance of the "dual carbon" goals, State Grid, acting as a pioneer in practicing corporate social responsibility, consciously shoulders the historical mission of promoting energy transformation and green development, and advances the construction of a clean, low-carbon, safe and efficient energy system.

讨论题
Discussions

(1)什么是"双碳"目标？它是在什么背景下提出的？

What are the "dual carbon" goals? In what context was it put forward?

(2)要实现"双碳"目标,中国能源企业面临的最大障碍是什么？

What is the biggest obstacle for China's energy enterprises to achieve the "dual carbon" goals?

(3)国有企业履行社会责任的作用有哪些？

What are the roles of state-Owned enterprises in fulfilling their social responsibilities?

资料来源

北方.国家电网:"碳达峰、碳中和"行动派的国企担当[EB/OL].[2023-02-28].http://www.eeo.com.cn/2021/0308/475235.shtml.

冉永平,赵秀芹,丁怡婷.国家电网的"双碳"行动(深度观察)[EB/OL].[2023-02-28].http://finance.people.com.cn/n1/2021/0428/c1004-32090097.htm.

高世楫,俞敏.中国提出"双碳"目标的历史背景、重大意义和变革路径[J].新经济导刊,2021(2):4-8.

References

Zhi Shi. State Grid: A state-Owned enterprise moving towards the goals of "peak carbon dioxide emissions and carbon neutrality" activists[EB/OL].[2023-02-28].http://www.eeo.com.cn/2021/0308/475235.shtml.

Ran Yongping, Zhao Xiuqin, Ding Yiting. The "dual carbon" action of State Grid (in-

案例 2.2　国家电网:"碳达峰""碳中和"行动派的国企担当

depth observation)[EB/OL].[2023-02-28]. http://finance.people.com.cn/n1/2021/0428/c1004-32090097.html.

Gao Shiji, Yu Min. The historical background, significance and transformation path of proposing the "dual carbon" goals by China[J]. New Economy Weekly, 20211(02):4-8.

案例2.3 文化的力量:百度人工智能革命透视
Case 2.3 The Power of Culture: Insights into Baidu's AI Revolution

教学目标
Teaching Objectives

百度是全球最大的中文搜索引擎,致力于向人们提供"简单可靠"的信息获取方式。由于人工智能转型推动百度的强劲增长,百度再次成为人们关注的焦点。而促使百度转型成功的内在原因包括对核心价值的承诺和组织适应能力的提高。本节通过案例分析,帮助学生理解组织文化的内容和重要性,了解组织文化的来源,以及如何通过组织变革、绩效考核、员工甄选与培养等制度和机制使组织文化得以延续与强化。同时,要求学生解读和评价代表性中国企业精神内核:使命驱动、诚信可靠、平等开放等,以及探讨中国传统文化与现代企业运作机制的有机融合。

As the largest Chinese search engine in the world, Baidu is dedi-

案例 2.3 文化的力量：百度人工智能革命透视

cated to providing people with "simple and reliable" ways to access information. With the strong growth driven by AI transformation, Baidu once again becomes the focus of attention. The internal reasons for the success of Baidu's transformation include its commitment to core values and the improvement of its organizational adaptability. Through case analysis, this section helps students understand the content and importance of organizational culture, the source of organizational culture, and how to continuously develop and strengthen organizational culture through organizational reform, performance appraisal, employee selection and training. Meanwhile, students are required to interpret and evaluate the spiritual implications of representative Chinese enterprises: mission-driven, honest and reliable, and equal and open, and to explore the organic integration of Chinese traditional culture with the modern enterprise operation mechanism.

案例涉及管理学原理中组织文化、职场精神、组织变革、绩效考核、员工招募等相关知识点。

The case involves organizational culture, professionalism, organizational reform, performance appraisal, recruitment and other related concepts in Principles of Management.

案例内容
Contents

2023年1月10日，百度 Create AI 开发者大会上，百度创始人、董事长兼首席执行官（CEO）李彦宏做出判断：随着技术应用门槛不断降低，创造者们将迎来属于人工智能的黄金 10 年（如图 2—3 所示）。由于人工智能转型推动百度的强劲增长，百度再次成为人们关注的焦点。如何摆脱我们的习惯性思维，点燃冲破界限的野心之火？

On January 10, 2023, at the Baidu Create AI for developers, Robin Li, founder, Chairman and CEO of Baidu, made a judgment that creators will usher in the golden 10 years of AI with the continuous lowering of the technology application threshold(as shown in Figure 2—3). The AI transformation which promotes the strong growth of Baidu, makes it once again the focus of attention. How to get rid of our habitual thinking and ignite the fire of our ambition that breaks through the boundaries?

图片来源：https://www.chinadaily.com.cn/a/202106/16/WS60c9a038a31024ad0bac97b2.html, 2023—02—25。

Source: https://www.chinadaily.com.cn/a/202106/16/WS60c9a038a31024ad0bac97b2.html, 2023—02—25.

图 2—3　在浙江温州博览会上孩子们正在与百度机器人互动
Figure 2—3　Children interact with the Baidu robot at the expo in Wenzhou, Zhejiang

案例 2.3 文化的力量:百度人工智能革命透视

故事必须从百度高管崔姗姗的回归说起,她在 2010 年 7 月离开百度照顾孩子,然后在 2017 年 12 月重新加入百度,在组织文化委员会任职。时隔 7 年,崔姗姗终于完成了一部 47 万字的长篇小说,讲述了西汉时期杰出的军事将领霍去病击败匈奴的英雄生平,对霍去病使命驱动的人格精神给予了高度认可,这也是她在百度不遗余力拓展的特质。

The story has to start from the return of Cui Shanshan, who left Baidu in July 2010 to look after her children and then rejoined the company in December 2017, serving in the Organizational Culture Committee. During the seven-year gap, Cui managed to finish a long novel of 470,000 words on Huo Qubing, a distinguished military general in the Western Han dynasty, giving high recognition to the general's attribute of being mission-driven, a trait that she goes great lengths to expand at Baidu.

崔姗姗经历了公司的早期发展阶段,帮助塑造了工程师文化。[①] 崔姗姗说,她是在响应内心的召唤,再次为百度工作,就和武将打败匈奴的决心一样。最重要的是,她传播了公司的核心价值:简单可靠。崔姗姗负责监管员工文化和组织效能,推出了一系列措施,以落实"简单可靠"的内涵,以及如何确保高标准的职业道德和进取精神。对她而言,这些努力并没有以任何新的方式改变百度,而是回到了巨人诞生时的最初愿景。崔姗姗全力以赴,从组织的角度审视百度的成长,

---

① 百度工程师文化的主要特征就是"用科技让复杂世界更简单",致力于为用户提供"简单可靠"的互联网搜索产品及服务,这也是它的使命。

Baidu's engineering culture is mainly characterized by "making the complex world simpler with technology", with a mission to provide users with "simple and reliable" Internet search products and services.

确保百度以最小的偏差走上正确的轨道。

Cui went through the company's early development stages and helped shape the engineers' culture. Cui said she was really answering the call of her heart to work for Baidu again, just like the military general's determination to defeat the Xiongnu nomadic tribe confederation. Most importantly, she truly shared the company's core value: Simple and Reliable. In her capacity, Cui has overseen employee culture and organizational effectiveness, launched a series of measures to bring to life what it means to be "Simple and Reliable" as well as how to ensure a high-standard work ethic and keep the enterprising spirit alive. These efforts, for her, were not changing Baidu in any new way, but going back to the original aspiration at the giant's birth. Cui has gone all out to scrutinize Baidu's growth from the organizational perspective and ensure it's on the right track with the least possible deviation.

一、改变想法或工作

Ⅰ. Change idea or job

回顾过去，百度为适应和创新而革新公司文化的努力源于移动互联网时代的严峻挑战，和微软或许有很多相似之处。这两家公司在个人电脑市场领域都是强有力的领导者，但它们行动缓慢，在移动互联网崛起时错失了市场机遇。在移动时代，百度作为核心信息中心的地位已经下降。

In retrospect, Baidu's efforts to renovate the company culture in order to be more adaptive and innovative originated from critical chal-

案例2.3 文化的力量：百度人工智能革命透视

lenges in the mobile Internet era, to which perhaps Microsoft has more similarities. Both companies were mighty leaders in the supremacy of the PC but they moved slowly and missed market opportunities when the mobile Internet rose. Baidu's position as a core information hub has declined in the mobile era.

在PC时代，搜索引擎的确是一种非常好的商业模式，但它非常简单，价值链相对较短：人们把关键字放在搜索框里，在互联网上免费查找信息，百度在这个过程中主要是作为一个连接器，带动相关网站的流量。在移动时代，网页上的信息越来越少，而更多的是由应用程序创建和存储的，因此百度连接网络信息的角色变得越来越弱化。

It's true that the search engine was a very good business model in the PC era, but it was very simple and had a relatively short value chain. People put keywords in the search box to find information free on the Internet as Baidu works mainly as a connector in the process, driving traffic to relevant websites. In the mobile era, information is less on the webpages and more created and stored by apps, so Baidu's role to connect web information became increasingly a mission impossible.

"遗憾的是，当时百度的搜索引擎服务业务表现不错。所以人们没有意识到（移动互联网兴起带来的）风险，认为一切都很好。"崔姗姗说。

"Unfortunately, at that time, Baidu's search engine service had a good business performance. So people were not aware of the risks (from the rise of mobile Internet) and thought everything was just fine," said Cui.

移动时代的商业模式相当复杂，价值链也更为复杂，这要求一家公司拥有相匹配的管理风格和组织能力。但崔姗姗表示,百度当时毫无准备,因为它的商业模式被设定为服务于较短的价值链。

Business models in the mobile era are rather sophisticated and have a more complex value chain, which naturally requires a company to have a proportionate management style and organizational capabilities. But Baidu was then unprepared since its business model was set to serve a short value chain, according to Cui.

当时的障碍还包括无效的组织结构,未能集中百度的优势。该公司有一名副总裁负责基本的搜索引擎服务,一名经理负责百度应用,一名副总裁负责迷你程序,一名副总裁负责业务和销售,一名技术负责人。这种松散的结构使其无法满足长价值链的要求。面对这样的挑战,公司不得不开始大规模重组。

At that time barriers also included an ineffective organizational structure that failed to pool Baidu's strengths together. The company had a VP responsible for the basic search engine service, a manager in charge of the Baidu app, another to lead mini-programs, another VP for business and sales, and different person for technology. This loose structure made it impossible to cope with the requirements of a long value chain. Facing such challenges, operationally and in organization, the company had to start a massive restructuring.

二、从意识到行动

Ⅱ. From awareness to action

在2019年的一次董事会议上,百度为移动时代制定了明确的战略。与会者共同持有的信念是:个人电脑黄金时代的消亡也宣告了以

案例2.3 文化的力量:百度人工智能革命透视

前免费开放网络时代的消亡,因此百度必须建立新的基础设施,确定业务领域,才能产生影响力。与会者达成共识,百度需要构建一个完整的移动生态系统,以增强用户体验,实现收入来源的多样化,并将自己的角色从过去摇摇欲坠的信息连接器大幅提升为横向和纵向提供闭环服务的综合平台,或者公司移动生态系统集团(MEG)的 $X+Y$ 战略。

In a meeting of directors in 2019, Baidu developed a clear strategy for the mobile era. The hard truth shared by participants was that the demise of PC also announced the death of the previous free and open web, so Baidu had to build new infrastructure and identify business areas to make an impact. It was also agreed that Baidu needed to construct an entire mobile ecosystem to enhance the user experience, diversify its income streams and dramatically renovate its role from a shaky information connector in the past to an integrated platform offering closed-loop services horizontally and vertically, or the $X+Y$ strategy of the company's Mobile Ecosystem Group (MEG).

在 $X+Y$ 战略中,横轴是指在不同场景下满足不同需求的用户门户,纵轴主要是为了扩大向用户提供的内容和服务范围。百度认为,这将有助于建立一个稳定、健康、可持续的商业模式,与过去单纯的信息链接完全不同。

In the $X+Y$ strategy, the horizontal axis refers to user portals that meet diverse needs in different scenarios, and the vertical axis is mainly aimed at expanding the range of content and services offered to users. Baidu believes this will help build a stable, healthy and sustainable business model that is completely different from its past role of simply connecting information.

三、将用户体验与业务目标集成

Ⅲ. Integrate the user experience with business goals

对于像百度这样的大公司来说,有必要形成正确的文化,让理念变为现实。10年前,百度向终端用户提供的免费服务和营利性的商业服务总是陷入争斗。似乎要么激怒了用户,要么牺牲了商业利益。

For a big company like Baidu, it's necessary to form the right culture to turn the idea into reality on the ground. Ten years ago, Baidu's free services to end users and for-profit business offerings were always locked in a fight. It seemed either users were pissed off or business interests had to sacrificed.

但是,$X+Y$ 的战略业务布局提供了一个全新的机会来容纳不同的关注点。百度将创作者、服务商和商家直接与生态系统中的相关用户联系起来,提供人性化的闭环服务。

But the strategic business layout of $X+Y$ offers a new chance to accommodate the different concerns. Baidu connects creators, service providers and merchants directly with relevant users in the ecosystem, calling it a humanization process. Baidu also provides users with closed-loop services.

百度管理层倡导将用户和企业放在首位的理念,强调了"所有员工都需要改变想法,尤其是管理人员,否则他们就会被取代"。从2019年1月到2020年4月是一个适应新战略和企业文化的完整过程。它从管理团队要求转变观念开始,明确了生态系统建设和收入多元化的目标,采取了轮换和改组等大规模措施,促进更广泛地接受新理念,塑

案例2.3　文化的力量：百度人工智能革命透视

造了符合新战略目标的文化,最终以$X+Y$战略的推出而告捷。

In advocating the mindset of taking both users and businesses to heart, Baidu's management has underlined the key message in the words of "all staff need to change their minds, especially the managers, otherwise they will be replaced". To summarize, the period from January 2019 to April 2020 saw a complete process of adaptation to the new strategy and company culture. It started from the management team's call for a change of mindset, made clear in the goal of building an ecosystem and diversifying revenue, undertook massive measures such as rotation and reshuffling to promote wider acceptance of the new idea, shaped a culture in line with new strategic objectives, and finally ended with the rollout of the $X+Y$ strategy.

对成功文化变革的研究显示了一个共同点：企业领导者需要将企业文化、战略和商业目标清晰地结合起来。否则，一个与公司文化背道而驰的战略必然会失败，模糊的文化价值观也很难让员工接受。从这个意义上说，百度无疑是一个成功的例子。

Studies of successful culture changes show one thing in common-business leaders need to clearly bind together corporate culture, strategy and business objectives. Otherwise, a strategy that runs counter to the company's culture is bound to fail, and vague culture value can be difficult for employees to embrace. Baidu is certainly a success story in this sense.

四、简单可靠成为基本原则
Ⅳ. Make simple and reliable the bedrock principle

重新加入百度后,崔姗姗全力以赴找出管理问题,在 2018 年组织了约 100 次会议,每次会议都会接待 5 至 7 名与会者。她对一些调查结果感到不满,比如让离职员工成为低绩效的替罪羊,或者让新员工承担沉重的责任。

After rejoining Baidu, Cui went all out to identify management problems by organizing about 100 meetings in 2018, with each session hosting five to seven participants. She was unhappy with some findings, such as making a departing employee a scapegoat for low performance or asking a new recruit to shoulder weighty responsibility.

百度的核心价值一向为"简单可靠"。"简单"意味着产品易于使用,以及有着纯粹的人际关系和直截了当沟通风格的工作环境。"可靠"意味着每个人都致力于工作,并且是可靠的,以一种让同事感到轻松的方式做事。

Baidu's core value has always been Simple and Reliable. Simple means that products are easy to use as well as a work environment that has healthy interpersonal relationships and a no-nonsense communication style. Reliable means everyone is committed to the work and is dependable, doing things in a way that puts colleagues at ease.

百度简单可靠的指导思想包含了至高无上的核心价值观,那就是不遗余力地高标准工作。这是毫不妥协的行为准则,引导着公司忠于其创建时的最初愿景。

案例 2.3 文化的力量：百度人工智能革命透视

Baidu's guiding faith of Simple and Reliable incorporates the paramount message of working to high standards with no exceptions. It's a stringent rule and an uncompromising code of conduct that steers the company to stay true to the original aspirations of its birth.

简单地说，以下四个方面让百度区别于其他企业：

Simply speaking, what sets Baidu apart from other enterprises is four-pronged：

1. 理性思维为基础，公司大多数人都受过科学教育，喜欢形式逻辑和演绎推理。

1. Rational thinking-based as most of the people in the company have an education background in science, and prefer formal logic and deductive reasoning.

2. 信奉技术，因为百度员工相信他们可以用技术改变世界，或者取得杰出成就。

2. Believe in technology as Baidu employees really believe that they can use technology to change the world or accomplish many achievements.

3. 百度支持平等，反对任何形式的官僚主义，甚至在谈话中禁止使用过分强调一个人的职位或引起不必要的人际关系亲密化的表达方式，比如用附加语称呼某人。

3. Supporter of equality as Baidu fights against any form of bureaucratic leadership and, in conversations, even bans the use of expressions that overemphasize a person's job title or beget unnecessary interpersonal closeness such as addressing someone with phatic additions.

4.对派系主义零容忍,因为百度认为内部派系和分裂是最大的禁忌。

4. Zero tolerance of factionalism because Baidu sees internal cliques and divisions as the biggest taboo.

百度创始人兼首席执行官李彦宏在求职面试中问求职者是否相信科技有改变世界的力量,这体现了大家对科技的共同信仰。百度的核心研发投入相当于其营收的21%左右,在业内处于较高水平。对于百度来说,核心价值观是指引具体行动的指南针,因此员工在回答我们做什么、如何与他人相处、什么构成企业文化等问题时,必须有确凿的证据来支持观点。

To give an example of the shared faith in technology, Baidu's founder and CEO Robin Li asked a candidate in a job interview if he believes technology has the power to change the world, which reflects a common belief in science and technology. Baidu's core R&D investment was equivalent to around 21 percent of its revenue, a high level in the industry. For Baidu, the core value is the guiding star to direct specific actions, so employees must be convinced by solid evidence in answering questions like what we do, how to get along with others and what constitutes the corporate culture.

公司仔细地阐述、探索并向全体员工展示了"简单可靠"的真正含义。百度在2018年从七个维度概述了这一定义,并在2020年制定了可衡量的行为准则,其中包括特别针对管理层的三个额外方面,从而形成了"7+3"文化框架。

What it really means to be Simple and Reliable has been carefully elaborated, explored and demonstrated to the entire staff. Baidu outlined the definition from seven dimensions in 2018, and then accompanied that with a measurable code of conduct in 2020, including three additional aspects especially for management, thus forming a "7+3" culture framework.

五、闭环管理系统
V. A closed-loop management system

公司文化既是企业做强的根源,也是其韧性的体现。百度的崛起源于逻辑思维和对技术的坚定信念。

A company's culture is both the root of growth and the ultimate demonstration of its resilience. Baidu has built its rise from logical thinking and a committed belief in technology.

崔姗姗说,在谈论公司文化时,有必要把抽象的想法具体化。她接着举例说明了这一点,把它比作空中重新造林,用机械方法在空中喷洒种子。"你不能只是喷洒种子然后停下来。你需要照顾这些树苗,确保它们的生存和茁壮成长,所以这需要一个闭环的方法。"

When talking about a company's culture, it's necessary to make abstract ideas concrete, said Cui. She went on to illustrate that by drawing an analogy with aerial reforestation, spraying seeds through the air by mechanical means. "You can't just spray the seeds and stop. You need to take care of the saplings and make sure they live and thrive, so this needs a closed-loop approach," said Cui.

坚持"简单可靠"的理念,需要的不仅仅是一个明确的定义。它必须包含在绩效评估中,就像阿里巴巴和华为的做法一样。在百度的绩效考核指标中,遵守公司文化作为重要指标,被赋予了一票否决权。

自2019年以来,评估系统经历了多次迭代。首先,自动选择同事和相关人员,对员工进行三个可能等级的评分：A. 榜样；B. 正常；C. 需要重新评估。在发现超过10%的人被评为A级后,崔姗姗认为这是"不正常"的比例,评估体系在2020年进行了更新,现在对于被评估人是否符合"简单可靠"这一价值的问题,选择题的答案已被"是"或"否"的回答取代。

Upholding the idea of "Simple and Reliable" needs more than a clear definition. It has to be included in the performance evaluation, just like Alibaba and Huawei have practiced. At Baidu, among performance evaluation indicators, compliance with the company culture has been given the veto power. The evaluation system has undergone several iterations since 2019. At first, colleagues and associates were automatically chosen to score a staff member with three possible grades: A. role model; B. majority; C. to be re-evaluated. After finding that over 10 percent were given grade A, an "abnormal" ratio in the view of Cui, the evaluation system was updated in 2020. Now for the question if the person being evaluated is in line with "Simple and Reliable", the multiple-choice answers have been replaced by a yes-or-no response.

如果一名精英不再自我驱动或完成新目标,那么无论他或她在过去多么成功,都应该被淘汰。对于一家面临激烈竞争的公司来说,这一点同样适用。在董事会上,李彦宏反复强调开拓新视角、跳出框框思考、以德服人的重要性。

If an elite is no longer self-driven or ambitious to accomplish new goals, then no matter how successful in the past he or she should leave a position. This also holds true for a company faced with fierce competition. At the director's meetings, Robin Li also repeatedly stressed the importance of developing new perspectives, thinking outside of the box, and following the example of the virtuous and wise.

点评
Comments

"简单可靠"是百度的核心价值观和精神密码。"百度"二字源于中国宋朝词人辛弃疾《青玉案》中的诗句"众里寻他千百度",象征着百度对中文信息检索技术的执着追求。百度的企业文化是在创业过程中逐渐形成的:为人们提供最便捷的信息获取方式。百度力求保持这种简洁的公司文化,并在实践过程中逐步形成以理性思维为基础,信赖技术、支持平等、公正开放的高效率文化特征。

"Simple and reliable" is Baidu's core values and spiritual code. "Baidu" originated from "hundreds and thousands of times I searched for her in the crowd", a line from the poem *Green Jade Cup* written by Xin Qiji, a Chinese poet living in the Song Dynasty. It symbolizes Baidu's persistent pursuit of Chinese information retrieval technology. Baidu's corporate culture is gradually developed in the entrepreneurial process: providing people with the most convenient access to information. Baidu strives to maintain this simple corporate culture, and in the process of practice, it has gradually developed an efficient cultural feature based on rational thinking, relying on technology, and supporting equality, fairness and openness.

从愿景到行动,百度的创业文化得以延续与重生。企业文化的最初来源通常反映了组织创建者的愿景。百度鲜明的工程师文化,和创始人李彦宏的工程师出身关系很大。一旦文化得以建立,一些特定的组织行为就有助于维持该文化。例如,李彦宏在求职面试中问求职者是否相信科技有改变世界的力量,这体现了公司对科技的高度重视。在员工甄选程序中,管理者通常不仅根据工作要求来评价求职者,还会根据求职者与本组织的价值观匹配程度来判断。其次,高层管理者的行为对组织的文化也会产生重大影响。百度高管崔姗姗深受西汉时期杰出的军事将领霍去病打败匈奴的使命感驱使,不遗余力带领百度进行组织变革与文化塑造。

From vision to action, Baidu's entrepreneurial culture has been perpetuated and reborn. The original source of corporate culture usually reflects the vision of the organization's founders. Baidu's distinctive engineering culture has a lot to do with the engineer background of Robin Li, the founder. Once a culture is established, some specific organizational behaviors will help to maintain it. For example, Robin Li once asked a candidate in a job interview if he believes technology has the power to change the world, which shows that the company attaches great importance to science and technology. When screening employees, managers usually evaluate job seekers according to both the job requirements and how they match the values of the organization. Besides, the behaviors of top managers also have significant impacts on the organizational culture. Cui Shanshan, an executive of Baidu, was deeply moved by the mission of Huo Qubing, an outstanding military general in the Western Han Dynasty, who defeated the

案例2.3 文化的力量：百度人工智能革命透视

Xiongnu, and spared no effort to lead Baidu in organizational reform and culture building.

讨论题
Discussions

(1) 请列出百度公司的企业文化和核心价值观，并解释这些价值观如何影响管理者的工作方式。

Please list Baidu's corporate culture and core values, and explain how these values affect the way managers work.

(2) 百度的企业文化是怎么形成的？又是如何维持的？

How is Baidu's corporate culture shaped and maintained?

(3) 面对瞬息万变的市场环境，企业如何支持创新文化、顾客响应文化？

In the face of the rapidly changing market environment, how can enterprises support the innovative culture and customer-responsive culture?

资料来源

文化的力量：百度人工智能革命透视[EB/OL]. [2023-02-25]. https://www.chinadaily.com.cn/a/202106/16/WS60c9a038a31024ad0bac97b2.html.

马英才. 百度还是"简单可依赖"吗[J]. 互联网经济, 2018(Z1):78.

References

The power of culture: Insights into Baidu's AI revolution[EB/OL]. [2023-02-25]. https://www.chinadaily.com.cn/a/202106/16/WS60c9a038a31024ad0bac97b2.html.

Ma Yingcai. Is Baidu as "simple and reliable" as before[J]. Internet Economy, 2018(Z1):78.

第三篇　战略管理

PART Ⅲ　STRATEGIC MANAGEMENT

案例 3.1　华为的品牌扩展战略
Case 3.1　Brand Expansion Strategy of Huawei

教学目标
Teaching Objectives

华为作为一家来自发展中国家的后起之秀,通过自己艰苦卓绝的努力,能够在这个高端市场站稳脚跟,并且经过近30年的发展超越爱立信、阿尔卡特等主要的西方巨头,登上通信领域世界第一的宝座,是难能可贵的,有很多值得开展全球化品牌塑造的其他企业学习借鉴的地方。本节通过对案例的分析,旨在让学生理解企业对利益相关者的责任、企业寻求增长战略的益处和风险,了解中国品牌走向全球市场的扩展策略,帮助大学生树立远大理想和人生抱负。

As a latecomer from a developing country, Huawei succeeded in gaining a firm foothold in the high-end market through its arduous efforts. After nearly 30 years of development, it has overtaken Ericsson, Alcatel and other major western giants to become the industry leader in telecommunications. Huawei's achievements are well worth praising, from which other enterprises should learn so as to carry out their own global brand building. Through the analysis of the case, this section aims to help students understand the responsibilities of enterprises towards stakeholders, the benefits and risks facing enterprises seeking growth strategies, and the expansion strategies of Chinese brands going global, so that they can establish lofty ideals and ambitions.

本案例涉及战略管理中的企业对利益相关者的社会责任、企业增长战略、品牌扩展战略、双品牌战略等相关知识点。

This case involves the corporate social responsibilities to stakeholders, corporate growth strategy, brand expansion strategy, dual brand strategy and other related concepts in strategic management.

案例内容
Contents

被誉为"现代营销学之父"的菲利普·科特勒认为,品牌是一种名称、术语、标记、符号或设计,或是它们的组合运用,其目的是借以辨认某个销售者或某群销售者的产品或服务,并使之同竞争对手的产品和服务区别开来。因此,品牌是企业获得消费者认可、声誉和忠诚度的根本途径。消费者对公司的主观感受会影响消费者的购买行为。

Philip Kotler, known as the "Father of Modern Marketing", believes that a brand is a name, term, mark, symbol or design, or a combination of them, intended to identify the goods and services of one

案例 3.1 华为的品牌扩展战略

seller or group of sellers and to differentiate them from those of the competitor. Therefore, brand is the fundamental way for enterprises to gain consumers' recognition, reputation and loyalty. Consumers' subjective feelings about the company will affect their purchasing behavior.

华为凭借其研发实力和资金实力,选择了商务人士这个细分市场,强调为商务人士服务的定位,从而确立了华为品牌的优势位置。在发展到一定阶段之后,华为又进行了产品的重新定位和渠道资源规划,在华为品牌的基础上,推出了荣耀品牌(现已出售),即开始实施双品牌战略。

With its R&D strength and deep pocket, Huawei has chosen the market segment of business people. By focusing on serving business people, Huawei has taken a dominant position in the market. After reaching a certain stage of development, it repositioned its products and re-planned the channel resources to launch another brand Honor (now sold), then the dual *Huawei and Honor* brand strategy began to be implemented.

华为品牌标识由扇形图标和"HUAWEI"英文组成,有竖版和横版两个版本,一般情况下使用竖版标识。标识中没有使用中文,体现了华为塑造全球化品牌的战略初衷。中文品牌名称"华为"的寓意是"中华有为"。该品牌标识的含义是聚焦、创新、稳健、和谐,体现了公司的理念。

Huawei's brand logo consists of a fan-shaped icon and "HUAWEI" in English, with vertical and horizontal versions. On most occasions, the vertical version is adopted. Chinese is not used in the logo, which reflects Huawei's original strategic purpose of shaping a global brand. Its Chinese name "Huawei" means "China will prosper". The brand Logo implies focus, innovation, stability and harmony, which embodies the company's philosophy.

一、华为国际化经营的现状

Ⅰ. Status quo of Huawei's international operation

华为技术有限公司是中国最具价值和影响力的IT企业。华为于1987年在深圳成立,连续9年在世界500强排名中不断上升,2017年进入百强企业,如表3－1所示。

Huawei Technologies Co., Ltd., the most valuable and influential IT enterprise in China, was founded in Shenzhen in 1987. After that, it had been rising in the ranking of the Fortune 500 companies for nine consecutive years. In 2017, it managed to rank among the top 100, as shown in Table 3－1.

表3－1　　　　　2012—2019年华为全球500强企业排名

Table 3－1　Huawei's Rankings Among Fortune Global 500 in 2012—2019

年份 Year	2012	2013	2014	2015	2016	2017	2018	2019
排名 Ranking	353	315	285	228	129	83	72	61

资料来源:《财富》中文网。

Source: fortunechina.com.

华为企业的产品主要涉及云、管道、终端三个部分。在云方面,华为为社会各界提供了多种服务和软件安装。其中,华为企业带来了从接入到承载、从承载到核心的全面智能网络体验。在终端方面,为消费者带来了令人满意的终端产品。华为的产品（涉及云、管道和终端业务的产品）在世界排名中位列前三,如表3—2所示。

Huawei's products mainly involve the cloud, pipe and device. In terms of cloud, Huawei provides various services and software installation for all sectors of society. Among them, it offers a comprehensive intelligent network experience from access to carrier and from carrier to core. For devices, it develops satisfactory device products for consumers. Huawei's products (involving cloud, pipe and device) rank among the top three in the world, as shown in Table 3—2.

表3—2　　2017年华为产品排名
Table 3—2　　Rankings of Huawei Products in 2017

华为的产品 Huawei Products	中国排名 Chinese Ranking	全球排名 Global Ranking
以太网交换机 Ethernet switch	1	2
数据中心交换机 Data center switch	1	3
企业路由器 Enterprise router	1	2
企业防火墙 Enterprise firewall	2	2

数据来源：互联网数据中心报告。

Source: reports from the Internet Data Center.

华为在通信网络、全球服务和终端产品三大业务领域逐步形成了比较优势。公司为消费者提供云、管道、中档产品和服务,帮助社会各界改善经营困难,提升网络竞争力水平,降低经营风险。近年来,华为业务总收入呈直线上升态势,如表3—3所示。

Huawei has gradually formed a comparative advantage in three business areas, including communication network, global service and device products. It provides consumers with cloud, pipe and medium-grade products and services, helping all sectors of society to improve their business difficulties, enhance their network competitiveness and reduce their business risks. In recent years, the total revenue of Huawei's business has been rising steadily, as shown in Table 3-3.

表 3—3 华为业务收入情况 单位:亿元
Table 3—3 Huawei's Revenue Unit:100 million yuan

	2015 年 2015	2016 年 2016	2017 年 2017
运营商业务 Operator business	2 351.49	2 905.67	2 978.51
公司业务 Enterprise business	276.18	407.23	549.48
消费者业务 Consumer business	1 252.69	1 798.74	2 372.31
其他 Miscellaneous	70.11	105.25	137.86
总计 Total	3 950.47	5 216.89	6 038.16

数据来源:华为年报。

Source:Huawei Annual Report.

二、华为品牌扩展的主要举措
Ⅱ. Major measures of Huawei brand expansion

(一)高性价比产品定位策略

(1)Cost-effective product positioning strategy

华为采用高性价比的产品定位方法。无论是高端产品还是低端

案例 3.1　华为的品牌扩展战略

产品,华为都追求最佳的性价比,满足消费者各个层次的需求。例如,华为 Mate 系列手机基本上都是大屏机,适合成功的商务人士使用;而荣耀系列则主打中低端用户,其性价比最高,但外形和质感方面一般。

Huawei adopts a cost-effective product positioning method. Whether it is a high-end or low-end product, Huawei always pursues the best cost performance to meet the needs of consumers at all levels. For example, Huawei Mate series are basically large-screen devices, suitable for successful business people. The Honor series focus on low-end users, with the highest cost performance, yet comparatively average shape and texture.

(二)客户群综合选择策略

(2)Comprehensive strategy for selecting customer groups

华为的客户群选择策略是全面的,它在市场上拥有不同层次的消费者。使用华为电信设备的电信公司遍布全球。作为企业生存发展的风向标,华为始终坚持消费者至上的理念,成立消费业务部,建立完整的消费业务官方网站。

Huawei has a comprehensive strategy for selecting customer groups, targeting different levels of consumers in the market. The telecommunication companies that use Huawei telecommunication equipment are all over the world. As a wind vane for the survival and development of enterprises, Huawei always adheres to the concept of consumer first. It has established a consumer business unit and a complete official website for consumer business.

(三)逆向选址策略

(3)Reverse location selection strategy

区位集中度的高低将对华为的外部扩展效应产生一系列影响。华为国际品牌扩展的区位选择是从俄罗斯开始,进而开拓亚洲、非洲、拉丁美洲市场,然后深入欧洲主流国家,最终进入美国。华为采取"农村包围城市"的区位战略。发展中国家为华为创造了几千万消费者。华为可以迅速提高在世界上的市场份额,推广华为的品牌。

The level of location concentration has a series of impacts on Huawei's external expansion effect. The location choice of Huawei's international brand expansion starts with Russia, followed by Asia, Africa and Latin America, then the major European countries, and finally the US. Huawei adopts the location strategy of "surrounding the cities from the countryside". The tens of millions of consumers in developing countries helped Huawei rapidly expand its market share in the world and promote its brand.

(四)狼营销策略

(4)Wolf marketing strategy

华为采用狼营销策略,具有"快、准、无情"的特点。华为狼营销的核心就是打造一支能征善战的营销铁军。华为人在营销过程中的进取精神、团队精神,都与狼群作战时的表现有着共同之处,因此,华为的营销被称为狼性营销。华为的狼性营销策略主要包括价格营销策略、渠道营销策略和促销营销策略三个方面。在价格营销策略方面,华为保证每一款产品都能满足消费者的基本需求或某一方面的特殊需求。其价格营销策略确保了华为稳定的客户资源,为其品牌扩展奠定了基础。华为正努力成为全球客户对主要IT品牌满意度的第一

案例 3.1 华为的品牌扩展战略

位,如表 3—4 所示。

Huawei adopts the wolf marketing strategy featuring "fast, accurate and ruthless". The core of this strategy is to build an invincible marketing army to win battles. It is the aggressiveness and team spirit of Huawei people in the marketing process that have something in common with the performance of wolves in combat. Therefore, what Huawei uses is a wolf marketing strategy, which mainly includes three parts: price marketing strategy, channel marketing strategy and promotion marketing strategy. In terms of price marketing strategy, Huawei guarantees that each product can meet the basic needs of consumers or the special needs of a certain aspect. This provides stable customer resources and lays the foundation for its brand expansion. Huawei is striving to become the brand with the highest satisfaction of global customers among major IT brands, as shown in Table 3—4.

表 3—4　　　　　2017 年全球 IT 品牌客户满意度指数
Table 3—4　　Customer Satisfaction Index of Global IT Brands in 2017

排名 Ranking	品牌 Brand	满意度 Degree of Satisfaction
1	华为 Huawei	80.7
2	苹果 Apple	79.7
3	魅族 Meizu	78.3
4	VIVO	78
5	觅乐 Millet	75.7

续表

排名 Ranking	品牌 Brand	满意度 Degree of Satisfaction
6	三星 Samsung	75.3

数据来源:中国质量协会评估结果。

Source: evaluation results of China Association for Quality.

在渠道营销策略方面,华为在品牌扩展方面采取全方位的渠道营销策略,如线上、离线整合、协助等。荣耀手机定位于面向年轻人的网上销售品牌策略,一经推出大获成功。2014年年底,全球销量超过2 000万部,进入全球60多个国家和地区;2015年全年出货量超过4 000万部。

Huawei adopts an all-round channel marketing strategy in brand expansion, such as online-offline integration and coordination. Honor, which adheres to a brand strategy of online sales for young people, has achieved a great success after its launch. By the end of 2014, its global sales volume had exceeded 20 million units and were sold in more than 60 countries and regions around the world. In 2015, its annual sales volume surpassed 40 million units.

在促销营销策略方面,华为率先开展饥饿营销。2017年保时捷新系列发布时,它抓住消费者的稀缺心理,采取饥饿营销策略,激发了消费者的购买欲望。

As for promotion marketing strategy, Huawei took the lead in hunger marketing. When the new Porsche model was launched in 2017, targeting consumers' mindset of "a thing is valued if it is rare", Huawei adopted the hunger marketing strategy to stimulate consumers to buy the product.

（五）公共关系联合战略

(5) Alliance strategy for public relations

华为以IT企业核心圈为基础,在公关上采取了产业联盟和商业联盟的战略。华为加入了各种产业联盟,积极与同一圈著名IT企业（如IBM)合作,实现双赢。已有越来越多的企业与华为合作。

Based on the core circle of IT enterprises, Huawei has adopted the strategy of industrial alliance and commercial alliance in public relations. Huawei has joined various industrial alliances and are actively cooperating with well-known IT companies (such as IBM) in the same circle to achieve win-win results. Now more and more companies are opting to partner with Huawei.

三、华为品牌扩展战略的启示

Ⅲ. Insights gained from Huawei's brand expansion strategy

（一）特色定位策略

(1) Characteristic positioning strategy

特色定位策略带来的启示有三点:第一,强调产品定位的突出特点。华为的产品定位有的体现在价格上,有的体现在质量上。华为的一些产品定位可以从产品实体上表现出来,比如荣耀8系列的镜面外观、Mate系列的核心处理器的性能、双摄像头的结构等。有些可以从消费者心理上反映出来,比如保时捷系列手机的豪华、X系列的简约、荣耀系列的时尚。第二,熟悉公司的竞争对手。在定位产品之前,华为充分了解了苹果、三星或电信设备制造商爱立信等竞争对手的产品特点,并将竞争对手定位在市场上。第三,整合企业资源。华为高性价比的产品定位是基于对华为优秀资源的整合。华为采取差异化的产品定位战略,推出华为和荣耀两大系列(如图3—1所示),带动了多个产品组合的发展。

There are three insights gained from Huawei's characteristic positioning strategy. First, it stresses the outstanding characteristics of product positioning. Huawei's product positioning is reflected in price and quality. For some of Huawei products, the positioning can be seen from the product itself, such as the mirror appearance of Honor 8 series, the performance of core processor of Mate series, and the structure of dual cameras. For other products, this can be reflected in catering to consumers' mindset, such as the luxury Porsche series, the simple X series and the fashionable Honor series. Second, it gets familiar with its competitors. Before positioning any products, Huawei fully understood the characteristics of products of competitors such as Apple, Samsung or Ericsson, a telecommunication equipment manufacturer, and identified their position in the market. Third, it integrates internal resources. Huawei positions its cost-effective product on the basis of integrating its outstanding resources. With a differentiated product positioning strategy, it launched two series, Huawei and Honor(as shown in Figure 3—1), which promoted the development of multiple product portfolios.

(二)客户群的多方位发展

(2)Multi-directional development of customer base

客户群的选择既重要又困难。我们从华为的经验中得到的启示是,以客户为本,为客户服务是企业的生存之道。华为全面开发客户

案例 3.1　华为的品牌扩展战略

图片来源：https://mp. ofweek. com/Upload/News/Img/member2576/202204/26102408216414. jpg,2023－02－20。

Source：https://mp. ofweek. com/Upload/News/Img/member2576/202204/26102408216414. jpg,2023－02－20.

图 3－1　华为与荣耀品牌

Figure 3－1　Huawei and Honor brands

资源，包括高端客户和低端客户。例如，为了满足不同偏好消费者的消费需求，华为手机制定了双品牌战略，荣耀是华为终端旗下独立运作的互联网品牌，于 2013 年 12 月 16 日发布。和华为手机在全球市场的高举高打不同，荣耀手机的主阵地则在互联网上，因此荣耀手机的营销策略是以快破局。

It's important yet difficult to select a customer base. What we learn from Huawei's experience is that customer-oriented service is the key to enterprises' survival. Huawei fully develops customer resources, including high-end customers and low-end customers. For example, in order to meet the consumption needs of consumers with different preferences, Huawei has adopted a dual-brand strategy for its

145

phones. Honor is an Internet brand independently operated by Huawei. It was first released on December 16, 2013. Unlike Huawei's high-profile mobile phones in the global market, Honor focuses on the Internet, so its marketing strategy is to quickly break the ice.

（三）区位选择的新颖性

(3) Innovative location selection

区位选择是影响跨国公司成功进行各种跨国经营的关键因素之一。在区位选择策略上，华为采取了"以城带乡"的扩展策略，这一扩展策略为其他IT企业如何进入国际市场提供了新的视角。华为选择从中国香港出发，它是深圳本土基地的近邻，最初进入外部约束较少的地区是为了积累经验，奠定坚实的基础。之后，华为凭借自己的经验、实力和良好的口碑，逐步打开了发达国家的市场。与直接进入发达国家市场相比，这一战略避免了不必要的风险和麻烦。

Location choice is one of the key factors that affect the success of international companies in their transnational operations. In terms of location selection strategy, Huawei has adopted the expansion strategy of "urban areas supporting rural development", which provides a new perspective for other IT enterprises to enter the international market. Huawei started from Hong Kong China, which is a close neighbor of Shenzhen headquarters. At first, it picked an area with less external constraints in order to accumulate experience and lay a solid foundation. After that, with its own experience, strength and good reputation, Huawei has gradually penetrated into the markets of developed countries. Compared with directly entering developed markets, this strategy has kept off unnecessary risks and troubles.

（四）采用差异化竞争方式

(4) Utilizing differentiated competition

当IT企业不具备与龙头企业竞争的实力时，可以采用差异化营销方式。在价格和渠道营销策略上，华为构建了不同于其他IT品牌的差异化竞争优势，并据此制定了具有华为特色的狼性营销计划。华为不仅推出高性价比的产品，而且推广高端产品，充分利用线上线下营销。

When IT enterprises do not have the strength to compete with leading enterprises, differentiated marketing methods can be adopted. For price and channel marketing strategy, Huawei has built a differentiated competitive edge, making it stand out from other IT brands. Based on that, Huawei formulated a wolf marketing strategy with Huawei characteristics. It not only introduces cost-effective products, but also promotes high-end products and makes full use of online and offline marketing.

（五）建立联盟公共关系

(5) Building alliance-based public relations

如果运用得当，公共关系就可以使企业品牌在国际上成功扩展，如鱼得水。IT企业不必在对外扩展的过程中一直处于困境，而是要通过多方面的合作来实现国际化扩展。华为在全球公关中扮演产业联盟和商业联盟双重角色的实践，对其他IT企业具有一定的启示价值。

If properly used, public relations can enable an enterprise brand to successfully expand in the world, like fish in water. IT enterprises can overcome obstacles in the process of going global through cooperation in various aspects. Huawei's practice of engaging in both industrial alliances and commercial alliances in global public relations has provided some insights for other IT enterprises.

点评
Comments

品牌不仅关乎企业的生存与发展,更是一个国家实力和核心竞争力的象征。中国把培育自己的品牌作为一项长期的国家战略来实施,而品牌的打造更需要有格局、有远大抱负、有社会责任的行业领军企业。

Brand is not only related to the survival and development of enterprises, but also a symbol of national strength and core competitiveness. China considers the cultivation of its own brand as a long-term national strategy, and brand building needs industry leaders with a broad and long-term view, ambitions and social responsibilities.

华为早在20世纪90年代便开始了海外的征程,通过努力发展自己,带着自己的产品赢得了世界各国的信任,也让世界各国对中国产品有了新的认知。华为深知自己的中国身份,也清楚地知道自己代表着中国形象,这有助于提升其在国际市场的主导地位。华为的中国身份给企业品牌注入了中国文化价值元素,例如"和谐""团结"和"尊重"。而这些正是中国企业要想在国际市场崭露头角所必需的元素。

As early as the 1990s, Huawei embarked on its journey of going global. Through its efforts for self-development, Huawei won the trust of the world with its own products, and also made the world have a new understanding of Chinese products. Huawei is well aware of its label as a Chinese company and that it represents the image of China, which helps to enhance its leading position in the international market. The identity of Huawei as a Chinese company has injected elements of Chinese culture into its brands, such as "harmony" "unity" and "respect", which are necessary for Chinese companies to distinguish themselves in the international market.

华为品牌扩展的案例给我们带来了这样的启示:中国不仅需要创造并建立自己的品牌,更需要将品牌意识的观念植入每一个国产企业。除了华为这样的高科技企业,其他中国企业同样可以从华为的成功之路中吸取宝贵经验。期待在世界经济舞台看到越来越多中国品牌的身影。

The case of Huawei's brand expansion has brought us such an insight that China not only needs to create and establish its own brand, but also implant the concept of brand awareness into every Chinese enterprise. Besides high-tech enterprises, other Chinese enterprises can also gain valuable experience from Huawei's success. We are looking forward to seeing more and more China brands on the global arena.

讨论题
Discussions

(1)你是如何理解国际品牌扩展的?
What do you think of the expansion of international brands?
(2)华为的国际品牌扩展战略给人们带来了怎样的启示?

What insights can people gain from Huawei's international brand expansion strategy?

(3)双品牌策略在企业具体营销中的优缺点有哪些?

What are the advantages and disadvantages of dual-brand strategy in the marketing practice of enterprises?

资料来源

吴哲伦,吴建功,侯奇,等."IT企业国际品牌扩张战略:华为的案例研究"[J].Procedia计算机科学,2021(183):733—744.

张景云.中国品牌全球化战略:华为的案例研究[J].品牌研究,2018(2):3—7.

贺杰,何颖,顾玉婷.中国智能手机企业多品牌战略研究——以华为公司为例[J].经济研究导刊,2020(2):132—135.

References

Zhelun Wu,Jiangong Wu,Qi Hou,et al.,"The strategy of international brand expansion of it enterprises:a case study based on Huawei"[J]. Procedia Computer Science,2021(183):733—744.

Zhang Jingyun. Globalization Strategy of Chinese Brands:A Case Study based on Huawei[J]. Journal of Brand Research,2018(02):3—7.

He Jie,He Ying,Gu Yuting. Research on the multi-brand strategy of Chinese smartphone companies-taking Huawei as an example[J]. Economic Research Guide,2020(02):132—135.

案例 3.2　小米公司的颠覆性创新战略
Case 3.2　Disruptive Innovation Strategy of Xiaomi

教学目标
Teaching Objectives

小米公司作为手机领域的后来者，充分利用互联网资源，成功实施颠覆性创新，重塑行业竞争规则，在众多竞争对手中脱颖而出。本节通过对小米公司的案例研究，分析其颠覆性创新的实施过程，以及对后发企业的成长提供的借鉴。本案例分析旨在让学生理解战略创新的核心问题是重新确定企业的经营目标，企业的核心能力是持久竞争优势的源泉，颠覆性创新模式具备适用性，让他们感受创新的魅力，体悟创业精神，帮助身处新时代的他们以创新为契机，不断开拓进取，勇攀高峰。

As a latecomer in the field of mobile phones, Xiaomi makes full use of Internet resources to rewrite industry competition rules and finally stand out among many competitors through successful disruptive innovation. Through the case study of Xiaomi, this section analyzes the implementation process of its disruptive innovation, which can be used as reference for the growth of latecomers. It aims to help students understand that the key to strategic innovation is redefining the business objectives of enterprises, stressing that the core competence of enterprises is the source of lasting competitive advantage. The applicability of the disruptive innovation mode allows students to experience the attractive innovation and understand the entrepreneurship, and helps them to take innovation as an opportunity to keep forging ahead and challenge a new height bravely in the new era.

本案例涉及战略管理中的战略创新、企业核心竞争力、颠覆性创新等相关知识点。

This case involves strategic innovation, core competitiveness of enterprises, disruptive innovation and other related concepts in strategic management.

案例内容
Contents

北京小米科技有限公司(简称小米公司)成立于 2010 年 4 月,是一家专注于自主研发基于安卓(Android)的高端智能手机的移动互联网公司。其核心业务是小米手机、米柚(MIUI)系统和米聊(MiTalk)。拥有小米一至五、青春版小米、红米等手机产品。自小米手机发布以来,凭借"为你而生,为小米而燃烧"的产品理念和性价比定位,小米手

案例 3.2 小米公司的颠覆性创新战略

机赢得了市场的青睐。

Founded in April 2010, Beijing Xiaomi Technology Co., Ltd. (Xiaomi for short) is a mobile Internet company focusing on independent research and development of high-end smartphones based on Android. Its core business includes Xiaomi mobile phone, MIUI system and MiTalk, covering Mi 1-Mi 5, Youth series, Redmi and other mobile phone products. Since the release of Xiaomi mobile phone products, they have gained great popularity in the market with its product concept and cost-effective positioning of "Born for You, Burn for MI".

2010年,小米手机正式上市时,34小时内就被订购了30万部。到2014年,小米手机销量增长到61.12亿部,年平均增长率在200%左右。总体而言,小米手机的市场份额呈持续爆发式增长,如表3—5所示。2014年第三季度,IDC和Strategy Analytics等多家调查机构宣布,小米手机在全球智能手机市场的份额排名仅次于苹果和三星。

In 2010, when Xiaomi's mobile phone product was officially launched, 300,000 units were ordered within 34 hours. By 2014, Xiaomi's mobile phone sales increased to 6.112 billion units, with an average annual growth rate of around 200%. Overall, the market share of Xiaomi's mobile phone products is growing exponentially, as shown in Table 3—5. In Q3 2014, several market survey institutions including IDC and Strategy Analytics announced that Xiaomi took the third largest share in the global smartphone market, following Apple and Samsung.

表 3—5　　　　　　　　　　2011—2014 年手机销量

Table 3—5　　　　　　　Sales of Mobile Phone in 2011—2014

年份 Year	销售额(万元) Sales(10,000 yuan)	增长率(%) Growth Rate(1%)	含税收入(亿元) Taxable Income(100,000,000 Yuan)
2011	30	—	—
2012	719	—	126
2013	1 870	160	316
2014	6 112	227	743

小米公司开发的小米手机的成功销售,不仅在中国手机市场引起震动,也成为学术界关注的焦点。作为中国手机行业的后发企业,小米公司虽然缺乏资源和技术,却占据了市场地位,成为中国领先的手机品牌。成功来自该公司在技术、市场、服务、内部组织管理等方面的创新。

The high sales of mobile phone products developed by Xiaomi not only shocked the mobile phone market in China, but also became the focus of academic attention. As a latecomer in China's mobile phone industry, Xiaomi has become a major market player and a leading mobile phone brand in China, despite its inadequate resources and technical strength. Its success comes from the innovation in technology, market, services and internal organization and management.

一、小米公司的技术创新

Ⅰ. Technological innovation of Xiaomi

在苹果、三星等外资品牌和华为、联想等国产品牌占据市场绝对优势的情况下,小米公司并没有选择正面进攻的策略,而是充分利用了自己软件开发团队的力量。公司首先开发了智能手机操作系统——MIUI系统,以此开拓市场。MIUI系统是基于Android系统,按照中国人的习惯开发的智能手机操作系统。系统改进项目200多项,力求打造最佳手机短信体验和原创主题系统。MIUI系统最大的优点是开放性。众所周知,IOS系统是不对外开放的,市场上使用Android的智能手机系统也是不对外开放的。但是MIUI系统的用户可以根据自己的需要随时进行动画设计(flash)。同时,MIUI系统的官方版本也保持每周更新一次的频率。这一独特的技术吸引了小米手机的定位客户手机爱好者。同时,这种技术的良好体验也得到了消费者的青睐。

With foreign brands such as Apple and Samsung and domestic brands such as Huawei and Lenovo taking the dominant position in the market, Xiaomi did not adopt the strategy of head-on attack, but made full use of the strength of its own software development team. At first, the company developed the smart phone operating system-MIUI system for market development. This smart phone operating system is based on Android and developed according to the using habits of Chinese people. With more than 200 system improvement items, it is designed to create the best SMS experience and original theme system. The biggest advantage of MIUI system is openness. As we all know, the IOS system is not available to the public, and neither are the Android-based smartphone systems in the market. However, users of MIUI system can flash at any time according to their own needs, and the official version of MIUI system is updated once a week. This unique technology has attracted fans of Xiaomi mobile phone products. At the same time, its good experience has also gained popularity among consumers.

其次,MIUI 系统有自己的管理团队来开发软件,最重要的是它充分利用了互联网,把技术创新的难度降到了最低。当时,MIUI 系统开发团队只有 20 多名员工,但他们在论坛上建立了一支 10 万人的互联网开发团队。

Secondly, MIUI system has its own management team for software development. The most important thing is that it makes full use of the Internet to minimize the difficulty in technological innovation. At that time, the MIUI system development team, with only 20 employees or so, established an Internet development team composed of 100,000 members on the forum.

二、小米公司市场创新

Ⅱ. Market innovation of Xiaomi

纵观中国智能手机市场,作为高端智能手机的代表,苹果和三星都在坚持创新,努力引领市场。产品更新换代快,性能好,功能更丰富。但高端智能手机的一些功能远远超出了大多数用户的需求。随着性能的提高,智能手机的价格也在快速上涨。用户越来越不愿意为持续的技术创新埋单。小米公司以低价、高性能进军市场,坚信利润不依赖硬件,而像互联网产品一样,未来由增值服务驱动。这一战略帮助其成功发展和巩固了市场地位。

Looking into the smart phone market in China, as high-end smart phone brands, both Apple and Samsung insist on innovation and strive to take the lead in the market. Their products are updated quickly for better performance and more functions, though some functions go far beyond what most users need. With the improvement of performance, the prices of smart phones are rising rapidly. Users are increasingly reluctant to pay for continuous technological innovation. Xiaomi entered the market with low price and high performance. The company firmly believes that profits do not come from hardware, but from value-added services like Internet products. This strategy has helped it successfully develop and consolidate its market position.

除了特殊的市场定位,小米公司还积极开发颠覆性的销售渠道。中国智能手机市场竞争激烈,无论是国外还是国内厂商的销售渠道都大同小异。当时手机厂商主要关注零售渠道、运营商渠道等线下渠道,显然小米公司无法与之竞争。因此,小米公司另辟蹊径,以互联网为主要销售渠道,采取口碑营销的方式。它最初通过论坛宣传自己的产品。成千上万的核心用户和粉丝免费为小米手机做广告,这对树立良好的口碑起到了很大的帮助。之后,小米公司充分利用QQ、微博、微信等,通过社交营销传播产品信息。在营销方面,小米再次充分利用互联网的力量,对传统的销售渠道和方式进行了颠覆性的创新,不仅降低了销售成本,而且赢得了市场的认可。

In addition to its special market positioning, Xiaomi also actively develops disruptive sales channels. The smart phone market in China is highly competitive, and the sales channels of both foreign and domestic manufacturers are similar. At that time, mobile phone manufacturers mainly focused on offline channels such as retail and operator channels. Obviously, Xiaomi has no advantage in these market segments. Therefore, Xiaomi has found another way, taking the Internet as the main sales channel for word-of-mouth marketing. In the beginning, it promoted its products through forums. Thousands of core users and fans popularized Xiaomi mobile phones for free, which greatly contributed to a good reputation. After that, Xiaomi spread product information through social media such as QQ, Weibo and WeChat. In marketing, Xiaomi once again utilized the power of the Internet and made disruptive innovations in traditional sales channels and methods. In this way, Xiaomi not only reduced its marketing costs, but also won the recognition of the market.

三、小米公司服务创新

Ⅲ. Service innovation of Xiaomi

在服务方面,小米公司也继承了其一贯的反传统作风,提出了超越传统标准化的非标准化服务模式。这意味着在标准化服务的基础上,小米公司提供了比预期更全面、更完善的服务。这一措施使其在售后服务中脱颖而出。其实小米公司的非标准模式有自己的标准。但是,这个标准并不是传统意义上的标准,它的目的是让用户不仅"满意",而且"快乐","满意"和"快乐"代表着两个截然不同的层次。传统的在位企业普遍采用效率高、质量好的标准化服务模式。这种模式虽然易于管理,但往往缺乏人与人之间的互动服务和温度。大多数消费者对他们的服务满意而不是快乐。非标准化服务就是基于这个标准,加上一些人性化的东西,让用户"开心",小米服务体系最大的特点就是用产品经理的思维做服务,为用户提供服务,同时也进行情感的交流和互动。小米公司在服务模式上的颠覆性创新,提高了客户的参与度和满意度,赢得了消费者的信任和认可。

案例 3.2　小米公司的颠覆性创新战略

In terms of service, Xiaomi adheres to its consistent anti-traditional style and puts forward a non-standardized service mode over the traditional standard one. This means that on the basis of standardized services, Xiaomi aims to provide more comprehensive and better services beyond expectation. It makes Xiaomi stand out in the after-sales service. In fact, Xiaomi's non-standardized mode has its own standards that are different from the traditional ones. It is designed to make users "satisfied" and "happy", which are two completely different feelings. Traditional enterprises generally adopt a standardized service mode with high efficiency and good quality. Although management becomes easier with this mode, interactive services and people-to-people warmth are always overlooked. Most consumers are satisfied but not happy with their services. Based on this standard, non-standardized services, with additional people-oriented features, are designed to make users "happy". The biggest feature of Xiaomi service system is serving users with the thinking of the product manager while making emotional exchanges and interactions. Its disruptive innovation in service mode has improved customer participation and satisfaction, and won the trust and recognition of consumers.

四、小米公司管理创新
Ⅳ. Management innovation of Xiaomi

后发企业颠覆性创新战略的制定和实施必然受到组织能力的影响。新兴企业的组织结构更有可能促进颠覆性创新的成功。成功的在位者拥有独特的企业文化，这成为企业的核心竞争力，也往往成为颠覆性创新成功的最大障碍。而这方面正是后来者企业的优势。首先,小米公司内部组织结构扁平化。其组织结构分为三个层次:核心创始人、领导者和部门员工。相对于成熟的大型企业来说,这种组织结构灵活、高效,具有独特的优势。其次,公司内部没有关键绩效指标(KPI)和复杂的规章制度。工作绩效是由用户决定的,这使得员工承担了更多的责任。此外,小米公司还有一个理念,就是利益必须与员工分享。公司成立时,鼓励员工参与投资计划,这给了他们很大的启发。

The formulation and implementation of disruptive innovation strategies of latecomers are bound to be influenced by the organization's capability. The organizational structure of an emerging enterprise is more likely to contribute to the success of disruptive innovation. Successful market leaders usually have a unique corporate culture, which is the core competitiveness of enterprises but often becomes the biggest obstacle to the success of disruptive innovation. Therefore, latecomers have advantages in this regard. First of all, Xiaomi has a flat internal organizational structure, which is divided into three levels, including core founders, leaders and department employees. Compared with mature large companies, this organizational structure is flexible and efficient with unique advantages. Secondly, there is no KPI, complicated rules and regulations within the company. Job performance is determined by users, which makes employees take on more responsibilities. In addition, Xiaomi also boasts a concept that benefits must be shared with employees. When the company was founded, employees were encouraged to participate in the investment plan, which made them greatly inspired.

公司始终追求快速创新的互联网文化,强调永无止境的创新创业精神,没有无聊的会议和冗长的过程。正是这种组织文化和能力使公司具备了开拓新思路、新渠道、新市场的能量和能力,敢于承担颠覆性创新的风险。管理创新使公司保持了持续发展的强劲势头和活力。

The company always pursues a fast and innovative Internet culture, stressing the spirit of endless innovation and entrepreneurship. There are no boring meetings and lengthy procedures. It is the unique organizational culture and capability that enables the company to have the energy and power to explore new ideas, new channels and new markets, and dare to take the risk of disruptive innovation. Management innovation has empowered the company to maintain its strong momentum and vitality in sustainable development.

点评
Comments

创新是引领发展的第一动力。抓创新就是抓发展,谋创新就是谋未来。随着以人工智能、量子信息、移动通信、物联网、区块链等为代表的新一代信息技术加速突破应用,只要进一步把握大势、抢占先机,瞄准世界科技前沿,中国就一定能推动制造业产业模式和企业形态发生根本性转变,以创新带动转型,以增量带动存量,促进中国产业迈向全球价值链中高端。

Innovation is the primary driving force for development. Focusing on innovation means stressing development and pursuing innovation stands for planning for the future. We have seen breakthroughs and application of a new generation of information technologies represented by artificial intelligence, quantum information, mobile communication, Internet of Things and blockchain. As long as we further grasp the general trend, seize the opportunities, and aim at the forefront of technologies in the world, China will definitely promote the fundamental transformation of the industrial modes and business forms of the manufacturing sector. By driving the transformation with innovation and solving existing problems with development, the industry in China can be advanced to take the medium and high positions in the global value chain.

颠覆性创新作为一种战略管理工具,最初是为了解决发达国家企业的创新困境而提出的。颠覆性创新理论以其非竞争性、低端的价值取向引导企业通过颠覆性创新占领市场。颠覆性创新理论为企业的快速发展开辟了新的思路,成为企业的重要战略选择,同时也为发展中国家后发企业的战略创新提供了新的视角。

Disruptive innovation, as a strategic management tool, was originally proposed to solve the innovation dilemma of enterprises in developed countries. Disruptive innovation theory guides enterprises to take over the market through disruptive innovation with its non-competitive and low-end value orientation. It has opened up a new way of thinking for the rapid development of enterprises, and thus has become their important strategic choice. At the same time, it also provides a new perspective for the strategic innovation of latecomers in developing countries.

案例 3.2 小米公司的颠覆性创新战略

小米的颠覆性创新是在顾客需求的基础上,开发差异化的产品或服务,实现自下向上的创新,最终占据主流市场的过程。然而,智能手机企业颠覆性创新的模式是否对其他行业的企业适用仍需进一步探索。

The disruptive innovation of Xiaomi is a process of developing differentiated products or services on the basis of customer demand, realizing bottom-up innovation, and finally occupying the mainstream market. However, whether the disruptive innovation mode of smart phone enterprises is applicable to those in other industries still needs further exploration.

讨论题

Discussions

(1)什么是颠覆性创新战略？

What is the disruptive innovation strategy?

(2)颠覆性创新所需的能力以及驱动力是什么？

What are the capabilities and driving forces required for the disruptive innovation?

(3)小米公司实施颠覆性创新战略带来了哪些启示？

What insights can we gain from Xiaomi's disruptive innovation strategy?

资料来源

Xiaoxu Yan. 后发企业的颠覆性创新战略——小米公司的案例研究[C]. 人文与社会

科学国际会议,2016:122—128.

董洁林,陈娟.无缝开放式创新:基于小米案例探讨互联网生态中的产品创新模式[J].科研管理,2014(12):76—84.

陈思睿,杨桂菊,王彤.后发企业的颠覆性创新机理模型——基于小米公司的探索性案例研究[J].管理案例研究与评论,2019(04):365—382.

References

Xiaoxu Yan. Research on the Latecomer Firms' Disruptive Innovation Strategy—A Case Study of Xiaomi Company[C]. International Conference on Humanity and Social Science,2016:122—128.

Dong Jielin,Chen Juan. Seamless open innovation:Exploring the product innovation mode in the Internet ecosystem based on the case of Xiaomi[J]. Science Research Management,2014(12):76—84.

Chen Sirui,Yang Guiju,Wang Tong. Disruptive innovation mechanism model of latecomers—an exploratory case study based on Xiaomi[J]. Journal of Management Case Studies,2019(04):365—382.

案例 3.3　上海迪士尼乐园本土化营销策略
Case 3.3　Localization Marketing Strategy of Shanghai Disney Resort

教学目标
Teaching Objectives

为了在中国市场有更加亮眼的表现,上海迪士尼乐园一直推行本土化,充分吸收中国元素,不遗余力地展现传统中国文化,"土""洋"结合,成功吸引众多中国游客。从目前的表现来看,本土化策略无疑在迪士尼乐园取得不俗业绩的过程中居功甚伟,而且可以预期的是,迪士尼乐园还将在本土化营销的道路上走得更远。本案例旨在让学生认识到建立文化自信的重要性,只有充分尊重民族文化,才能有力量推进国家的伟大建设;同时引导学生正确地从世界的角度看待外来文化,包容和尊重不同的文化,吸收人类最优秀的文明成果。

In order to have a better performance in China, Shanghai Disney Resort has been promoting the localization strategy. It has successfully attracted numerous Chinese visitors by fully using Chinese elements, sparing no effort to show traditional Chinese culture, and combining "local" and "foreign" elements. According to current performance, the localization strategy has undoubtedly made great contributions to its good results. Moreover, it can be expected that Shanghai Disney Resort will go further in localization marketing. This case, aims to help students realize the importance of building cultural confidence. Only by fully respecting a nation's culture can people have the strength to advance the great construction of their own country. Meanwhile, it will guide students to correctly look at foreign cultures from the perspective of the international community as a whole, tolerate and respect different cultures, and learn from the best achievements of human civilizations.

本案例涉及战略管理中的国际本土化战略、本土化营销策略等相关知识点。

This case involves International localization strategy, localization marketing strategy and other related concepts in strategic management.

案例内容
Contents

上海迪士尼项目于2011年4月8日在浦东新区川沙镇破土动工,历经5年多的建设,2016年6月16日,作为迪士尼家族在中国内地的首座乐园,也是中国第二座、亚洲第三座、世界第六座迪士尼神奇

案例 3.3　上海迪士尼乐园本土化营销策略

主题公园,上海迪士尼乐园开园迎客。

The Shanghai Disney Resort project commenced construction in Chuansha Town, Pudong New Area on April 8, 2011. After more than five years of construction, Shanghai Disney Resort opened to the public on June 16, 2016. It is the first Disney Resort in Chinese mainland and the second Disney Magic Kingdom Theme Park in China (the third in Asia and the sixth in the world).

为了在中国市场取得更好的成绩,迪士尼公司一直在上海迪士尼乐园中实行本土化营销策略,积极将中国文化元素和美国文化元素相结合,设计出符合游客文化习惯的主题乐园。上海迪士尼乐园于2011年动工时,董事长兼首席执行官罗伯特·艾格就宣布"原汁原味迪士尼,别具一格中国风"的理念。从园区景观设计、施工到故事策划、主题表演、餐饮服务等环节都植入了中国元素,在展现迪士尼乐园一贯的梦幻、传奇、快乐风格的同时,人们还能体验到浓厚的中国韵味。

In order to better achieve results in the Chinese market, the Walt Disney Company has been implementing the localization marketing strategy in Shanghai Disney Resort. By actively combining Chinese cultural elements with American ones, it designs theme parks that conform to visitors' cultural habits. When Shanghai Disney Resort started construction in 2011, Chairman and CEO Robert A. Iger described it as "authentically Disney and distinctly Chinese". Chinese elements were implanted in different aspects of the park from landscape design, construction, to story planning, theme performance and catering service. While showing the consistent dream-like, legendary and joyous style of Disney Resort, it also provides visitors with a great opportunity to experience the lasting appeal of Chinese culture.

一、产品策略的本土化
Ⅰ. Localization of product strategy

从基本概念上讲,产品策略意味着企业要注重产品开发的功能,使产品有独特的卖点,把产品的功能诉求放在第一位。上海迪士尼乐园的产品策略本土化体现在视觉符号表现、主题表演、餐饮服务体验等方面。

Basically speaking, product strategy means that enterprises should pay attention to the function of product development, so as to provide products with unique selling points while putting the fundamental requirements of products over anything else. The localization of product strategy of Shanghai Disney Resort is reflected in visual symbols, theme performance, catering service experience and so forth.

(一)视觉符号表现中国化
(1)Chinese visual symbols

上海迪士尼乐园本土化最重要、最基础的一环当属在整个园区融入中国元素,实现中国文化在园区落地。园区的建筑、景观、标识、文字、图案等各种可视化的载体在保持原汁原味的基础之上,巧妙融入各种中国元素,并且是随处可见(如图3-2所示)。通过这种方式,游客得以直接体验到本土化所带来的观感冲击。

The most significant and basic part of the localization of Shanghai Disney Resort is to integrate Chinese elements into the whole park to show Chinese culture. Various visual carriers such as buildings,

案例 3.3　上海迪士尼乐园本土化营销策略

landscapes, signs, characters and patterns in the park are ingeniously blended with Chinese elements that can be seen everywhere on the basis of maintaining the original style(as shown in Figure 3－2). In this way, visitors can directly experience the visual impact brought by localization.

图片来源：http://mmbiz.qpic.cn/mmbiz/X0CpvXARbP4ibNPAlw7zfT2ficj1apPAJ8I2pXqZ36szohhr9JMBYyCjAkc6rmwjtVCUFVun7NhicNv3exfAvZmAg/640?wx_fmt=png&wxfrom=5&wx_lazy=1&wx_co=1,2023－02－23。

Source: http://mmbiz.qpic.cn/mmbiz/X0CpvXARbP4ibNPAlw7zfT2ficj1apPAJ8I2pXqZ36szohhr9JMBYyCjAkc6rmwjtVCUFVun7NhicNv3exfAvZmAg/640?wx_fmt=png&wxfrom=5&wx_lazy=1&wx_co=1,2023－02－23.

图 3－2　上海迪斯尼园区的建筑

Figure 3－2　Buildings in the Shanghai Disney Resort

在上海迪士尼乐园内部，游客随时随地都可以看到自己熟悉的建筑风格。从乐园的门口设计到正中央的迪士尼城堡，每一处的建筑都让游客感觉似乎和自身本土设计一样，但似乎又比本土设计多了些什么。

169

Inside Shanghai Disney Resort, visitors can see their familiar architectural styles anytime and anywhere. From the entrance design of the park to the Disney Castle in the center, every building brings visitors the same feel as the local design, but there seems to be something more.

在上海迪士尼的乐园入口处，迪士尼的设计师将上海本土的石库门建筑和迪士尼传统的城堡风格相结合，设计出了带有上海迪士尼特色的乐园入口。相较于生硬的"拼凑风"，迪士尼的设计师在将两种建筑风格融合到一起的时候不断寻找二者的共同点和不同点，努力让它们的融合变得自然。除了融合之外，设计师还在原有的风格上进行了创新，设计出钟表式的门楼。这种设计代表着游客一旦进入迪士尼，他们的快乐时光也即将开启。

At the entrance, designers combined the local Shikumen architecture with Disney's traditional castle style, presenting unique characteristics of Shanghai Disney Resort. Compared with the blunt "patchwork style", Disney designers were constantly looking for similarities and differences between the two styles when they combined the two architectural styles together, so as to make the integration as natural as possible. In addition to integration, they also innovated based on the original style and designed a clock-style gatehouse. This means happy hours are coming once visitors enter the Disney Resort.

奇幻童话城堡最高的塔尖图案是中国名花——牡丹，而在另外的塔尖上还能够看到上海市市花白玉兰的图案，除此之外还有中国传统的祥云、莲花等。游客入园之后，会发现类似这样的可视化符号俯拾皆是，亲近感、熟悉感油然而生，很快就会产生继续游玩下去的欲望和

案例3.3 上海迪士尼乐园本土化营销策略

兴趣。

On the highest spire of the Enchanted Storybook Castle, visitors can find a pattern featuring peony, a famous flower in China. On other spires, there are patterns of Magnolia denudata, the flower of Shanghai city, as well as the traditional auspicious clouds and lotus flowers of China. After entering the park, visitors will see visual symbols like this everywhere. With a sense of closeness and familiarity arising spontaneously inside, they will soon have the desire and interest to further explore the resort.

迪士尼还针对中国游客特别设计了"十二朋友园",从迪士尼经典的动画中挑选出十二个动画明星,与中国的十二生肖相契合。别出新意的融合方式虽略显简单,但不可否认形象的视觉识别符号能带来文化关联,较容易帮助游客找到文化共鸣。

Disney also specially designed the "Garden of the Twelve Friends" for Chinese visitors. Twelve animated stars are selected from Disney's classic animations to match twelve Chinese zodiac signs. Although the way of innovative integration is somewhat simple, it is without doubt that the visual identification symbols of images can bring cultural connection, which makes it easier for visitors to find cultural resonance.

(二)主题表演洋溢中国风

(2) Theme performance with Chinese style

作为吸引游客最主要的方式,主题公园的娱乐表演大多会以个性化的方式呈现。其中,最打动游客的莫过于各地的经典文化和故事。在上海迪士尼乐园中,大部分娱乐节目由中国演员表演,并且表演所用语言主要是中文和英文。除此之外,上海迪士尼还在相关节目中融入了传统的中式元素。《花木兰》中利用传统的中国故事来讲述中美两国文化的优秀精神——勇敢、独立和忠诚。在《唐氏太极》节目中,身穿唐装的中国演员和唐老鸭一起向游客展示了中华太极的魅力。久演不衰的《狮子王》中出现孙悟空、皮影戏等中国经典的角色和艺术,土狼操着东北口音,剧中还揉进许多本土化的台词;《人猿泰山》则是在表演中渗透了中国传统的杂技,再加上川剧喷火表演,中国特色文化有机融入。最值得注意的是,在上海迪士尼的每一种娱乐表演背后都配备了优秀的中国艺术家为演出设计造型、编写歌曲。

As the most important way to attract visitors, a majority of entertainment performances in the theme park are presented in a personalized way. The most touching part for visitors is the classic cultural stories from all over the world. In Shanghai Disney Resort, most of the entertainment programs are performed by Chinese actors, mainly in Chinese and English. In addition, Shanghai Disney Resort has also incorporated traditional Chinese elements into related programs. Mulan adopts the traditional story of China to tell the excellent qualities shared by both Chinese and American cultures, such as courage, independence and loyalty. In Tai Chi with Donald Duck, Chinese actors in Tang suits and Donald Duck jointly show the visitors how charmful the Chinese Tai Chi is. The Monkey King, shadow play and other classic Chinese characters and art forms appear in the long-running The Lion King. There are hyenas speaking with a northeastern China accent, and many localized lines are included into the play. Tarzan the Ape Man absorbs China's traditional acrobatics and Sichuan Opera's fire-breathing show, organically integrating China's characteristic culture. Most notably, behind every entertainment performance in Shanghai Disney Resort, outstanding Chinese artists are always prepared for designing characters and writing songs.

（三）餐饮服务体验中国味

(3) Experience Chinese flavor in catering service

迪士尼上海乐园的餐饮服务因地制宜，更加贴近本土游客的消费习惯。中国和亚洲传统菜式在园区的各大主题餐厅都能轻易找到，如传统的中国包子以及川、粤、湘等多种菜系，游客能在园区根据个人的口味偏好选择消费。从数量上看，中式餐饮的比重达到70%，占绝大多数。迪士尼为了更贴近本土消费者的口味，配备了700多人的厨师团队，仅有3人来自海外，其余全部来自全国各地，能够满足八大菜系的要求。落户上海，迪士尼也充分融入上海传统菜式，比如上海的烧麦、小笼包等传统美食。

The catering service of Shanghai Disney Resort is adapted according to local conditions to better meet the consumption habits of local visitors. Chinese and Asian traditional cuisines can be easily found in the major theme restaurants in the resort, such as traditional steamed stuffed buns, and Sichuan, Guangdong and Hunan cuisines and so forth. Therefore, visitors can choose food according to their preferences. In terms of quantity, Chinese restaurants account for 70%, taking a dominant place. In order to better meet the tastes of local consumers, Disney has a team of more than 700 chefs, only three of whom are foreigners, and the others are Chinese from all over China, capable of serving eight major cuisines of China. As it is located in

Shanghai, Disney also fully incorporates the traditional Shanghai cuisine, such as Shanghai-style shaomai, xiaolongbao (soup dumplings) and other traditional delicacies.

餐饮本土化的同时,迪士尼也没有摈弃"原汁原味"的初心,结合中国传统和迪士尼形象,创新性推出各种中国口味的迪士尼菜式,比如米奇肉包、米奇红豆包等,结合迪士尼的创意和本土口味创造性地开发出多种菜式,外在与内涵的融合再一次彰显了文化创新的强大张力。

While localizing catering services, Disney doesn't abandon its original aspiration of "Disney flavor". Combining Chinese traditions and Disney images, it has innovatively launched different kinds of Disney dishes with Chinese flavor, such as Mickey Mouse Meat Stuffed Bun and Mickey Mouse Red Bean Bun, and creatively developed a wide variety of dishes integrating Disney's creativity and local taste. The integration of the inside and the outside shows once again the great power of cultural innovation.

二、宣传策略本土化

Ⅱ. Localization of publicity strategies

宣传策略是指企业利用各种信息载体与目标市场进行自身宣传的传播活动,包括广告、人员推销、营业推广与公共关系等方面。在上海迪士尼乐园中,宣传策略包括宣传片传播、名人效应、企业合作等途径。

The publicity strategy refers to the communication activities that enterprises use various information carriers and target markets to promote themselves, including advertising, personal promotion, marketing and public relations. At Shanghai Disney Resort, publicity

案例 3.3　上海迪士尼乐园本土化营销策略

strategies include propaganda film dissemination, celebrity effect, business cooperation and so forth.

（一）以"家"文化为主的宣传片广告

(1) Propaganda film featuring "home" culture

"家"文化概念在中国源远流长。上海迪士尼的开业宣传片正是将重点集中在"家"文化概念上。从宣传片中的家庭成员人物形象，到后来的广告宣传语"无论你是谁，无论你多大年纪，只要你充满童心，请接受我们的邀请，带上家人好友，一起点亮心中奇幻之梦"。所有的元素都在向游客传递一种讯息：上海迪士尼会为他们提供一个享受家庭亲情的场所，任何人都可以在上海迪士尼乐园中与家人一起追求梦想，享受快乐时光。而在最新的宣传片中，上海迪士尼同样将宣传的重点聚焦于"家庭"和"快乐"。

The cultural concept of "home" has a long history in China. It is a key part of the propaganda film for the opening ceremony of Shanghai Disney Resort. From the characters of family members in the propaganda film to the advertising slogan "No matter who or how old you are, as long as you are full of childlike innocence, please accept our invitation to bring your family members and friends here to jointly light up your magic dreams", all elements are sending a message to visitors that Shanghai Disney Resort will be a fantastic place for them to enjoy family affection. Anyone can pursue their dreams and enjoy a happy time with their families at Shanghai Disney Resort. In the latest propaganda film, Shanghai Disney Resort once again focuses on "family" and "happiness".

(二)本土名人的正能量效应

(2) Positive energy effect of local celebrities

随着时代的不断发展,消费者的观念也在不断发生变化,即由过去重视物质消费到现在重视精神消费,因此,名人的正能量效应对于主题公园的发展也起到了一定的推动作用。2016年9月,上海迪士尼在开业的第三个月邀请了中国著名跳水冠军吴敏霞到乐园内参观游玩,并且还打出了"欢迎奥运跳水冠军吴敏霞回家!"的横幅。这一举措不仅提升了上海迪士尼的知名度,还借助中国本土名人的形象拉近了乐园与中国游客的距离。此后,上海迪士尼经常邀请本土名人来乐园做客。中国本土演员邓超、体操运动员李小鹏、中国台湾明星林志玲等人的身影都曾在上海迪士尼出现过。从上海迪士尼邀请的名人名单上可以看出,这些名人都在专业领域取得过优异成绩,拥有良好的品质。这种邀请本土名人的做法也在无形中表明上海迪士尼乐园不仅是一个为游客提供快乐的地方,还是一个充满正能量的乐园。

With the continuous development of the times, consumers' ideas are constantly changing. Now they prefer spiritual consumption over material consumption. Therefore, the positive energy effect of celebrities also plays a certain role in promoting the development of theme parks. In September 2016, Shanghai Disney Resort invited Wu Minxia, a Chinese diving champion, to visit the park in the third month after its opening, and put up a banner saying "Welcome home! Olympic diving champion Wu Minxia!". This move not only enhanced the popularity of Shanghai Disney Resort, but also made it get closer to Chinese visitors supported by the image of local celebrities in China. Since then, local celebrities who have achieved excellent results in their careers with good qualities have been frequently invited to visit the resort, including Chinese actor Deng Chao, gymnastics champion Li Xiaopeng, and Chinese Taiwan actress Lin Chi-ling. This practice of inviting local celebrities also indicates that Shanghai Disney Resort can provide both happiness and positive energy for visitors.

点评
Comments

文化是一个国家、一个民族的灵魂。一个国家、一个民族只有树立高度的文化自信，才能锻造出坚持坚守的定力、奋起奋发的勇气、创新创造的活力，让国家和民族的精神大厦巍然耸立。

Culture is the soul of a country or a nation. Only by establishing a high degree of cultural confidence can a country or a nation have the willpower for persistence, the courage for hard work and the vitality of innovation and creation to create a spiritual building that will stand tall.

中国消费者一方面需要领略迪士尼文化所蕴含的梦幻色彩，另一方面更希望能看到中国文化在乐园的集中体现。失去前者，乐园就没有了灵魂；没有了后者，就难以得到中国消费者的高度认同。

For Chinese consumers, on the one hand, they should learn to appreciate the magic colors embedded in Disney culture. On the other hand, they hope to see the concentrated expressions of Chinese culture there. Without the former, the resort will lose its soul, while without the latter, it will be difficult for the resort to be widely received among Chinese consumers.

上海迪士尼乐园所应用的本土化营销策略的确是主题公园国际化发展的一种十分有效的方式。该乐园既坚持"迪士尼化"的全球统一标准,又借鉴和吸收本土元素的营销策略,创造欢乐,树立品牌,提高建设、管理和营销水平,贯彻"全球化思维"的理念,从而建成具有中国特色的主题公园,促进了中国主题公园的健康发展。

The localization marketing strategy adopted by Shanghai Disney Resort is indeed a highly effective way for theme parks to go global. While adhering to the global standard of Disney, Shanghai Disney Resort learns from and absorbs local elements. It aims to create joyful experiences, establish corporate brand, improve construction, management and marketing level, and implement the concept of "global mindset", thus building a theme park with Chinese characteristics and promoting the healthy development of theme parks in China.

讨论题

Discussions

(1)上海迪士尼的营销策略包括哪些方面的内容?

What aspects does the marketing strategy of Shanghai Disney Resort include?

(2)你对上海迪士尼本土化营销战略的做法有何评价?

What do you think of the localization marketing strategy of Shanghai Disney Resort?

(3)上海迪士尼的本土化营销战略有哪些启示?

案例 3.3　上海迪士尼乐园本土化营销策略

What insights gained from the localization marketing strategy of Shanghai Disney Resort?

资料来源

郑红,李毅峰.上海迪士尼主题乐园本土化营销策略中的第三文化研究[J].文化学刊,2019(07):14—16.

杨金宏.上海迪士尼本土化营销策略研究[J].中国商论,2018(02):54—56.

Jia Yao.市场营销战略研究:迪士尼的案例研究[C].第二届经济与工商管理国际会议,2017:473—481.

References

Zheng Hong,Li Yifeng. Research on third culture in the localization marketing strategy of Shanghai Disney Resort[J]. Culture Journal,2019(07):14—16.

Yang Jinhong. Research on the localization marketing strategy of Shanghai Disney Resort[J]. China Journal of Commerce,2018(02):54—56.

Jia Yao. Research on marketing strategy:case study of Disneyland[C]. Second International Conference on Economic and Business Management,2017:473—481.

第四篇　市场营销
PART Ⅳ　MARKETING

案例 4.1 "人民需要什么,五菱就造什么"
——五菱汽车营销案例
Case 4.1 "Wuling Makes Whatever People Need"
—Marketing Case of Wuling Motors

教学目标
Teaching Objectives

2020年年初,新冠疫情爆发。为控制疫情蔓延,公共社交场所要求民众佩戴口罩。口罩一度成为稀缺资源。一家生产汽车的企业——上汽通用五菱——因转产生产口罩迅速走红,将一盒盒印着"人民需要什么,五菱就造什么"的"五菱牌口罩"送往疫区。通过学习本案例,学生不仅能了解分析企业精湛的营销能力、品牌传播与提升能力,同时也能感受到企业打造中国品牌的社会责任感。

At the beginning of 2020, COVID-19 broke out. In order to control the spread of the epidemic, people at public places were required to wear face masks that once became a scarce resource. SAIC-GM-

Wuling, a company that used to manufacture automobiles, went viral as it started to make masks. It sent boxes of "Wuling masks" printed with "Wuling makes whatever people need" to epidemic-affected areas. Through the analysis of this case, students can not only understand and analyze the excellent marketing, brand communication and promotion capabilities of enterprises, but also feel their social responsibility in building a Chinese brand.

案例涉及国际营销中关于品牌营销、用户需求、宏观环境影响等相关知识点。

The case covers relevant knowledge points in International Marketing, such as brand marketing, user demand, and macro environmental impact.

案例内容
Contents

2020年年初,新冠疫情爆发。世界各国多个城市相继采取封城隔离措施,抑制疫情发展蔓延。公共社交场所要求民众佩戴口罩。口罩一度成为稀缺资源。

In early 2020, COVID-19 broke out. Many cities around the world had successively taken measures such as lockdown to curb the spread of the epidemic. People at public places were required to wear face masks that once became a scarce resource.

案例4.1 "人民需要什么,五菱就造什么"——五菱汽车营销案例

图片来源:https://baijiahao.baidu.com/s?id=16834974066300461378&wfr=spider&for=pc,2023-02-20。

Source: https://baijiahao.baidu.com/s?id=16834974066300461378&wfr=spider&for=pc,2023-02-20.

图4-1 新冠疫情期间"一罩难求"五菱汽车转产生产口罩送往疫区

Figure 4-1 Wuling Motors began to manufacture masks and sent them to the affected area during the epidemic when the masks were in shortage

疫情防控期间,一盒盒印着"人民需要什么,五菱就造什么"的"五菱牌口罩"送往疫区(如图4-1所示)。这让一家生产汽车的企业因转产生产口罩而迅速走红,人们对五菱汽车也有了新的认识。一时间,五菱汽车的国民口碑达到了巅峰。五菱企业不仅展示了其精湛的营销能力,也向社会证实了中国品牌的社会责任感!

185

During the epidemic, boxes of "Wuling masks" printed with "Wuling makes whatever people need" were sent to the epidemic-affected areas(as shown in Figure 4—1). In this way, a company that used to produce automobiles went viral as it started to manufacture masks, and people had a new understanding of Wuling Motors. For a time, the reputation of Wuling Motors reached its peak. While demonstrating its excellent marketing capability, it showed the social responsibilities of a Chinese brand to the public!

一、"人民需要什么 五菱就造什么"

Ⅰ. "Wuling makes whatever people need"

上汽通用五菱主要生产销售6万~8万元的商用MPV(多用途汽车),因为坚实耐用、价格低廉,一直深受消费者的喜爱,更是长期盘踞销量前列。疫情防控时期,在口罩物资供不应求的情况下,上汽通用五菱宣布改造口罩生产线,所生产的口罩"只赠不卖",全部捐赠广西柳州政府,统一调配。如表4—1所示。

SAIC-GM-Wuling mainly produces and sells commercial MPV (multi-purpose vehicle) at 60,000—80,000 yuan. Thanks to its durability and low price, it has always been widely a favorite among consumers, ranking at the top for a long time. During the special period of the epidemic, considering that face masks were in short supply, SAIC-GM-Wuling announced transformation of mask production lines, and all the masks produced would be donated to the Liuzhou government of Guangxi Zhuang Autonomous Region for unified distribution. As shown in Table 4—1.

案例 4.1 "人民需要什么,五菱就造什么"——五菱汽车营销案例

表 4—1 　　　　　　2020 年上汽通用五菱改造口罩生产线
Table 4—1　SAIC-GM-Wuling's Transformation of Mask Production Lines in 2020

时间 Date	改造进展 Progress in Transformation
2月5日 February 5	五菱从海外购买 2 万只医用口罩送给一线。 Wuling bought 20,000 medical masks from overseas and sent them to the front-line medical staff.
2月6日 February 6	五菱计划联合供应商造口罩,改造供应商 12 条生产线,日产量计划当月底达 170 万个。 Wuling planned to cooperate with suppliers to manufacture masks and transform 12 production lines of suppliers. The daily output was expected to reach 1.7 million pieces by the end of the month.
2月8日 February 8	第一批 20 只口罩下线,符合民用标准,医用口罩正在准备中。 The first batch of 20 masks were successfully produced, which met civil standards. Medical masks were being prepared.
2月10日 February 10	五菱发现产能还不够,决定自己也要生产口罩。 It was found that the production capacity was not adequate and wuling decided to produce masks itself.
2月13日 February 13	五菱自己生产的口罩出货,50 万只/天。 Wuling's face masks were officially produced, with a daily output of 500,000 pieces.
2月14日 February 14	第 100 万只口罩下线,一部分交给政府,一部分送给一线医护人员。 The millionth mask went off the production line, part of which was given to the government, and the rest were sent to the front-line medical staff.
2月19日 February 19	五菱第一台口罩机下线,仅仅用了 76 小时,意味着:五菱不仅要生产口罩,还要生产口罩机器…… It took only 76 hours for Wuling's first face mask machine to be produced which meant that Wuling would produce mask machines in addition to masks…
2月20日 February 20	五菱交给政府一批智能移动测温车,可以在 2 米内对大面积移动人群进行测温…… Wuling handed over a batch of intelligent mobile temperature measuring vehicles to the government, which can measure the temperature of a large group of moving individuals within a range of 2 meters…
……	

2020年,五菱仅仅在半个月时间内,从一个外购口罩捐献给一线的车企,开始计划生产口罩,生产出口罩机、智能移动测温车/床,并捐献给一线医护人员和政府。这一举措赢得了社会与群众的广泛赞誉,一时间,社交媒体上全部是"五菱牌口罩"的新闻。五菱站在了营销的高地上。

In 2020, within half a month, as an auto producer used to donate purchased masks to the front-line medical staff, Wuling began to produce masks, mask machines and intelligent mobile temperature measuring vehicles/beds, and donated them to front-line medical staff and the government. This activity won nationwide acclaim from the public. At that time, news of "Wuling masks" swept over social media, putting Wuling in a favorable position in marketing.

五菱究竟是如何抓住这次营销机遇的?众多履行企业社会责任的品牌为何没有达到效果?"五菱牌口罩"又是如何深入人心的?

How did Wuling seize this marketing opportunity? Why did so many brands that fulfill corporate social responsibilities fail to do so? How did the "Wuling masks" win popularity among the people?

二、新冠疫情困境下的抉择
II. Choice made during COVID-19

中国汽车市场受疫情影响,2020年销售局面十分严峻。中国汽车工业协会公布的数据显示,2020年1月销量为194.1万辆,同比下降18%。对于汽车这样的大型消费品而言,传统销售模式面临挑战:消费者缺少实际体验,购买意愿下降。

Affected by the epidemic, the auto market of China faced severe

案例 4.1 "人民需要什么，五菱就造什么"——五菱汽车营销案例

sales situation in 2020. According to the data released by China Association of Automobile Manufacturers, the sales volume in January 2020 was 1.941 million, decrease 18% year on year. For large consumer goods like automobiles, the traditional sales model faced challenges: consumers lacked actual experiences, leading to decreased willingness in purchasing.

如何在疫情特殊时期做好营销成为车企重点考虑的方面。

How to effectively conduct marketing in the special period of epidemic has become a key concern for auto makers.

作为汽车生产企业，五菱面对的消费群众是以中小生意为主的商用群体，在上半年疫情形势严重的影响下，这一群体购买力大幅下降。各汽车企业都基本处于无生意可做的状态，面临销售供应大于需求的严峻现实。五菱也难以幸免，在现有生产线的产品生产方面，其生产能力远大于市场所需，造成生产线产力盈余。也就是说，五菱的生产线无需满负荷生产也完全满足市场对其产品的需求。

As an auto maker, Wuling's customers are small and medium-sized business owners. Influenced by the severe epidemic in the first half of the year, the purchasing power of the target group dropped sharply. All types of auto makers hardly had business, facing the grim reality that supply exceeded demand, neither did Wuling. If it manufactured with existing production lines, its productivity was far greater than the market demand, resulting in a surplus of production capacity. In other words, Wuling's production line could fully meet the market demand even if it was not operating under full load.

供求关系的改变，使得五菱所面对的问题并非生产，而是销售。

需要考虑的重点就是如何利用现有资源转化优势,为下半年销售做好铺垫与准备,提升品牌认知度。

With changes in supply-demand relationship, the problem facing Wuling was not production but sales. The major concern to be considered was how to make full use of existing resources to pave the way for sales in the second half of the year and enhance brand awareness.

三、创新营销提升品牌形象
Ⅲ. Innovative marketing for improving brand image

五菱采取了五方面行动:

Wuling adopted a five-pronged approach:

1. 在不影响本业生产的前提下,充分发挥可利用资源优势,改造生产线:现有富余生产能力可否改造生产除汽车以外的其他产品?

1. Given that its auto manufacturing would not be affected, it gave full play to its available resources and transformed its production lines. Could its surplus production capacity be used to make products other than automobiles?

2. 提出朗朗上口的营销口号:"人民需要什么,五菱就造什么。"

2. It proposed a catchy marketing slogan "Wuling makes whatever people need".

其实在五菱之前,已经有比亚迪、富士康、五菱汽车、中石化、佛慈制药等企业,以及水星家纺、华纺股份、报喜鸟、爹地宝贝、三枪内衣、红豆服饰、雅戈尔等上市公司或子公司发布公告临时改线转产口罩、医用防护服等产品。但是,只有"五菱牌口罩"被消费者广为知晓,这主要得益于其朗朗上口的传播口号"人民需要什么,五菱就造什么"。

案例4.1 "人民需要什么,五菱就造什么"——五菱汽车营销案例

虽然其他企业在公益与企业社会责任方面也担起了重任,是为国家和社会付出的标杆企业,但从营销方面来看却没有五菱成功。

In fact, before Wuling, BYD, Foxconn, Sinopec, Foci Pharmaceutical and other enterprises, as well as listed companies or their subsidiaries such as Mercury Home Textiles, Huafang, Saint Angelo, Daddy Baby, THREEGUN, HODO, YOUNGOR, etc. released announcements about their temporary shift to produce medical products including masks and medical protective clothing. However, only "Wuling masks" was widely known among consumers thanks to its catchy communication slogan "Wuling makes whatever people need". Other benchmark enterprises serving the country and the public were not as successful as Wuling in marketing, though they also shouldered heavy duties in public welfare and corporate social responsibilities.

3. 涟漪效应,促使新媒体自发讨论:微博、微信、抖音、快手纷纷为其免费传播……

3. Ripple effect: new media like Weibo, WeChat, TikTok and Kuaishou discussed the topic spontaneously and spread it for free…

社交媒体大量转发"五菱牌口罩"新闻,很多并非由五菱企业设置,而是媒体与营销号主动的行为。之所以形成了免费的传播,关键在于五菱的营销口号为社会提供了足够引发关注与讨论的话题:在口罩紧缺状态下改造生产线,用于缓解物资紧张。当"五菱"(汽车生产企业)与"口罩"两个词组合在一起的时候,很难不引发关注。

Social media forwarded a large number of news about "Wuling masks", many of which were not promoted by Wuling, but by the media and marketing accounts themselves. The key to the free communication was that Wuling's marketing slogan provided an attractive topic for the public to conduct heated discussion: transforming its production lines to alleviate the problem of mask shortage. When the words "Wuling" (auto maker) and "mask" are bundled together, it is quite easy to attract attention.

4."只赠不卖"反转行为,提升品牌形象。

4. The practice of "giving away but not for sale" improved its brand image.

不谈改造生产线的投入,就仅仅由于疫情特殊时期无形中提高的原材料费用与人力成本,口罩的价格也会小幅增长。那么"五菱牌口罩"究竟会卖多少钱呢?

The price of masks rose slightly because of the inevitable increase in raw materials and labor costs during the special period of the epidemic, let alone Wuling's investment in transforming its production lines. So at what price should the "Wuling masks" be sold?

"只赠不卖"打破了人们的传统思维,作为柳州市的龙头企业,五菱将全部口罩捐赠广西柳州政府统一调配。"只赠不卖"不仅再一次提升了五菱的品牌高度,更为五菱赢得了当地政府与消费者良好的口碑,为其今后在当地的发展打下了良好的基础。2020年6月3日,港股五菱汽车午后大幅拉升,最高涨幅达126.13%,报0.45港元/股。

"Giving away but not for sale" changed people's traditional thinking. As a leading enterprise in Liuzhou, Wuling donated all masks to the Liuzhou government of Guangxi Zhuang Autonomous Region for unified distribution. "Giving away but not for sale" improved the brand image of Wuling once again, and won it a good repu-

案例4.1 "人民需要什么,五菱就造什么"——五菱汽车营销案例

tation among the local government and consumers, laying a solid foundation for its future development in Liuzhou. On June 3, 2020, Wuling Motors Stocks listed in Hong Kong rose sharply in the afternoon, with the highest increase of 126.13% to 0.45 HKD per share.

5. 易于二次创作的"人民需要体"。

5. The "style of whatever people need" is easy for recreation.

"人民需要什么,五菱就造什么"话题在多个营销账号的引导下,引发全网讨论与跟进,并以"人民需要××,五菱就造××"为句式造句,一时间,各种千奇百怪的物品被提及,如"我需要个锤子,五菱你造不造""我需要大补鸳鸯锅,五菱你造不造"等,不得不佩服网民的脑洞之大。无论多么正向的传播,如果仅仅停留在单向传播上,受众是无法参与进来的。只有形成互动,才能进一步引发受众的参与,让受众"玩"在其中。

Under the guidance of several marketing accounts, the topic "Wuling makes whatever people need" sparked discussion all over the internet. People started to draft sentences following "if people need ××, Wuling makes ××". For a time, all kinds of strange items were mentioned, such as "if I need a hammer, can Wuling make one" "if I need a two-flavor hotpot to replenish my energy, can Wuling make one" and so forth. We have to admit that netizens are full of imagination. However, the audience can never join in a one-way communication, no matter how positive it is. Only when there are interactions can we get the audience more involved and let them "enjoy" it.

四、总结

Ⅳ. Summary

在 2020 年上半年销售难以达成预期的局面下,为下半年打好销售铺垫是重点;五菱改造口罩生产线,生产"五菱牌口罩",只赠不卖;用"人民需要什么,五菱就造什么"这一极具号召力与感染力的口号进行传播,引发社会讨论与关注;2 月 15 日,央视新闻联播报道《战疫情中国制造跑出中国速度》点赞五菱之举。牛年除夕夜那天,一张张色彩鲜艳、图案喜庆的央视春晚+五菱汽车联名款春晚红色口罩,出现在了春晚的大屏中,上汽通用五菱也成为国内首个以跨界产品在春节联欢晚会中亮相的汽车品牌,收获了满满的人气和口碑。

Given the fact that it was difficult to achieve expected sales in the first half of 2020, laying a solid foundation for the second half was crucial. Wuling transformed its production lines to make "Wuling masks", which were only given away but not for sale. Communicating with the slogan of "Wuling makes whatever people need" aroused discussion and concern among the public. On February 15, the report of CCTV news titled Made in China Achieved China Speed in Fighting COVID-19 highly praised Wuling's actions. On New Year's Eve of 2021, red masks with Chinese characters of "CCTV Spring Festival Gala" and "Wuling Motors" in bright colors and festive patterns appeared on the large screen of the Spring Festival Gala, making SAIC-GM-Wuling the first Chinese auto brand showing up in the Spring Festival Gala with its cross-industry product. In this way, Wuling gained great popularity and reputation in China.

案例 4.1 "人民需要什么,五菱就造什么"——五菱汽车营销案例

如果企业采取捐款的方式,社会的关注点仅仅在于数字,一个数字最终会被另一个更高的数字替代,存留在人们脑海中的,还会剩下什么?而"人民需要什么,五菱就造什么"的"五菱牌口罩"传播性却远远不是简单的捐款所能达到的。

If enterprises make donations, the public only focuses on "figures". One figure will eventually be replaced by another larger one, and what will remain in people's minds? However, the popularity gained by "Wuling masks" with the help of "Wuling makes whatever people need" slogan goes far beyond donations.

点评
Comments

好品牌一定要被消费者认知和接受。"人民需要什么,五菱就造什么"这句口号究竟好在哪里?接地气,易理解。当品牌的受众群体整体认知水平并不高的时候,企业更需要以通俗易懂、贴近大众情感的方式宣传。如果说一句"众志成城,抗击疫情",就平淡无奇,很难打动消费者。而"人民需要什么,五菱就造什么"表达的是"倾其所有"的奉献精神,用朴实的言语表达,极具号召力与感染力。所传达的信息符合营销策略目标,能够让受众感知五菱的品牌文化。像是一个就在你身边的人,在你遇到困难的时候,五菱是站在"人民"身边的兄弟,或许文化程度不高,也不善言辞,不会附庸风雅,却有无私奉献的心。这句口号传递出了五菱始终站在消费者身边这一理念。

A good brand must be recognized and accepted by consumers. What's the point in the slogan "Wuling makes whatever people need"? It is down to earth and easy to understand. When the brand audience is not well aware of the brand, the enterprise needs to promote it in a way that is easy to understand and close to the public. By contrast, the slogan "work as one to fight the epidemic" is "flat and passionless" and cannot impress consumers. "Wuling makes whatever people need" expresses the dedication of "giving everything". The words are simple but have great appeal. The information conveyed is in line with its marketing strategy objectives and can make the audience perceive the brand culture of Wuling. Like someone who is always there with you, Wuling acts like a brother who stands with the "people" when people are in trouble. Perhaps he is not well educated, not talkative and not arty-crafty, but he devoted himself to fighting the epidemic selflessly. This slogan conveys the idea that Wuling always stands with consumers.

"精准洞察用户需求,深度传递品牌价值。"从营销的角度说,五菱精彩跨界的行动抓住了品牌营销的本质,即用户需求。"人民需要什么,五菱就造什么"并不是简单的品牌口号,而是能够满足消费者需求的核心价值:在疫情防控时期,相比汽车,消费者更需求的是口罩。未来品牌营销的成败,取决于"用户需求"。精准洞察用户需求,以用户需求为驱动,这才是品牌营销的根本。

"Accurate insights into user demand and in-depth delivery of brand value." From the marketing point of view, Wuling's outstanding cross-industry moves reflected the essence of brand marketing, namely the user demand. "Wuling makes whatever people need" is not a simple brand slogan, but a core value that can meet the needs of

案例 4.1 "人民需要什么，五菱就造什么"——五菱汽车营销案例

consumers. During the epidemic, consumers need masks more than cars. The success or failure of brand marketing in the future depends on "user demand". Accurate insights into user demand and operation driven by user demand are fundamental issues in brand marketing.

产品营销必须与宏观环境相适应。五菱基于当时大环境，根据自身能力开展公关工作，生产口罩，既满足了自身需求，如缓解了用工荒、开发了新的业务线等，又体现了企业的社会责任感，最终不仅得到直接、间接消费者的关注与认同，更在很大程度上提升了品牌的知名度和美誉度。

Product marketing must adapt to the macro-environment. Taking into account the external environment at that time, Wuling carried out a public relations campaign and produced masks according to its own capability, which not only met its own needs, such as alleviating the labor shortage and developing new business lines, but also showed its sense of social responsibility. While winning the attention and recognition of the direct and indirect consumers, it enhanced its brand popularity and reputation to a great extent.

讨论题

Discussions

(1)什么是品牌营销？品牌营销的核心是什么？

What is brand marketing? What is the core of brand marketing?

(2)企业发展是要营利的，当企业发展目标与企业社会责任冲突时，应该如何处理？

As the enterprises seek for profit, how to deal with the conflict between corporate development goals and corporate social responsibility?

(3)如何理解品牌营销与价值观二者之间的关系？

How to understand the relationship between brand marketing and values?

资料来源

人民需要什么，五菱就造什么：五菱再刷屏的营销秘籍[EB/OL]. [2023-02-20]. https://www.digitaling.com/articles/262569.html.

人民需要什么，五菱就造什么[EB/OL]. [2023-02-20]. https://baijiahao.baidu.com/s?id=1660565076214464753&wfr=spider&for=pc.

上汽通用五菱年度总结，人民需要什么就造什么的它，有哪些成绩？[EB/OL]. [2023-02-20]. https://www.163.com/dy/article/GTMJ0QQM0552D2XT.html.

References

Wuling makes whatever people need: The key to regain popularity for Wuling through marketing[EB/OL]. [2023-02-20]. https://www.digitaling.com/articles/262569.html.

Wuling makes whatever people need[EB/OL]. [2023-02-20]. https://baijiahao.baidu.com/s?id=1660565076214464753&wfr=spider&for=pc.

Annual summary of SAIC-GM-Wuling. What performance have the company making whatever people need achieved? [EB/OL]. [2023-02-20]. https://www.163.com/dy/article/GTMJ0QQM0552D2XT.html.

案例 4.2 做有温度的品牌：
民宿鼻祖 Airbnb(爱彼迎)与中国民宿
Case 4.2 A Brand with Warmth: Airbnb, the Originator of B&B, and Chinese B&B

教学目标
Teaching Objectives

Airbnb 是 AirBed and Breakfast("Air-b-n-b")的缩写,中文译为"爱彼迎"。爱彼迎成立于 2008 年 8 月,总部设在美国加州旧金山。Airbnb 是一个旅行房屋租赁社区,用户通过网络或手机应用程序发布、搜索度假房屋租赁信息并完成在线预订程序。这是一家联系旅游人士和家有空房出租房主的服务型网站平台,为用户提供多样的住宿信息。该社区平台在 191 个国家、65 000 个城市为世界各国旅行者们提供数以百万计的独特入住选择。目前在世界旅游界已享有盛名。

Airbnb is the abbreviation of AirBed and Breakfast ("Air-b-n-b"), which is called "爱彼迎" in Chinese. It was founded in August

2008, with its headquarters in San Francisco, California, USA. Airbnb is a vacation homes rental community, where users can post and search vacation homes rental information and complete online booking procedures through the Internet or mobile phone apps. It is a service-oriented website platform that connects tourists and homeowners with vacant rooms and provides users with a variety of accommodation information. This community platform offers millions of unique accommodation options for travelers from all over the world in 65,000 cities of 191 countries. At present, it enjoys a good reputation in the global tourism industry.

同样，在中国，度假日租房租赁市场也开始逐渐发展，主要提供与Airbnb类似服务和商业模式的网站有"乐日租"（Lerizu）。中国领先的房产家居网站搜房网也推出了"游天下"，提供类似的服务和商业模式。除此之外，中国农家乐的形式更为普遍。不过，农家乐的经营却不尽如人意。究其原因，中国农家乐无论从影响力、服务质量及品牌效应方面都有提高的空间。

Similarly, the vacation house rental market is also gradually developing in China. Lerizu is a website that mainly provides services and business models similar to Airbnb. SouFun, China's leading property website, also launched "YOUTIANXIA" to provide similar services and business models. In addition, agritainment is more widely accepted in China. However, its management is not satisfactory, as there is great room for its improvement in terms of influence, service quality and brand effect.

本节关注的重点是让学生通过学习本案例，从"品牌""产品质量"

案例 4.2 做有温度的品牌:民宿鼻祖 Airbnb(爱彼迎)与中国民宿

"服务"的角度理解该行业未来的发展。

This section aims to help students understand the future development of this industry from the perspectives of "brand" "product quality" and "service" by studying this case.

案例涉及国际营销中关于品牌、产品、服务、产品本土化等相关知识点。

The case involves brand, product, service and product localization and other related concepts in International Marketing.

案例内容

Contents

2022 年 6 月 3 日,Airbnb(爱彼迎)发布了房东/房源迁移计划,表示已与中国美团民宿、小猪/飞猪、途家民宿达成合作,可将大部分房东信息及房源信息迁移至合作民宿平台,并为符合条件的迁移房东/房源争取并推出了多项补贴权益。

On June 3, 2022, Airbnb released its house owner/housing relocation plan, indicating that it had reached cooperation with Meituan Homestay, Piglet/Flying Pig and Tujia Homestay from China. According to the plan, most of the information about house owners and houses would be transferred to the platform of its B&B partners, and a number of subsidies had been introduced for eligible relocated house owners/houses.

作为全球著名民宿鼻祖,Airbnb 对全球旅游者的吸引力无疑是巨大的。该公司曾官宣用全球远程、同工同酬的方式彻底结束办公室时代,瞬间吸引了 80 万求职者挤爆招聘官网。因此,分析 Airbnb 的经营模式就显得非常有意义了。

As the world-famous originator of B&B, Airbnb has undoubtedly great appeal to global tourists. It used to officially announce that it would put an end to the office era by means of working from home globally and equal pay for equal work, which instantly attracted 800,000 job seekers to rush onto its official website. Therefore, it is quite meaningful to analyze Airbnb's business mode.

一、Airbnb 加拿大住宿体验

I. Airbnb accommodation experience in Canada

有游客在网上分享了其通过 Airbnb 在加拿大住宿的体验:

Some tourists shared their experience of staying in Canada through Airbnb online:

游客通过"Airbnb"(爱彼迎)提前订好了包括加拿大蒙特利尔和魁北克城在内的全部住宿,在这两个城市住的都是公寓。通过"Airbnb"预订,价钱只有旅馆的一半左右,住宿条件"超值"!

The tourists booked all their accommodations in advance in Montreal and Quebec in Canada through Airbnb. They lived in apartments in both cities. By booking through "Airbnb", it cost about half the price of the hotel, with "excellent" accommodation conditions!

该游客在魁北克古城附近的 Levis 小镇住的是一套两室一厅的公寓。房东是位 20 几岁的女孩子,毕业于魁北克大学艺术系,酷爱旅游。当租客一行 4 人于 2015 年 7 月 14 日晚上 9 点多钟到达 Levis 小镇,进入公寓后,大家的表情皆有些惊愕,因为没想到公寓布置得很有品位,干

案例 4.2　做有温度的品牌：民宿鼻祖 Airbnb(爱彼迎)与中国民宿

净整洁。房间的装修材料并不昂贵,但无论是客厅、卧室,还是厨房、走廊,都有些让人意想不到的设计和点缀,构思巧妙,匠心独运。

The tourists lived in a two-bedroom apartment in Levis town near the ancient city of Quebec. The house owner was a girl in her twenties. She graduated from the Art Department of the University of Quebec and loves traveling. When the four tourists arrived in Levis town at 9:00 p. m. or so on July 14, 2015, everyone was somewhat stunned after entering the apartment, because they didn't expect the apartment to be so tasteful and clean. The decoration materials were not expensive, but unexpected innovative and ingenious designs and decorations could be found here and there in the living room, bedroom, kitchen and corridor.

爱彼迎是一家联系游客与房东的服务型平台。留宿后,房东与房客可以在平台网站上互相评价,这些评价将为今后房东和房客相互之间做出选择提供客观可信的依据。Levis 小镇公寓的房东得到该中国游客的好评,而后这位游客也看到了出租人对他们的评价：respectful(好人)。"评价"在某种程度上规范了房东与房客的行为,是相互制约又相互信任的好方式。Airbnb 之所以能够得到快速发展,一方面是因为它方便了人们的生活,另一方面则是它设计了这种巧妙的游戏规则。

Airbnb is a service platform that binds tourists and house owners. After staying, the house owners and tenants can evaluate each other on the platform website, which will provide objective and reliable information for the future choices between them. Surely, the house owner of Levis Town Apartment was well received among the

Chinese tourists. Then, the tourists also saw the owner's evaluation on them: respectful. The "evaluation" that regulates the behaviors of house owners and tenants to some extent is a good way for them to supervise each other and build mutual trust. Airbnb's rapid development lies in that it not only facilitates people's lives, but also developed such ingenious rules of the game.

游客与房东并不见面,一般房东会提前将居住方式、房间使用等留下告知方式,以方便游客安心便利居住。如该游客的房东留下字条,告知 Wi-Fi 密码、房东联系电话,以及眼罩可供使用等,给人感觉非常贴心。

Tourists and house owners don't have to meet each other. Usually, house owners leave a note describing the resident manner and how to use the room in advance, so that tourists can live with peace and convenience. In this case, the house owner left the tourist a note, saying the Wi-Fi password, the contact number of the house owner, and the availability of sleeping masks, which was very considerate.

小结:这种通过 Airbnb 订房的住宿体验,给旅游者留下了非常美好的印象。

Summary: The accommodation experience gained by booking houses through Airbnb has left a great impression on tourists.

二、中国民宿现状

Ⅱ. Status quo of B&B in China

民宿最早在我国台湾地区兴起,随后在杭州西湖、云南大理等一些著名景区,逐渐出现了利用当地居民自宅空余房屋为游客提供住宿

案例 4.2 做有温度的品牌：民宿鼻祖 Airbnb（爱彼迎）与中国民宿

和餐饮服务的乡村旅游接待设施。它以家庭方式经营，随着乡村经济不断发展，有部分景点开始将住宿服务作为主要经营项目。民宿从江浙开始逐渐向全国普及。

B&B first emerged in Taiwan Province, China, and then in some famous scenic spots such as West Lake in Hangzhou and Dali in Yunnan, where rural tourism reception facilities gradually appeared, providing accommodation and catering services for tourists with the vacant houses of local residents in the household-based operation mode. With the continuous development of rural economy, some scenic spots began to bring accommodation services into their main business scope. B&B has gradually spread nationwide from Jiangsu and Zhejiang.

中国民宿最初是农家乐、农村旅馆的形式。伴随旅游业的快速发展，民宿也发生了诸多变化，居民大多利用自家的房屋，为前来观光的游客提供简单的住宿，并提供早餐。民宿包含了传统的客栈、农家乐等概念。居住者不仅可以体验农村氛围的宁静，享受当地的美食和传统美食的多样性，还可以了解当地的习俗以及传统的游戏和活动。我国民宿经历了民宅、农庄、农舍、城市短租、家庭旅馆、农家乐、精品民宿、品牌连锁运营等不同阶段。

B&B in China originally took the form of agritainment and rural hostel. With the rapid development of tourism, many changes have taken place in homestays. Most residents use their own houses to provide simple accommodation and breakfast for tourists. "B&B" involves traditional concepts such as hostel and agritainment. Tourists can experience the tranquility of the countryside, enjoy the diversity of local and traditional food, and learn about local customs and traditional games and activities. B&B in China has gone through different stages, such as residence, farm, farmhouse, urban short-term tenancy, family lodge, agritainment, boutique homestay, brand chain operation, etc.

旅游业被各地视为推进乡村振兴的重要引擎,是实现乡村振兴的特色路径。因此,具有中国特色的民宿旅游对各地乡村振兴也起到了重要的推动作用,民宿作为一个新兴的业态,其规模、市场、覆盖范围在几年内迅速扩大(如图4—2所示)。

Tourism is regarded as a vital engine to promote rural revitalization and also a characteristic path to realize rural revitalization nationwide. Therefore, homestay tourism with Chinese characteristics has played an important role in promoting the revitalization of rural areas around China. As a new form of business, it has expanded rapidly in scale, market share and coverage within a few years(as shown in Figure 4—2).

但是,我国民宿在迅速扩大的发展过程中,仍出现较多问题。主要表现在以下几个方面:

However, in the process of rapid expansion, there are still lots of problems, mainly in the following aspects:

一是民宿产业地区发展不均衡。东部沿海地区民宿产业发展较迅猛。而西部地区民宿产业发展缓慢,虽然西部有得天独厚的少数民族文化资源,但成规模的民宿度假区较少。

First, B&B industry features unbalanced development nationwide, with rapid growth in the eastern coastal regions and slow growth in the west. In spite of unique cultural resources of ethnic minorities, there are few large-scale B&B resorts in the west.

案例 4.2　做有温度的品牌：民宿鼻祖 Airbnb(爱彼迎)与中国民宿

图片来源：https://www.sohu.com/a/492212675_393312，2023—02—22。
Source：https://www.sohu.com/a/492212675_393312，2023—02—22.

图 4—2　陕西宝鸡南由古城民宿

Figure 4—2　B&B in the ancient city of Nanyou, Baoji, Shaanxi

二是缺少文化特色。民宿产业的经营特点就是使游客能够切身感受到当地的文化特色。然而我国的民宿在建设过程中往往忽略了这一点，商业化、同质化严重，导致很多民宿在建筑风格、经营模式上千篇一律，缺乏经营特色。"家庭式"的民宿服务氛围并不浓厚，相应的特色体验项目、文化体验活动并不完善，缺乏个性，无法展现区域文化的特色，降低了民宿的吸引力。

Second, there is a lack of cultural characteristics. The business characteristics of the homestay industry are reflected by enabling tourists to feel the local cultural features, which is often overlooked in the development of homestays in China. Being seriously commercialized and homogenized, the homestays in China show similarity in architectural style and business mode, and lack business characteristics. The homestay service atmosphere is not "home-like" enough, and the related characteristic experience items and cultural experience activities are not perfect. Lack of uniqueness and failing to show the characteristics of regional culture reduce the attractiveness of the homestays.

三是硬件设施不足。基础硬件设施的缺乏是多数地区民宿产业发展面临的实际问题。比如有地区民宿的周边环境不成熟，晚上一片漆黑，没有地方可供休闲娱乐，留不住客人，自然民宿也就无法经营。

Third, the hardware facilities are insufficient. The lack of basic hardware facilities is a practical problem facing the development of B&B industry in most regions. For example, in some regions, due to the undeveloped environment nearby, it is completely dark at night and there is no place for leisure and entertainment, so guests are unwilling to stay and it is impossible for homestays to survive.

四是缺少全国性的指导规范，导致各地民宿质量参差不齐。比如，莫干山的民宿评价极高，而云南的民宿却常有顾客投诉。部分地区民众素质偏低，没有将服务意识、诚信意识融入民宿业态。民宿在法律监管上尚存在立法不足、主体缺失、惩罚机制不足的问题。

Fourth, the lack of national guideline regulation has led to uneven quality of homestays around the country. For example, the homestays in Mogan Mountain are highly rated, while those in Yunnan are often complained by customers. In some areas, since the qualities of local residents diathesis are still not very high awarencss of service and integrity have not been integrated into the business form of homestays.

案例 4.2 做有温度的品牌：民宿鼻祖 Airbnb（爱彼迎）与中国民宿

There are still some problems in the legal supervision of homestays, such as insufficient legislation, absence of regulators and inadequate punishment mechanism.

五是缺乏品牌意识。随机的、碎片化的建设和运营较为普遍。

Fifth, lack of brand awareness contributes to widespread random and fragmented construction and operation.

六是缺乏平台的运营推动。国内民宿的前身是客栈，而民宿的兴起需要有相应的贩卖文化生活的特色产品，民宿缺少专业的平台进行运营、推广，游客缺乏了解和寻找民宿的渠道。

Sixth, lack of platform operation promotion. The former form of domestic homestays is hostel. The rise of homestays needs to be supported by characteristic products reflecting local cultural life. But the fact is that they have no platform specialized in operation and promotion, and thus no channels are available to tourists to understand and find homestays.

三、总结

Ⅲ. Summary

Airbnb 和中国民宿对比鲜明，Airbnb 通过对其核心产品——住宿体验，以及附加产品——住宿服务等统一规范，加强管理，逐渐创造出独特的品牌。用户熟知度高，在系列营销中确立了品牌标志性的营销手段。Airbnb 的发展大致可分为三个阶段：

Airbnb and B&B in China are in sharp contrast. Airbnb has gradually created its unique brand by unifying and standardizing its core product of accommodation experience and its additional product of accommodation service, with high user familiarity. It has established an iconic marketing method of the brand in a series of marketing campaigns. The development of Airbnb can be roughly divided into three stages:

第一阶段:打响品牌知名度。将新的认知、对旅行新的定义分享给消费者,让他们了解到有归属感的旅行方式是什么样子。第二阶段:品牌本土化。Airbnb深耕世界各国当地市场,打造品牌的本土化形象。从本土消费者心理需求出发,创造更多的场景和兴趣点来推动他们的旅行意愿和频次。第三阶段:深入对话。抓住当地市场内的每一个细分消费群体的需求,更深入地与他们逐一对话。将"旅行不止是千篇一律的打卡"这一旅行方式深植每个旅行者的心智。

The first stage is creating brand awareness. Share the new cognition and a new definition of travel with consumers, and let them know what it is like to travel with a sense of belonging. The second stage is about to brand localization. Airbnb is deeply involved in local markets around the world to create a localized image of the brand. Starting from the mental needs of local consumers, it aims to create more scenes and points of interest to enhance their willingness and frequency of travel. The third stage includes in-depth dialogue. It means grasping the demands of every consumer segment in the local market and having an in-depth dialogue with them one by one. The travel mode that "traveling is more than coming and taking photos" is deeply rooted in the heart of every traveler.

中国民宿产业虽然发展迅速,但仍面临法律规范不完善、行业协会力量较为薄弱、民宿经营服务不够精细化、专业管理人员短缺、国际

案例 4.2　做有温度的品牌：民宿鼻祖 Airbnb（爱彼迎）与中国民宿

化程度有限等问题。

Although the B&B industry in China has seen rapid development, it still faces some problems, such as imperfect laws and regulations, weak industry associations, inadequately meticulous homestay management services, shortage of professional managers, and limited internationalization and soon.

由此可见：通过本案例的学习，我们应该清晰认识到在产品质量内容为王的今天，好的内容营销就是成功地打造并推广出有独特核心内容的知名品牌。Airbnb 秉持初心，通过重新定义旅行，创造了一个更有归属感的世界，打造了一个有温度的品牌。中国民宿要创立自己的民族品牌走向世界，还有一段很长的路要走。

It can be seen that through learning this case, we have to clearly realize that product quality and content are foremost these days, and good content marketing strategy means successfully creating and promoting well-known brands with unique core content. Airbnb adheres to its original aspiration, and by redefining travel, it has created a world with a stronger sense of belonging and a brand with warmth. Chinese homestays still have a long way to go to create its own national brand and go global.

点评

　　Comments

与其说 Airbnb 提供了房屋住宿服务，不如说它提供的是一种生活方式。对 Airbnb 来说,民宿的定义不限于住宿的地方。民宿之所以有魅力,是因为人与人之间的交往足够温馨,旅行当地的风土人情足够引人入胜,文化赋予的内涵足够丰富多彩。很多人选择爱彼迎,是因为能够在不同的民宿中获得归属感,感受到原汁原味的本土文化魅力,收获与众不同的体验。

Airbnb provides a lifestyle rather than just housing services. For Airbnb, the definition of B&B is not limited to places to stay. The reason why B&B is attractive depends on the fact that the people-to-people communication is warm enough, the local conditions and customs are fascinating enough, and the connotation given by culture is rich enough. Many people choose Airbnb because they can get a sense of belonging in various homestays, feel the original charm of local culture, and gain a unique experience.

Airbnb 迎合了新一代消费力量的生活方式,通过这些与众不同的住宿体验和具有互动性、沉浸式的旅行方式带给用户美好体验。Airbnb 在全球范围内推出了成千上万的本土化体验项目。例如,积极成立房东和租客社群,提供住宿服务,让房东推荐餐厅和当地美食,鼓励租客参与瑜伽、陶艺等项目,吸引租客参与社群活动。在更为亲密的情感链接中,爱彼迎培养出具有高粘合性的用户群体。

Airbnb caters to the lifestyle of a new generation of consumers, offering them a wonderful experience through these unique accommodation experiences and interactive, immersive travel options. Airbnb has launched thousands of localized experience projects around the world. For example, it has actively established a house owner-tourist community, provides accommodation services, ask house owners rec-

案例 4.2　做有温度的品牌：民宿鼻祖 Airbnb（爱彼迎）与中国民宿

ommend restaurants and local cuisine, encourages tourists to participate in yoga, pottery and other activities, and encourage tourists to participate in community activities. With a more intimate emotional link, Airbnb has cultivated a user group with strong loyalty.

Airbnb 改变了人们的租住意识。Airbnb 重塑了酒店行业，人们可以从个人手中租住一间房屋，而不是在一家酒店中租住。大多数情况下，人们不愿意让陌生人住进自己家里，安全、隐私等各种问题一直让房东们望而却步。可见改变观念和培养市场并不是容易的事情，而 Airbnb 成功地教育了市场，培养了用户，其成功的重要原因在于其通过核心产品塑造了强有力的品牌，并且通过规范化的服务得到了消费者的认可。

Airbnb has changed people's consciousness of renting houses, and reshaped the hotel industry, where people can rent a house from individuals instead of doing so from a hotel. In most cases, people don't like strangers to live in their own houses. Security, privacy and other issues have always been discouraging house owners. It can be seen that it is not easy to change the concept and cultivate the market, but Airbnb has successfully educated the market and cultivated users. The important reason for its success is that it has built a strong brand through its core products, and has been recognized by consumers through standardized services.

相比而言，国内民宿发展迅速，但在规模、品牌效应、服务质量及行业规范、管理约束等方面还有较大的改进和提升空间。目前，Airbnb 与美团民宿、小猪/飞猪、途家民宿等多个合作平台沟通，为符合条件的迁移房东、房源争取并推出了多项补贴权益，这对未来中国民宿发展进一步塑造品牌、做好规范化管理及产品服务等方面或许能带来较大的发展机遇和提升空间。

In comparison, Chinese homestays have developed rapidly, but there is still long way to improve in terms of scale, brand effect, service quality, industry norms, and management constraints. At present, Airbnb is in discussions with a number of cooperation platforms such as Meituan Homestay, Piglet/Flying Pig and Tujia Homestay, and plans to subsidies for eligible relocated house owners/houses, which may bring greater opportunities and promotion room for the future development of the Chinese B&B industry in in-depth brand building, standardized management and product services.

讨论题

Discussions

(1)什么是产品？民宿产品的核心功能是什么？

What is a product? What are the core functions of B&B products?

(2)什么是品牌？如何做好品牌管理？

What is a brand? How to conduct brand management?

(3)比较美国的 Airbnb 和中国的农家乐，它们有什么不同，造成这些不同点的关键原因是什么？

What are the differences between Airbnb in the US and agritainments in China? What are the key reasons for these differences?

(4)列出几家 Airbnb 在美国和中国的竞争对手，看看它们的网案例 4.2　做有温度的品牌:民宿鼻祖 Airbnb(爱彼迎)与中国民宿站。Airbnb 如何将自己与竞争对手区分开来?

List several competitors of Airbnb in the US and China, an visit their websites. How does Airbnb distinguish itself from its competitors?

资料来源

做有温度的品牌:民宿鼻祖 Airbnb 爱彼迎的营销策略[EB/OL].[2023-02-21]. https://baijiahao.baidu.com/s?id=1676230598438527081&wfr=spider&for=pc.

《加拿大见闻·经历》住宿——AIRBNB:爱彼迎[EB/OL].[2023-02-21]. http://www.360doc.com/showweb/0/0/1092793619.aspx.

王丽丽.中国民宿建设形态发展现状[J].中外建筑,2019(05):78-80.

李梦娟,胡晓.近十年中国民宿发展研究综述[J].技术与市场,2022(05):145-148.

刘冰冰.我国民宿法律监管中的问题及对策[J].乡村科技,2019(14):13-14.

任嘉浩.生态旅游视域下中国民宿行业发展的困境与突围[J].人文天下,2018(11):64-71.

曾经风靡一时的农家乐,为何变成了"农家哭",看完明白了[EB/OL].[2023-02-21]. https://baijiahao.baidu.com/s?id=1677599816787288080&wfr=spider&for=pc.

曾经红火的农家乐变"农家哭",为何短短几年就"无人问津"了?[EB/OL].[2023-02-21]. http://k.sina.com.cn/article_7453483255_1bc4320f700102cqor.html.

希拉皮克·内森.全球化:爱彼迎的多市场扩张教训[EB/OL].[2023-02-22]. https://www.getblend.com/blog/global-multi-market-expansion-lessons-from-airbnb.

爱彼迎与途家进行系统对接 9成优质房源已接入途家[EB/OL].[2023-02-22]. https://baijiahao.baidu.com/s?id=1734596973879245647.

爱彼迎中国房东大迁移 国内民宿平台抢房源+抢流量[EB/OL].[2023-02-22]. http://www.chinadevelopment.com.cn/news/cj/2022/06/1781280.shtml.

《加拿大见闻·经历》住宿——AIRBNB:爱彼迎[EB/OL].[2023-02-22]. http://www.360doc.com/showweb/0/0/1092793619.aspx.

References

A brand with warmth: Marketing strategy of Airbnb, the originator of B&B[EB/OL]. [2023-02-21]. https://baijiahao.baidu.com/s? id=1676230598438527081&wfr=spider&for=pc.

What is Airbnb? Let's see my Canadian accommodation experience[EB/OL]. [2023-02-21]. http://www.360doc.com/showweb/0/0/1092793619.aspx.

Wang Lili. Current status of development of B&B construction form in China[J]. Chinese & Overseas Architecture, 2019(05):78-80.

Li Mengjuan, Hu Xiao. A review of research on the development of B&B in China over the past decade[J]. Technology and Market, 2022(05):145-148.

Liu Bingbing. Problems and Countermeasures in the Legal Supervision of B&B in China[J]. Rural Science and Technology, 2019(14):13-14.

Ren Jiahao. Dilemma and breakout of the B&B industry in China from the perspective of eco-tourism[J]. Renwen Tianxia, 2018(11):64-71.

You'll see why the once popular agritainment declines after reading this article[EB/OL]. [2023-02-21]. https://baijiahao.baidu.com/s? id=1677599816787288080&wfr=spider&for=pc.

Why does the once popular agritainment decline in just several years? [EB/OL]. [2023-02-21]. http://k.sina.com.cn/article_7453483255_1bc4320f700102cqor.html.

ShiraPik-Nathan. Going Global: Multi-Market Expansion Lessons from Airbnb[EB/OL]. [2023-02-22]. https://www.getblend.com/blog/global-multi-market-expansion-lessons-from-airbnb.

Airbnb and Tujia connect their systems to provide 90% of high-quality properties for Tujia[EB/OL]. [2023-02-22]. https://baijiahao.baidu.com/s? id=1734596973879245647.

House owners of Airbnb in China start a great migration. Domestic B&B platforms compete for properties and traffic[EB/OL]. [2023-02-22]. http://www.chinadevelopment.com.cn/news/cj/2022/06/1781280.shtml.

案例 4.2　做有温度的品牌：民宿鼻祖 Airbnb(爱彼迎)与中国民宿

What I saw and heard in Canada·Experience Accommodation—AIRBNB[EB/OL].[2023－02－22]. http://www.360doc.com/showweb/0/0/1092793619.aspx.

案例 4.3 2022 年上海疫情防控期间的团购与物流配送

Case 4.3 Group Purchase and its Logistics & Distribution During the COVID-19 in Shanghai in 2022

教学目标

Teaching Objectives

2022 年 4—5 月,上海疫情防控期间,市民居家,商品物流配送出现较大问题。居民的日常生活必需品难以送达。国际营销中 4Ps 营销理论中的"Place"即指如何在方便消费者可及的地方提供产品。这个"Place"是商家期望能够找到客户的地方,也是实现销售的地方。

During the epidemic in Shanghai (from April to May, 2022), there was a severe situation in commodity logistics and distribution facing local residents due to travel ban. It was quite difficult for residents to obtain daily necessities. The "Place" in the 4Ps marketing

案例 4.3　2022 年上海疫情防控期间的团购与物流配送

theory refers to a place where it is convenient and accessible for consumers to get products. This "Place" is where businesses expect to find customers and sell their products.

本案例学习将明晰如何运用国际营销中物流渠道理论分析疫情防控期间出现的各小区团购现象。

By studying this case, we will learn how to use the logistics channel theory in international marketing to analyze the phenomenon of group purchase in various communities during the epidemic.

案例涉及国际营销中的 place、物流渠道等知识点。

This case includes place, logistics channels and other related concepts in International Marketing.

案例内容

Contents

2022 年 4 月 11 日,上海新增本土新冠肺炎确诊病例 994 例,无症状感染者 22 348 例。多轮封控措施之下,大部分上海居民遵循非必要不外出的原则,不出小区、不下楼、不出家门。线下出不了门,线上电商平台抢不到菜,谁都不会预测到 2022 年 4—5 月的上海会发生一场热闹空前的社区团购"百团大战"。各种细分品类的团购群上线,从"牛奶团""蔬菜团""肉蛋团"再到"薯片团""冰淇淋团""生活用纸团"以及"宠物粮团"等购物方式成了不少居住在上海的人获得物资的重要方式。团购突然间就火了(如图 4—3 所示)。

By April 11, 2022, there had been 994 new COVID-19 confirmed cases and 22,348 asymptomatic carriers. Under several rounds of

图片来源：https://baijiahao.baidu.com/s?id=1730155970713509626&wfr=spider&for=pc,2023-03-02。

Source: https://baijiahao.baidu.com/s?id=1730155970713509626&wfr=spider&for=pc,2023-03-02.

图 4—3 上海疫情防控期间生鲜快消供应链受压，社区团购成为主要自助方式

Figure 4—3 Community group purchase became the main way for self-help when the fresh food and FNCG supply chain in Shanghai was under pressure during the epidemic

lockdown, most Shanghai residents followed the proposals of not going out unless necessary, not leaving the neighborhood, not going downstairs and not leaving the house. The residents were unable to go out and get food on e-commerce platforms online. No one could predict that there would be an unprecedentedly bustling "campaign of one hundred Group online purchases" in Shanghai from April to May

案例 4.3　2022 年上海疫情防控期间的团购与物流配送

in 2022. The groups for purchasing various supplies, including milk groups, vegetable groups, meat and eggs groups as well as potato chips groups, ice cream groups, tissue paper groups and pet food groups, became an important way for numerous Shanghai residents to obtain supplies. Group purchase went viral overnight (as shown in Figure 4—3).

一、我在上海做"团长"

Ⅰ. Being a "group purchase leader" in Shanghai

故事 1 "张哥！什么时候开团？"

Story 1:"Brother Zhang! When will the group purchase start?"

坐标:浦东新区曹路镇

Location:Caolu Town, Pudong New Area

团长:张先生　银丰苑小区志愿者防疫战队队长

Group leader:Mr. Zhang, leader of the epidemic prevention team of volunteers in Yinfengyuan Neighborhood

"太疯狂了。"4 月 11 日晚上 9:30,张先生在业主群里发起了牛肉团购,仅仅 30 秒,60 份牛肉一扫而光。没抢到的业主望肉兴叹,一犹豫就与牛肉失之交臂。张先生,一名 85 后,现任上海爱元通公司高管,是银丰苑小区里的"元老级"业主,也是小区志愿者防疫战队队长,近期最知名的身份就是"团长"。从 3 月 30 日到 4 月 11 日,他已成功组团 18 次。

"It's crazy." At 9:30 p.m. on April 11, Mr. Zhang launched a beef group purchase among the property owners. Within just 30 seconds, 60 pieces of beef were sold out. The owners who failed to get the beef could do nothing but looked at the picture of beef and sighed, saying that they just missed the beef in an instant hesitation. Mr. Zhang, born after 1985, was an executive of Shanghai Aiyuantong Technology Co., Ltd. He was one of the first property owner of Yinfengyuan Neighborhood, and also the leader of the neighborhood epidemic prevention team of volunteers. At that time, his most well-known title was the "group leader". From March 30 to April 11, he successfully organized 18 group purchases.

"一开始没有经验,难免手忙脚乱。"不过,接下来张先生很快就对小程序运用自如,开团、统计、下单……每天都很忙。如何成功组团?张先生总结了四大要素:信任、质量、效率、实惠。"信任是非常重要的。在组团的过程中,我直接把交易记录发给大家。对方什么价格,我就给大家什么价格。"这一公开透明的关键之举直接稳固了张先生"团长"的地位,却也让他首单亏本。

"Being inexperienced at first, inevitably, I found myself in a hurry scurry." However, soon Mr. Zhang was able to utilize the applet freely. Starting a group purchase, counting number, placing orders and so forth, he was terribly busy every day. How to organize a group purchase successfully? Mr. Zhang concluded with four key words: trust, quality, efficiency and cost-effectiveness. "Trust is very important. In the process of organizing the group purchase, I sent the transaction records directly to everyone. I showed the price that the supplier offered to my neighbors." This behavior of openness and honest directly consolidated Zhang's position as the "group purchase leader", but it also made him lose money in his first order.

案例4.3　2022年上海疫情防控期间的团购与物流配送

原来,初期大家对鸡蛋和蔬菜的需求都非常高。通过浦东发布及新曹路公众号,张先生很快找到了物资提供平台。蔬菜和鸡蛋的组合套餐,张先生直接以43元的进价开团,很快173人下单并成功收货。沉浸在喜悦中的张先生在首单结束后,才注意到平台需要手续费。开团即亏损的局面如何扭转?小区志愿者人手紧张,如何解决最后100米配送难题?为释放运力,他在群中发起征询,提出开团每单增加2元配送费给志愿者、超过一定金额增加提现费的建议,得到了业主一致认可。

Here is the story. There used to be strong demand for eggs and vegetables at first. From Pudong Release and the WeChat official account of Xincao Road, Zhang quickly found a platform of supplies. For the combined package of vegetables and eggs, he launched a group purchase directly at the price of 43 yuan. 173 orders were placed and packages were delivered successfully. Mr. Zhang, immersed in joy, didn't notice the service charge of the platform until the first order was finished. So how to reverse the situation of losing money when starting a group purchase? As there were not enough volunteers in the neighborhood, how to deliver supplies to the final users? In order to gain manpower, he initiated an opinion solicitation in the WeChat group, and proposed an extra delivery fee of 2 yuan to the volunteers for each group purchase, and a cash withdrawal fee beyond a certain amount, which was unanimously agreed by the owners.

以牛奶为例,一箱牛奶成本价50元,加2元运费,再加0.5元提现费,张先生以每箱牛奶52.5元的价格开团。所有的问题迎刃而解后,张先生又相继开了不少团,三黄鸡、羊肉、猪肉、蔬菜包、色拉油等团购先后成团。考虑到大家对时令蔬菜的需求较为强烈,4月6日,经过多轮筛选,他再度开启蔬菜团,里面包括了卷心菜、韭菜、辣椒、西红柿等新鲜蔬菜。此次也是跟团人数最多的一单,高达 305 单。

Take the milk as an example. One case of milk costs 50 yuan, plus a freight fee of 2 yuan and a cash withdrawal fee of 0.5 yuan. Mr. Zhang started the group purchase at the price of 52.5 yuan per case of milk. After all the problems were solved, he launched numerous group purchases one after another, including Sanhuang chicken, mutton, pork, vegetable packages and salad oil. Considering the strong demand for fresh vegetables, on April 6, after several rounds of choice, he once again started the group purchase of vegetables, including cabbage, leeks, peppers and tomatoes, making it the group purchase with the largest number of orders, up to 305.

故事 2:讲述人:钱女士 互联网公司高管 上海徐汇区

Story 2: Narrator: Ms. Qian, an executive of an Internet company, Xuhui District, Shanghai

我是徐汇区一个老小区的"团长",服务近 200 人。我盘活了整个小区的物资。5 年前,我从北京到上海工作,在这里租了间一居室,从没和邻居打过交道。2022 年 4 月 1 日,我所在的小区正式进入封控状态。起初我并未成为志愿者。后来,牛奶喝完了,我在业主群发起牛奶团购。我觉得自己能做点什么来改变物资紧缺的情况,而不是被动等待别人的帮助。渐渐地,我成了整个小区的"团长",负责日常物资的采买。小区里几位有医学背景的居民报名成为志愿者,一些腿脚灵便的老人家也协助他们做消杀和分发,加在一起有十余人。小区里的秩序没有乱过。几乎每隔几天,都有货车把物资配送到小区门口。消杀一小时后,志愿者以栋为单位把物资分配下去,再逐户分发。我的

案例 4.3　2022 年上海疫情防控期间的团购与物流配送

任务是对接货源,盘活需求,再用一套表格管理好团购的每个环节。

I am the head of an old neighborhood in Xuhui District, serving nearly 200 residents. I was responsible for supplies of the entire neighborhood. Five years ago, I left Beijing for Shanghai to work, and rented a one-bedroom apartment here. I never made contact with my neighbors. On April 1, 2022, my neighborhood was officially locked down. I didn't apply to be a volunteer at first. Later, when the milk was empty, I propose to organize a milk group purchase among the owners. I thought I could do something to the shortage of supplies instead of passively waiting for others' help. Gradually, I became the "leader" of the neighborhood, responsible for the purchase of daily necessities. Several residents with medical background in the neighborhood joined us as volunteers, and some healthy elderly people also helped us with disinfection and distribution, these aged volunteers were more than ten volunteers. The neighborhood was always kept in good order. Almost every few days, there were trucks delivering supplies to the gate of the community. One hour after disinfection, volunteers would distribute the supplies building by building and then door by door. My task was to ensure the supply of goods, find out the demand, and then control every link of group purchase with a set of tables.

我跟另外一个朋友组建了上海"团长"微信群,做供货资源分享,目前约有 300 个"团长"在群里互助。作为"团长",最难的是对接物流。一次,配送牛奶的司机在晚上 12:30 给我打电话,叫我找人取货。我睡着了,没有接到电话。第二天回拨的时候,对方告诉我不确定下次什么时候会送过来。一些专门做面包的企业在物流上也不太熟练,总是要晚上一两天。最差的情况是,在配送途中,菜品不知为何烂掉了。每当配送失败或者延迟,"团长"群里就会有人崩溃:"我们小区都是一帮老头老太太,这怎么可以?"刚开始做"团长"时,也有居民在群里指责我找的渠道不靠谱,总是延期。但渐渐地,大家就都理解并信任我了。我几乎把所有精力都放在了团购上。我加了二十来个供货群,牛奶、面包、蔬菜、五花肉……整个小区的口粮都依赖线上交易。一次团购周期三到五天,从发货到配送,我需要时刻在线盯着电脑。我用 Excel 表格登记好每份团购背后的门牌号和采购数量。开始配送后,每位"团长"收到物资后都会拍张照片发到群里。

A friend of mine and I created a WeChat group named "group purchase leaders" in Shanghai to share supply resources. Then, there were about 300 "group purchase leaders" helping each other in the group. As a "group purchase leader", the most difficult part is matchmaking with logistics. Once, the milk delivery driver called me at 12:30 in the morning, trying to ask me to find someone to pick up the milk. I fell asleep and missed the call. When I called back the next day, the driver told me that he was not sure when it would be delivered next time. Some bakeries were not very good at logistics, and their delivery was always delayed for one day or two. In the worst case, the vegetables somehow rotted during the delivery. Whenever the delivery failed or was delayed, someone in the "group purchase" group would collapse, "Our neighborhood are mostly old people, how could this happen?" When I first became the "group purchase leader", some residents in the group accused me of finding unreliable channels and frequent delays. But gradually, everyone tried to understand and trust me. I almost devote myself into group purchase. I joined more than 20 supply groups, including milk, bread, vegetables and pork belly…The supplies of the whole community depend on online trading. A group purchase cycle lasted for three to five days. From delivery to distribution, I needed to stare at the computer all the time. I used Excel tables to register the house number and purchase quantity of each group purchase order. when the distribution began to deliver, each "group purchase leader" would take a photo and send it to the group after receiving the supplies.

我们都希望上海早日解封,生活恢复正常,这一共识让以团购为形式的物资保障顺利地进行下去。

We all hoped that Shanghai would be lifted out of lockdown as soon as possible and people's life would return to normal. This consensus made the supplies guarantee in the form of group purchase to go on smoothly.

二、社区团购因疫情而迅速发展

Ⅱ. Community group purchase developed rapidly due to the epidemic

2016 年,"你我您"开创了目前社区团购主要的经营模式,相较于早期的手抄单发布团购消息,"你我您"利用了线上电商的优势,大大提高了团购的效率和便捷性。此后,行业快速爆发,盒马、京东、苏宁、永辉等巨头均开始探索赛道。至于年轻的团购创业公司,更是呈星火燎原之势。2018 年,社区团购的赛道融资额就高达 40 亿元。到了

2019年,随着风口之后的泡沫挤压,以亏损换市场的快速扩张模式遭遇融资遇冷,各公司迎来了自我造血能力和业务模式构建上的考验期,并购、调整、关店成了社区团购行业的主题,而拥有充足资本能力的头部公司仍在快速扩张。

In 2016,"Niwoning" initiated the main business model of community group purchase ("Niwoning"-means "you-I-you", a kind of platform of community purchasing). Compared with the early form of handwritten lists for releasing group purchase information, "Niwoning" took advantage of online e-commerce and greatly improved the efficiency and convenience of group purchase. Since then, the industry boomed rapidly, and giants such as Hema Fresh, JD.com, Suning and Yonghui began to explore the market segment. Meanwhile, the group-purchase startups sprang up one after another. In 2018, the funding for community group purchases reached up to 4 billion yuan. In 2019, with the bursting of the economic bubble after the booming, it was quite difficult for the enterprise rapid expansion mode featuring exchanging losses to obtain financing, and companies involved found themselves facing the challenge of independent operation for profit and business mode rebuilding. During this period, mergers and acquisitions, adjustment and outlet closure became an overwhelming trend in the community group purchase industry, while the industry leaders with strong financial strength were still expanding rapidly.

到了2020年,新冠疫情深刻改变了用户的消费习惯和信息获取习惯。社区团购迎来自身爆发式增长,美团、京东、拼多多、阿里、滴滴等相继将社区团购作为重点拓展业务,资本的投入大大提升了社区团购行业的发展速度,社区团购开始在全国范围内拓展。比如美团就将社区团购业务定为一级战略项目。对于美团而言,社区团购在体量上可比肩外卖,同时,其核心覆盖人群与美团现有人群有较好的互补性,有利于下沉市场的拓展。

By 2020, COVID-19 had profoundly changed consumers' consumption pattern and information acquisition habits. Community group purchase sees its own explosive growth. Meituan, JD. com, Pinduoduo, Alibaba, DiDi, etc. successively switched their focus to community group purchase to expand their business. The capital investment greatly accelerated the development of the community group purchase industry, allowing it to expand nationwide. For example, Meituan designated the community group purchase business as a top-level strategic project. As far as Meituan is concerned, community group purchase is comparable to take-out in volume, and meanwhile, its core target groups and existing customer base are mutually complementary, which is favourable for the development of markets in lower-tier cities.

三、总结

Ⅲ. Summary

产业的进化,就是不断地自我更新。过去,不少中小企业面临的最大困难,就是自身和消费者都难以踏出线上消费的第一步。但在社区团购高适应性、低损耗、低配送成本、需求精准性高的冲击下,这一切都在悄然改变。2022年上海疫情下的各社区自发组织了团购,团长更加积极拥抱商家,自觉主动地维系社群,悄然改变用户的消费习惯。在疫情的危机中,社区团购也更加重视自身产业的可控性,更加重视社群消费的可适应性。这为物流配送更多的线下业态发挥其流量优势和供应链优势,开拓了新的成长路径。

The evolution of an industry features constant self-renewal. In the past, the biggest trouble facing numerous small and medium-sized enterprises was the difficulty for themselves and consumers to take the first step in online consumption. However, under the impacts of the community group purchase with high adaptability, low losses, low distribution cost and high demand accuracy, everything was changing unnoticedly. In 2022, the communities in Shanghai had to voluntarily organize group purchases due to the epidemic, and the group purchase leaders contacted the suppliers more actively and maintained the order in the community consciously and proactively, which changed the consumption patterns of users unnoticedly. In the crisis of the epidemic, community group purchase pays more attention to the controllability of the industry and the adaptability of community consumption. This opens up a new growth path for the offline business forms with more logistics and distribution services available to give full play to their advantages in purchase quantity and supply chain.

点评
Comments

疫情防控期间突然流行的社区团购模式,对快消企业是千载难逢的好机会。从供应链管理角度看,这种直接对接团长的方式,可以快

案例 4.3　2022 年上海疫情防控期间的团购与物流配送

速提升企业的实物流、资金流和信息流。

The popularity of community group purchase model during the epidemic was a golden opportunity for FMCG enterprises. From the perspective of supply chain management, directly contacting the group purchase leaders can quickly improve the physical flow, capital flow and information flow of the enterprise.

从实物流看,运输配送的总路线缩短了,以前的模式是商品配送到电商平台的仓库,消费者在线下单,由骑手完成最后 3～5 千米的配送。如果有 10 个消费者下单,骑手配送的总里程最高可达 50 千米。这对于社会资源是一种浪费。现在团购直接配送到小区门口,把零散订单汇总在一起,极大地降低了社会物流负担,也帮助快消企业减少了运输成本。

In terms of physical flow, the total length of transportation and distribution route was shortened. In the previous model, goods were delivered to the warehouses of e-commerce platform, and consumers placed orders online before the delivery drivers cover the last 3－5 km distance of distribution. If 10 consumers place orders, the total mileage of the delivery drivers can reach up to 50 km, which is a huge waste of social resources. Now with the group purchase, goods are delivered directly to the gate of the community, and the scattered orders are gathered, which greatly lowers the social logistics burden and transportation costs for FMCG enterprises.

从资金流看,以前快消企业是销售给经销商或电商,回款并不是很及时。现在团购模式是先收款后发货,现金循环周期大幅缩短,显著地改善了企业的现金流。

For capital flow, in the past, FMCG enterprises dealt with dealers or e-commerce merchants, and the payment was not done in a timely manner. At present, with the group purchase mode, money is collected first and then comes the delivery, which greatly shortens the cash cycle and significantly improves the cash flow of enterprises.

最后看信息流,它从3个方面帮助企业提高供应链能力。一是直接获取客户信息。传统模式下,快消企业很难获取到终端客户的信息:商品卖给了哪些人? 他们的购买偏好是怎样的? 这些关键信息都掌握在平台手上。现在社区团购对接的是一个个鲜活的消费者,企业就能够得到第一手的顾客画像。二是提高预测准确性。由于社区直接成团,是真实的订单而不是预测,可以降低需求和预测的偏差,提高预测的准确性。三是降低运营成本。在疫情发生之前,市场竞争过于激烈,使得品牌的获客成本越来越高。但在疫情防控期间,市民急缺物资,官方媒体也在发布各类团购信息,有可能是免费推广的,这等于是帮助快消企业免费打了一波广告。

Finally, let's look at information flow. It helps enterprises improve their supply chain capabilities from three aspects. First, customer information is obtained directly. In the traditional mode, it is difficult for FMCG enterprises to obtain the information of end users, like who are the buyers and what are their purchasing preferences. The key information is controlled by the platform. Now as the community group purchase directly reaches consumers, enterprises can get first-hand customer information. Second, the accuracy of forecast is improved. As the group purchase is directly done at the community level, it is a real order rather than a forecast, which can reduce the de-

案例 4.3　2022 年上海疫情防控期间的团购与物流配送

viation between demand and forecast and improve the accuracy of forecast. Third, operating costs are reduced. Before the outbreak of the pandemic, due to the fierce market competition, the cost of user acquisition was getting higher and higher. However, during the epidemic, local residents were short of supplies, and the official media were also releasing all kinds of group purchase information for promotion, which advertised for FMCG enterprises free of charge to some extent.

讨论题
Discussions

(1)订单暴增、交通封控,上海疫情下的团购是如何运转的?

How did the group purchase work during the epidemic in Shanghai facing the surge in orders and the city locked down?

(2)请用 4Ps 营销理论讨论社区团购中的营销策略。

Please discuss the marketing strategy adopted in the community group purchase with 4Ps marketing theory.

(3)离开了疫情,社区团购将来的发展趋势在哪里?

Where is the trend of community group purchase in the post-pandemic era?

资料来源

叶心冉. 潮退潮起 上海疫情中异化的社区团购[EB/OL]. [2023-03-02]. https://baijiahao. baidu. com/s? id=17308039131351259907&wfr=spider&for=pc.

石润乔,徐雪飞,杨柳. 上海疫情防控期间,"社区团购"成为不少人获得物资的重要方式[EB/OL]. [2023-03-02]. https://baijiahao.baidu.com/s? id=1730035721590242398&wfr=spider&for=pc.

弘毅供应链. 上海疫情期间,社区团购是消费品企业弯道超车的机会[EB/OL]. [2023-03-02]. http://www.360doc.com/content/22/0410/08/77881800_1025679132.shtml.

石润乔,徐雪飞,杨柳. 我在上海做"团长"[EB/OL]. [2023-03-02]. https://baijiahao.baidu.com/s? id=1729925582548018208&wfr=spider&for=pc.

董志雯,葛俊俊,陈晨,等. 我在上海做"团长"——来自上海社区的抗疫故事(上)[EB/OL]. [2023-03-02]. http://sh.people.com.cn/n2/2022/0415/c134768-35224743.htm.

References

Ye Xinran. Ebb and flow: Alienated community group purchase in Shanghai during the epidemic[EB/OL]. [2023-03-02]. https://baijiahao.baidu.com/s? id=1730803913135125990&wfr=spider&for=pc.

Shi Runqiao, Xu Xuefei, Yang Liu. "Community group purchase" became an important way for many people to obtain supplies in Shanghai during the period of epidemic prevention and control[EB/OL]. [2023-03-02]. https://baijiahao.baidu.com/s? id=1730035721590242398&wfr=spider&for=pc.

Hongyi Supply Chain. Community group purchase became an opportunity for consumer goods manufacturers to overtake others in Shanghai during the epidemic[EB/OL]. [2023-03-02]. http://www.360doc.com/content/22/0410/08/77881800_1025679132.shtml.

Shi Runqiao, Xu Xuefei, Yang Liu. I am a "group purchase leader" in Shanghai[EB/OL]. [2023-03-02]. https://baijiahao.baidu.com/s? id=1729925582548018208&wfr=spider&for=pc.

案例4.3 2022年上海疫情防控期间的团购与物流配送

Dong Zhiwen,Ge Junjun,Chen Chen,et al. I am a "group purchase leader" in Shanghai-anti-epidemic stories from communities in Shanghai (Part 1)[EB/OL].[2023－03－02]. http://sh.people.com.cn/n2/2022/0415/c134768-35224743.html.

第五篇 物流管理
PART Ⅴ　LOGISTICS MANAGEMENT

案例 5.1　爱回收:小回收做成大生意
Case 5.1　Aihuishou:Small Recycling Business Makes Big Difference

教学目标

Teaching Objectives

爱回收是一个二手电子设备 C2B 交易平台。用户通过多种方式向平台提交旧设备,经过平台方的质检评估后,进入 B 端交易系统。作为中国最大的电子产品回收及以旧换新平台之一,爱回收 2018 年的年交易额超过 70 亿元,处理了约 1 000 万台二手电子产品。2018 年 7 月 12 日,爱回收宣布完成 1.5 亿美元新一轮融资,这是迄今为止全球电子产品回收领域最大的单笔融资。手机回收是一个长尾行业,用户转化慢、使用频次低,烧钱买流量的互联网模式很难生存。爱回收从前端入手,培养用户回收习惯,通过搭建不同场景扩充流量来源,抢占渠道,构建线上线下的服务闭环,最终突出重围,把看似不起眼的小生意做成了大买卖。本节通过案例分析,帮助学生更好地理解回收物流与逆向物流的概念和内涵、实现逆向物流的途径和方法,让学生明白回收物流的重要意义:电子产品的回收利用不仅能够变废为宝、增加收益,还对保护环境起到重要作用,达到经济与生态的双赢。

Aihuishou is a C2B trading platform for second-hand electronic equipment. Users can submit old equipment to the platform in various ways, and after quality inspection and evaluation, they enter the B-side trading system. As one of the largest electronic product recycling and trade-in platforms in China, Aihuishou had an annual transaction volume of more than 7 billion yuan and handled about 10 million second-hand electronic devices in 2018. On July 12, 2018, Aihuishou announced it completed a new round of financing of 150 million US dollars, which was by then the largest-scale single financing in the field of electronic device recycling globally. Mobile phone recycling is a long-tail industry, featuring slow user conversion and low frequency of use, therefore, it is hard for the Internet mode of heavy investment in buying traffic to survive. Aihuishou starts from the front end to cultivate users' recycling habits and develop traffic sources by constructing different scenarios in order to seize channels and build a closed loop of online and offline services. Finally, it made breakthroughs, making seemingly insignificant small businesses into big deals. Through case analysis, this section will help students better understand the concepts and connotations of recycling logistics and reverse logistics, the ways and methods to realize reverse logistics, and the significance of recycling logistics: the recycling of electronic products can not only turn waste into treasure and increase income, but also play an important role in protecting

案例 5.1 爱回收：小回收做成大生意

the environment and achieving a balance between economy and ecology.

案例涉及物流与供应链管理中回收物流、逆向物流、选址、外包、众包等相关知识点。

The case involves recycling logistics, reverse logistics, site selection, outsourcing, crowdsourcing and other related concepts in Logistics and Supply Chain Management.

案例内容
Contents

随着电子产品更新速度不断加快，我国废弃电子产品的数量持续增长。废弃电子产品处理不当，会给自然环境以及我们的身体健康带来极大的危害。而废旧电子产品的回收利用能够变废为宝、增加收益，达到经济与生态的双赢。

With the increasingly rapid upgrading of electronic products, the quantity of discarded electronic products in China continues to grow. Improper disposal of discarded electronic products will bring great harm to the natural environment and our health, while their recycling can turn waste into treasure, increase income and achieve a win-win situation between economy and ecology.

爱回收成立于 2011 年。最初，其只能通过线上下单和估价，并提供免费邮寄。但不久后，爱回收就发现，在对回收的电子产品做专业检测时，往往容易因为线上交易，在品质和价格方面产生用户纠纷。另外，线上交易的模式使爱回收遭到两面夹击，一面是逐渐入局在线二手电子产品回收行业的众多公司,另一面是遍布在华强北和中关村等电脑城的二手回收散户们。

Aihuishou was established in 2011. Initially, the used products could only be submitted and valued online, enjoying free shipping. But before long, Aihuishou found that when doing specialized testing on recycled electronic products, disputes with users in terms of quality and price often occurred for online transactions. In addition, the online trading mode left Aihuishou in a situation under attack from two sides, i. e. the companies entering the online second-hand electronic product recycling industry one after another, and the second-hand product recycling retails that could be found all over the computer cities such as Huaqiang North and Zhongguancun.

一、开拓多渠道引流

Ⅰ. Develop multiple channels to gain customers

"鼓励建立线上线下融合的回收渠道",爱回收除了有线上交易模式,也是二手3C行业中最先开设线下门店的[3C行业是指计算机、通信、消费电子一体化的信息家电产业,3C是指电脑(Computer)、通信(Communication)和消费性电子(Consumer Electronic)],门店场景可以让店员和顾客完成充分的沟通,减少因信息不对称产生的投诉。2013年,爱回收开始做线下门店,与客户进行线上线下的交流。受到商场里ATM以及一些互动屏的启发,爱回收没有租用整个店面,而是选择在商场的走道位置租下一面墙或是一根立柱,只要能摆得下一台电脑,或能安装两三面触摸屏就够了。与传统手机门店相比,这种站点式的门店开起来速度快、成本小,一次性硬件投入7万元,每个月的运营成本(含员工工资)大约 3 万元。

"It promoted the establishment of recycling channels integrating online and offline resources". In addition to online trading mode, Aihuishou is the first to run offline stores in the second-hand 3C industry (3C industry refers to the information household appliances industry integrating computer, communication and consumer electronics, and 3C stands for Computer, Communication and Consumer Electronics). Physical stores can allow shop assistants and customers to complete full communication and reduce customer complaints caused by information asymmetry. In 2013, Aihuishou began to run offline stores, communicating with customers both online and offline. Inspired by the ATMs and some interactive screens in the shopping mall, Aihuishou chose to rent a wall or even a column in the aisle of the shopping mall instead of renting the whole store, as long as it can accommodate a computer, or two or three touch screens. Compared with traditional mobile phone stores, this kind of site-based store is easy to open at a low cost, with a one-time hardware investment of 70,000 yuan and a monthly operating cost (including staff salary) of about 30,000 yuan.

二、精心选址

Ⅱ. Careful site selection

选址是个大问题。爱回收得出的经验是:要选择贴近用户的中高端商场,覆盖周边三到五千米范围内的用户,用户群年轻化、基数大。商场层次太低,覆盖范围小,用户年龄偏老;商场层次太高,流量又太少。爱回收在上海做了几家门店进行尝试后,发现咨询量和转化率不错,后在北京、杭州、深圳等城市先后布局门店。黄白相间的装修风格,以及内嵌在墙面上的触摸屏幕,令其引人注目。门店的存在除了增加回收量外,一个更重要的作用是宣传品牌,路过的人即便当时没有回收需求,也会忍不住多看两眼。在用户心里留下了爱回收可以回收手机的印象,是培养他们回收习惯的第一步,也是最重要的一步(如图5—1所示)。

Site selection is a big problem. The experience gained by Aihuishou was that it should choose mid-to-high end shopping malls close to users within the range of three to five kilometers around, with a large base of young users. Low-end shopping mall features a small coverage and more elderly users, while if the shopping mall is too high-end, there will be only a small number of customers. After trying several stores in Shanghai, Aihuishou found that the consultation volume and conversion rate were good, and then it opened outlets in Beijing, Hangzhou, Shenzhen and other cities. The yellow and white decoration style and the touch screen embedded in the wall make the outlet eye-catching. In addition to increasing the recycling volume, the outlets play a more important role in promoting the brand. Even if there is no recycling demand at that time, people passing by can't help gazing at it. It was the first and most important step to cultivate users' recycling habits by leaving an impression on them that Aihuishou can recycle their mobile phones(as shown in Fignre 5—1).

在线下,爱回收在超30多个城市布局了300余家门店,几乎都位于大型城市的核心商圈。同时,为了进一步让交易场景贴近用户,爱

案例 5.1 爱回收：小回收做成大生意

图片来源：https://www.sohu.com/a/473686767_121124374c,2023-02-02。
Source：https://www.sohu.com/a/473686767_121124374c,2023-02-02.

图 5—1 爱回收

Figure 5—1　Aihuishou

回收增加了自助回收服务，并入驻丰巢、速递易等渠道，覆盖了 20 余万线下回收网点。除了不断完善自有回收渠道，爱回收在线上还与三星、小米、华为、OPPO、vivo 等品牌商合作，提供电子产品回收服务。借着二手经济的爆发之势，又接入了京东、闲鱼、芝麻信用等平台，不断寻找新的场景以扩充线上流量来源，抢占精准渠道。比如，在京东上购买手机的用户可以一键提交旧手机抵价需求，接着就由爱回收介入完成服务，这种方式在促进京东商城新机销售的同时，也大大提升了爱回收业务量。

Offline,Aihuishou has more than 300 outlets in more than 30 cities,almost all of which are located in the core business districts of major cities. Meanwhile, in order to make the trading scene closer to users, Aihuishou began to provide DIY recycling services by joining hands with HIVE BOX, Sposter and other channels, covering more than 200,000 offline recycling outlets. While constantly improving its own recycling channels, Aihuishou cooperated with brands such as Samsung, Xiaomi, Huawei, OPPO and vivo online to provide electronic product recycling services. With the outbreak of the second-hand economy, it also worked with platforms such as JD. com, Goofish, and Sesame Credit to keep seeking for new scenarios to expand online traffic sources and seize accurate channels. For example, users who intend to buy mobile phones on JD. com can submit their demand for used mobile phones with a single click before Aihuishou completes the service. This not only promotes the sales of new products in JD Mall, but also greatly enhances the business volume of Aihuishou.

三、用众包模式打开中小城市市场

Ⅲ. Develop the market in small and medium-sized cities with crowdsourcing model

2017年，爱回收已在全国各大城市打开市场，开在大型商场和超市的门店中，八成实现盈利。但要下沉到中小城市，照搬在一线商超里开直营店的套路显然过重。中小城市的消费水平难以支撑爱回收的线下门店，客单价较低，用户的消费习惯也没有培养起来。因此，爱回收最终选择以线下众多零售实体店为目标，用众包的形式开展回收业务，成立独立品牌"爱机汇"。具体操作就是爱回收与零售商签合同，零售商在消费者实名认证后回收旧手机，赚取利润转给爱回收。

案例 5.1　爱回收：小回收做成大生意

In 2017, Aihuishou had set foot in major cities across China, running stores in large shopping malls and supermarkets, 80% of which already made profits. However, in order to enter small and medium-sized cities, it is obviously too costly if it follows the mode of operating retail stores in supermarkets in many large cities. It was difficult for the consumption capacity of small and medium-sized cities to support offline stores of Aihuishou, as the per customer transaction was small in amount, and the consumption habits of users had not been cultivated. Therefore, Aihuishou finally chose to work with numerous offline retail stores to carry out recycling business in the form of crowdsourcing, and set up an independent brand "Aijihui". Specifically, Aihuishou signed contracts with the retailers who recycled the used mobile phones after the consumer had finished real-name authentication prior to earning profits and transferring them to Aihuishou.

"爱机汇"的做法是：让商家先收购旧机，再转给爱回收。它们给线下渠道提供一套检测、回收手机的工具和流程，并给商家一部分利润，让线下渠道自发推动旧机的回收。商家也乐于去推动旧机的回收——既有钱赚，又能加快手机的流通和换代速度。商家在这个过程中，不再只是一个收租的角色，而是参与了交易，要承担错误估价带来的风险，验机流程再也不能随意。而从外观到拆机检验，"爱机汇"都会提供一套完整的流程和定价标准。为了说服商家参与交易，"爱机汇"提供回收金额的 10%～15% 作为提成，而其他企业的比例通常是 8% 左右。同时，约定商家亏损额度，超过这个数字，"爱机汇"会承担一部分损失；如果亏损得更多，双方就会中止合作。

"Aijihui" requests merchants to buy used machines first, and then transfers them to Aihuishou for recycling. It provides offline channels with a set of tools and processes for detecting and recycling mobile phones, and surrenders part of profits to merchants, so that offline channels can spontaneously promote the recycling of used phones. Merchants are also willing to promote the recycling of used machines as it can both make money and speed up the circulation and replacement of mobile phones. In this process, in addition to collecting money, the merchants participate in the transaction and have to bear the risks brought by wrong valuation. Therefore, the inspection cannot be done at will. From appearance to disassembly inspection, "Aijihui" provides a complete set of processes and pricing standards. In order to persuade merchants to participate in the transaction, "Aijihui" provides 10%~15% of the recycling amount as a commission, compared to around 8% given by other enterprises. Meanwhile, the losses are set to a certain limit so that once the limit is exceeded, "Aijihui" will bear part of the losses. If the losses are excessively high, both sides will terminate their cooperation.

四、推出标准回收体系

Ⅳ. Launch a standard recycling system

非标准化是二手手机交易的一大痛点,所谓新旧程度很主观,电池等不可见的零件的损耗程度难以评估。同时,是不是翻新机、是否进过水等问题,都需要专业考证,导致定价复杂、不容易给出让用户满意的价格。此外,数据安全、流程麻烦也是阻碍用户交易的关键因素。正因如此,爱回收总结了回收行业多年的经验,制定了"隐私深度清

案例 5.1 爱回收：小回收做成大生意

除""产品透明估价"和"产品环保处理"三大标准体系。

Non-standardization is a major pain spot in second-hand mobile phone transactions. The concept of used and new is subjective, and the loss degree of invisible parts such as batteries is difficult to evaluate. Meanwhile, specialized inspection is required to check whether it is a refurbished device or has dropped in the water, etc., which leads to complicated pricing and difficulty in offering a satisfactory price to users. In addition, data security and complex processes are also key factors that hinder the transactions with users. For these reasons, Aihuishou has summarized its experience gained over the past years in the recycling industry, and formulated three standard systems: deep clearance of private information, transparent product valuation and green disposal of products.

首先是隐私深度清除。爱回收主要运用 Blancco 技术做深度隐私擦除。Blancco 曾获得 10 余个国家安防安全认证，被 Blancco 做过"根除式"清理的电子设备中，被删除的信息基本无法恢复。目前，爱回收在全国各大运营中心都设置了隐私清除实验室，明确了最高规格的隐私清除步骤与流程。当爱回收完成一台二手设备的隐私清除工作后，运营中心就会向设备的卖方实时报告进度，并最终提供一份详尽的隐私清除报告。

The first is the deep clearance of private information. Aihuishou mainly uses Blancco technology to achieve this purpose. Blancco has obtained the security certifications of more than 10 countries. The deleted information is basically unrecoverable in the electronic equipment that Blancco has done "eradication" clearance. At present,

Aihuishou has set up private information clearance laboratories in major operation centers all over China, and defined the highest-standard private information clearance steps and processes. When Aihuishou completes the private information clearance of a second-hand device, the operation center will report the progress to the seller of the device in real time, and finally provide a detailed report of the clearance.

其次是做到价格透明。一个信息高度不对称的市场,需要有一套被交易各方认同的公允定价机制,爱回收充当了这一角色。对 B 端,爱回收提供了一套相对标准化的检测评估流程,综合评估设备内外状况后,给出一个从 S 级到 K 级的评级意见,这成为回收商报价的参照。对 C 端,爱回收反过来采集 B 端的报价数据,并结合一些外部数据推算市场价格。市场价格和回收商报价之间的差价成为爱回收的利润空间之一。这套市场价格推算系统基于海量数据的处理和若干复杂模型的搭建,并且具有自学习的特性。透明的价格信息有效地提高了平台的定价公信力。

The second is to ensure transparent pricing. A highly asymmetric information market needs a fair pricing mechanism recognized by all parties involved in the transaction, in which Aihuishou plays the major role. For B-end, Aihuishou provides a relatively standardized testing and evaluation process. After comprehensively evaluating the internal and external conditions of the device, it gives ratings on a scale from S to K, which is the basis for recyclers' pricing. For the C-end, Aihuishou collects the pricing data of the B-end in turn, and calculates the market price by taking into account some external data. The difference between the market price and the price offered by the recycler has become part of the profits of Aihuishou. This market price calculation system is based on the processing of massive data and the construction of several complex models, featuring self-learning. Transparent price information effectively improves the pricing credibility of the platform.

最后,在产品环保处理体系上,对于回收至爱回收后台的二手产品,将有三种处理办法:具有较高残余价值的二手产品经过爱回收的检测清理后将再次出现在其二手售卖平台"口袋优品"上;仍具有使用价值的低残值二手产品会被周转至部分海外市场;而无法使用的二手产品将提取功能运作正常的硬件,用于二手维修,剩下的部分将交由具有环保资质的回收机构,拆解提取重金属,用以二次利用。针对回收来的手机,爱回收会进行身份信息以及手机串号的验证,数据与公安机关联网;如果是失窃手机,即便顺利卖给爱回收,后期也有极大可能被找回并追究来源,一般小偷不会铤而走险,这也在很大程度上杜绝了失窃手机的灰色流通链。

Finally, in the green product disposal system, there are three ways to deal with the recycled second-hand products. The second-hand products with high residual value will reappear on the second-hand sales platform "Koudaiyoupin" after being tested and utilized by Aihuishou. Those with low residual value but with use value will be turned over to some overseas markets. The unusable second-hand products will be handed by extracting the hardware that is still working for second-hand maintenance, and the rest will be handed over to recycling institutions with environmental protection qualifications for dismantling and extracting heavy metals for secondary use. For the recycled mobile phones, Aihuishou will verify their identity information and serial number, and the data will be networked with the public security organs. If it is a stolen mobile phone that has been successfully sold to Aihuishou, it is very likely that it will be recovered and traced back to the source later. In this way, thieves usually don't take risks, which largely eliminates the gray circulation chain of stolen mobile phones.

五、开拓 B2B 市场，稳住 C2B 根基
V. Develop B2B market and stabilize C2B foundation

2018 年 6 月，爱回收宣布建立 B2B 模式下的二手电子产品代拍平台"拍机堂"，以此试水全球市场。爱回收力图通过搭建一个全球化的二手贸易平台，通过对诸如印度 Cashify 以及巴西 Trocafone 等二手交易平台的投资，在世界各地建立全球运输中心，进行全球范围内的贸易和资源调配，实现货品跨区域的快速流通。经过大半年的运营，"拍机堂"已积累了众多上下游商家，单月商品总销量（GMV）环比增长 20%～30%。

In June 2018, Aihuishou announced the establishment of a second-hand electronic product auction platform "Paijitang" adopting the B2B mode to set foot in the global market. Aihuishou tried to build a global second-hand trading platform, and establish global transportation centers around the world by investing in second-hand trading platforms such as Cashify in India and Trocafone in Brazil for global trading and resource allocation, so as to realize rapid circulation of goods across regions. After half a year's operation, "Paijitang" has accumulated numerous upstream and downstream businesses, with its monthly GMV (Gross Merchandise Volume) up by 20%～30% from the previous month.

开拓新业务的同时,爱回收也在传统的 C2B 中推进渠道建设,比如与链家、中国联通、京东无界零售等网点合作,在其门店中铺设自助回收机,配合芝麻信用的风控体系,当场预付部分回收款,三天内完成质检流程并为用户转完尾款。

While developing new business, Aihuishou also promoted channel construction under the traditional C2B mode, such as cooperating with outlets such as Lianjia, China Unicom and JD. com Unbounded Retail, and installing self-service recycling machines in the outlets. Working with the risk control system of Sesame Credit, it prepaid part of the recycling price on the spot, and completed the quality inspection process within three days and then transferred the final payment to users.

爱回收为消费者提供便捷安全的线上线下融合的交易渠道,为更多消费者提供专业和安全的交易渠道,让绿色消费更便捷。

Aihuishou provides consumers with accessible, professional and secure online and offline trading channels, making green consumption more convenient.

点评
Comments

发展循环经济是中国经济社会发展的一项重大战略。"十四五"

时期中国进入新发展阶段,大力发展循环经济,推进资源节约集约利用,构建资源循环型产业体系和废旧物资循环利用体系,对保障国家资源安全,推动实现"碳达峰""碳中和",促进生态文明建设具有重大意义。

Developing circular economy is an important strategy for China's economic and social development. During the "14th Five-Year Plan" period, China entered a new stage of development. It is of great significance to vigorously develop circular economy, promote resource conservation and intensive utilization, and build a resource-recycling industrial system and a recycling system for waste materials. They will ensure national resource security, advance the realization of peak carbon dioxide emissions and carbon neutrality, and push forward the construction of ecological civilization.

从消费规模和结构看,中国开始进入消费全面升级转型阶段,这也是绿色消费与生活方式的窗口机遇期。坚持发展绿色经济,正是贯彻落实科学发展观,实现经济发展与资源环境保护双赢的必然选择。此次《"十四五"循环经济发展规划》的发布,给循环经济行业带来了长期利好,也给予了企业发展的充分动力与信心,万物新生将持续发挥"让闲置不用,都物尽其用"的企业使命,秉承"让二手商品流通全球"的愿景,持续助力循环经济发展。爱回收将企业社会责任和可持续商业实践融入企业日常运营当中,不仅提升了行业的规范化和规模化水平,还通过技术手段和供应链能力,促进了二手行业的可持续发展。

From the scale and structure of consumption, China began to enter the stage featuring all-round upgrade and transformation of consumption, which is also the window period of an opportunity for green consumption and lifestyle. Adhering to the development of green economy is an inevitable choice to implement Scientific Outlook on Development and achieve win-win results for economic development and resource and environmental protection. The release of the 14th Five-Year Plan for Circular Economy Development has brought long-term benefits to the circular economy industry, and also fully motivated and boosted the development of enterprises. ATRenew will continue to adhere to its corporate mission of "making the most of everything idle" and its vision of "making second-hand goods circulate around the world" to support the development of circular economy. Aihuishou integrates corporate social responsibility and sustainable business practices into its daily operation, which not only improves the standardization and scale of the industry, but also promotes the sustainable development of the second-hand industry through technical means and supply chain capacity.

讨论题
Discussions

(1)讨论回收物流与循环物流的概念、必要性、发展趋势预测。

Discuss the concept, necessity and development trend forecast of recycling logistics and circular logistics.

(2)物流设施选址的方法有哪些？请设计校园手机回收网络。

What are the methods for location selection of logistics facilities? Please design a mobile phone recycling network on campus.

(3)描述标准化的含义和意义。

Describe the meaning and significance of standardization.

资料来源

卢岳. 爱回收:以技术手段和供应链能力助力行业发展[N]. 消费日报,2021－07－20.

丁毓. 爱回收:小回收做成大生意[J]. 上海信息化,2019(02):71－74.

References

Lu Yue. Aihuishou:Promoting industry development with technical means and supply chain capabilities[N]. Consumption Daily,2021－07－20.

Ding Yu. Aihuishou:Small recycling business makes big difference[J]. Shanghai Informatization,2019(02):71－74.

案例 5.2 菜鸟绿色物流，打造中国绿色物流新样本
Case 5.2 Cainiao Green Logistics Sets a New Example of Green Logistics in China

教学目标
Teaching Objectives

海量网购消费带来的绿色快递需求巨大，使得企业绿色物流能力瓶颈凸显。菜鸟网络于 2016 年 6 月携手 32 家全球物流合作伙伴共同启动"绿动计划"，正式宣告开展绿色物流实践。菜鸟网络绿色计划包括减量化、再使用、再循环。菜鸟网络的绿色物流实践，体现了循环经济的减量化、再使用、再循环原则，对拓展企业绿色物流能力具有示范作用。本节通过案例分析，帮助学生更好地理解企业物流与绿色物流的概念和内涵，实现绿色物流的途径和方法，以及企业承担社会责任的必要性和重要意义，提升学生的社会责任感和主人翁精神。

A huge demand for green express delivery has been brought by massive online shopping consumption, which highlights the bottleneck of green logistics capacity of enterprises. In June 2016, Cainiao Network joined hands with 32 global logistics partners to launch the "Green Plan" and officially announced to carry out the green logistics practice. The green plan includes reduce, reuse and recycle. The green logistics practice which embodies the principles of reducing, reusing and recycling of circular economy has a demonstration role in expanding the green logistics capacity of enterprises. Through case analysis, this section helps students better understand the concepts and connotations of corporate logistics and green logistics, the ways and methods to realize green logistics, and the necessity and significance of shouldering corporate social responsibility, so as to enhance their sense of social responsibility and ownership.

案例涉及物流与供应链管理中企业物流、绿色物流、物流技术、绿色仓储、绿色包装等相关知识点。

The case involves corporate logistics, green logistics, logistics technology, green warehousing, green packaging and other related concepts in Logistics and Supply Chain Management.

案例内容
Contents

自改革开放以来，物流业快速发展，为经济社会持续发展奠定了坚实基础，中国也逐步成为全球最大物流市场。但物流业的高速发展也给我国资源、环境、社会带来巨大压力，仅快递行业每年就会面临千

案例 5.2 菜鸟绿色物流，打造中国绿色物流新样本

亿包裹的垃圾负担。所以，绿色物流发展刻不容缓，愈发受政府、物流行业及企业等广泛重视，是现代物流发展的必然趋势。

Since the reform and opening up, the rapid development of the logistics industry has laid a solid foundation for sustainable economic and social development. China has gradually become the largest logistics market in the world. Nevertheless, the fast development of the logistics industry has also put China's resources, environment and society under huge pressure. The express delivery industry alone has to dispose of the garbage caused by hundreds of billions of parcels every year. Therefore, as an urgently needed development trend of modern logistics, green logistics has attracted increasing attention from the government, logistics industry and enterprises.

一、绿色物流的概念

Ⅰ. Concept of green logistics

绿色物流已成为我国物流流通领域变革的新主题，并被视作新的增长点。绿色物流指以降低对环境的污染、减少资源消耗、提高运行效率为目的，利用先进物流技术规划和实施的运输、储存、装卸、流通加工等物流活动，是连接绿色供给主体和绿色需求主体，克服空间和时间阻碍的有效、快速的绿色商品和服务流动的绿色经济管理活动过程，也可称为"环保物流"，国外称之为"生态物流"或"环境物流"。早于 20 世纪 80 年代，这一概念便随可持续发展概念的兴起而被提出。"环保""生态""低碳"等高频词也折射出绿色物流的核心在于"生态环保和低碳节约"。

Green logistics which has become a new theme in the reform of

China's logistics and circulation sectors is regarded as a new growth point. Green logistics refers to logistics activities such as transportation, storage, loading and unloading, and distribution processing, which are planned and implemented with advanced logistics technology for the purpose of reducing environmental pollution, minimizing resource consumption, and improving operating efficiency. It is an effective and rapid green economic management process for green goods and service flow that connects green suppliers and green users, and overcomes the obstacles of time and space. It can also be called "environmental-friendly logistics", and "ecological logistics" or "environmental logistics" abroad. As early as the 1980s, it was put forward with the rise of the concept of sustainable development. Frequently-used words such as "environmental protection" "ecology" and "low carbon" also reflect that the key to green logistics lies in "ecological environmental protection and low carbon saving".

物流业虽是国民经济发展的基础、先导及战略性产业,但也属于高耗能、高碳排放产业。自2009年国务院刊发《物流业调整和振兴规划的通知》至今,国家及相关行业主管部门都提出要大力发展绿色物流,物流企业等纷纷开展物流绿色实践,其中脱胎于阿里巴巴的菜鸟网络便是领先企业样本。

As the fundamental, pioneering and strategic industry for national economic development, logistics industry features high energy consumption and high carbon emission. Since the State Council issued the Notice on the Adjustment and Revitalization Planning of Logistics Industry in 2009, the state and relevant industry regulators have pro-

案例 5.2　菜鸟绿色物流,打造中国绿色物流新样本

posed to vigorously develop green logistics, and then logistics enterprises have carried out green logistics practices one after another, among which Cainiao Network under Alibaba set an example of leading enterprises.

二、菜鸟绿色物流

Ⅱ. Cainiao green logistics

"菜鸟是中国快递物流行业中最早发起绿色行动的企业之一,比如率先联合中华环境保护基金会设立了菜鸟绿色联盟公益基金,并持续引领绿色探索和实践。"菜鸟绿色行动负责人牛智敬还对外表示,菜鸟通过推广电子面单、装箱算法、智能路径规划、环保袋、循环箱、绿色回收箱、太阳能物流园等,已构建起从订单生成到包裹送达的全链路绿色物流解决方案,覆盖仓储、包装、配送及回收等上下游各环节。

"Cainiao took the lead in China's express logistics industry to launch green initiatives, such as setting up the Cainiao Green Alliance Foundation with China Environmental Protection Foundation, and continuously leading green exploration and practice." Niu Zhijing, the head of the Cainiao Green Initiative, said that Cainiao has built a full-link green logistics solution from order generation to package delivery by promoting electronic express sheets, packing algorithms, intelligent path planning, environmental protection bags, recycling bins, green recycling bins, solar logistics parks, etc. , covering all upstream and downstream links such as warehousing, packaging, distribution and recycling.

2021 年 11 月 11 日(在中国称为"双 11"购物节),菜鸟全链路绿

图片来源:https://new.qq.com/omn/20211116/20211116A06NFS00.html,2023-03-10。

Source: https://new.qq.com/omn/20211116/20211116A06NFS00.html, 2023-03-10.

图 5—2　菜鸟推进"双 11"减碳计划

Figure 5-2　Cainiao promotes the carbon reduction plans during "Double 11"

色物流解决方案全面发力(如图 5—2 所示)。据《2021"双 11"菜鸟绿色物流报告》显示,11 月 1—14 日,包括使用电子面单、原箱发货、装箱算法、驿站绿色回收和寄件等行为,基于菜鸟绿色物流全链路,菜鸟、商家和消费者合计产生 18 亿次绿色行为,为全社会减碳 5.3 万吨。

On November 11, 2021 (known as "Double 11" shopping festival in China), Cainiao's full-link green logistics solution was fully launched(as shown in Figure 5-2). According to the "Double 11" Cainiao Green Logistics Report in 2021, from November 1 to 14, Cainiao, the merchants and consumers generated 1.8 billion green actions

案例 5.2　菜鸟绿色物流,打造中国绿色物流新样本

in total based on the whole link of Cainiao green logistics, including the use of electronic express sheets, original package delivery, packing algorithm, green recycling and mailing at express outlets, saving 53,000 tons of carbon for the whole society.

(一) 绿色仓储

(1) Green warehousing

自2017年起,菜鸟网络就开始在上海、广州、杭州、武汉、东莞的智慧物流园区内建设屋顶太阳能光伏发电站,将清洁能源应用于物流园区以降低能耗。2020年菜鸟物流园区实现年发电量超过2 000万度,相当于节省8 000吨煤炭。以上海嘉定园区为例,2021年,该园区总发电量预计331万度,若烧煤发电,所产生的二氧化碳需要480棵树吸收1整年,现在园区不仅实现了用电自给自足,每年还能为上海市政电网输送100万度的绿色能源。

Since 2017, Cainiao Network has started to build rooftop solar photovoltaic power stations in smart logistics parks in Shanghai, Guangzhou, Hangzhou, Wuhan and Dongguan, and applied clean energy to logistics parks to reduce energy consumption. In 2020, the Cainiao logistics parks achieved an annual power generation of more than 20 million kwh, saving 8,000 tons of coal. In 2021, Shanghai Jiading Park was expected to generate power of 3.31 million kWh. If coal-fired power generation is adopted, the carbon dioxide emissions need to be absorbed by 480 trees for a whole year. Now the park realizing self-sufficiency in electricity consumption contributes 1 million kWh of green energy to Shanghai municipal power grid every year.

(二)绿色包装和周转
(2) Green packaging and recycling

菜鸟通过装箱算法、电子面单、纸箱复用、循环箱等解决方案从源头实现了包材减量、环保及流通安全、高效等。例如菜鸟通过装箱算法,能直接让"大材小用、过度包装"的现象大幅减少。据统计,通过优化箱型和推荐合理的装箱方案,2021年"双11"仅在菜鸟仓内"瘦身"的包裹就达2.5亿个,如今这一技术已经在全行业推广。再比如,在2014年就已率先上线的菜鸟电子面单,截至2021年累计服务了1 000多亿个快递包裹,帮助全行业节省纸张5 000亿张,节约成本200亿元。值得一提的是,菜鸟电子面单自诞生以来,已逐渐取代传统纸质面单,推动快递业数字化进程的同时,也帮助行业减排增效。2021年11月1—14日,全行业使用菜鸟绿色一联单的包裹量达16亿件,相较于传统纸质五联单,可省下的纸张相当于少砍伐3 700平方米的森林。

Cainiao has achieved reduction in packaging materials, environmental protection, safe circulation and high efficiency from the sources through packing algorithm, electronic express sheets, carton reuse and recycled cartons. For example, Cainiao greatly reduced "overqualified and over-packaged" cases through the packing algorithm. According to statistics, in 2021, by optimizing the carton type and recommending a reasonable packing scheme, "Double 11" "cut down" 250 million packages in the Cainiao warehouses alone, and now this technology has been promoted across the industry. Another example is the Cainiao electronic express sheet, which was first launched in 2014. It had been applied to more than 100 billion express

案例 5.2 菜鸟绿色物流,打造中国绿色物流新样本

parcels by 2021, helping the whole industry save 500 billion sheets of paper worth 20 billion yuan. It is worth mentioning that the Cainiao electronic express sheet has gradually replaced the traditional paper express sheet, which not only promotes the digitalization process of the express delivery industry, but also helps the industry reduce emissions and increase efficiency. From November 1 to 14, 2021, the number of packages using the green one-part sheet of Cainiao in the entire industry reached 1.6 billion. By replacing the traditional five-part paper sheet, it saved 3,700 m^2 of forest.

而对于包装箱选取,菜鸟联手天猫超市等推广"原箱+回收纸箱发货",实现 70% 的包裹发货不再用新纸箱。这种"零"新增包材的创新模式,与国家提倡的减少电商快件二次包装的方向相一致,并在菜鸟推动下渐成趋势。目前,杭州萧山菜鸟仓已实行大规模回收箱发货,并建立了一整套回收箱使用标准和工作流程。另一方面,菜鸟自 2017 年起便推动绿色"回箱计划",在全国 31 个省区市 300 多个城市的菜鸟驿站和快递网点铺设绿色回收箱,鼓励消费者取件后将快递纸箱、包装填充物投入回收箱。2021 年"双 11",菜鸟在全国范围内再新增 1.3 万个回收箱,预计每年可循环再利用上亿个快递纸箱。与此同时,菜鸟自 2018 年起启用循环箱发货,每个循环箱自带 RFID 识别,"双 11"期间,单个菜鸟仓使用的循环箱每日便可以替代超过 20 万个纸箱和塑料包材,此模式目前正计划向北京等其他城市推广。

For the selection of packing cartons, Cainiao teamed up with Tmall Supermarket to promote "original package + recycled carton delivery", and 70% of the parcels were delivered without additional cartons. This innovative model of "zero" new packaging materials was consistent with the practice advocated by the state to reduce the secondary packaging of e-commerce express mails, and it gradually became a trend under the promotion of Cainiao. Currently, Hangzhou Xiaoshan Cainiao Warehouse has implemented large-scale recycling carton delivery, and established a set of recycling carton usage standards and workflows. On the other hand, since 2017, Cainiao has been promoting the green "carton recycling plan", setting up green recycling bins in Cainiao posthouses and express outlets in more than 300 cities in 31 provinces, autonomous regions and municipalities across China. It encourages consumers to put express cartons and packaging fillers into the recycling bins after picking up the packages. During "Double 11" in 2021, Cainiao added 13,000 recycling bins nationwide, and it is estimated that hundreds of millions of express cartons can be recycled every year. Meanwhile, Cainiao began to use recyclable cartons for delivery in 2018, and each of them has its own RFID. During "Double 11", the recyclable cartons used by a single Cainiao warehouse can replace more than 200,000 cartons and related plastic packaging materials every day. This model is planned to be promoted to other cities such as Beijing.

(三)菜鸟包裹全链路绿色化

(3) Green packages along the entire link of Cainiao

此外,菜鸟还通过新能源车、环保寄件袋、智能分仓、智能路径规划等实现绿色、高效配送。

In addition, Cainiao achieves green and efficient distribution through new energy vehicles, green mailing packages, intelligent

案例 5.2 菜鸟绿色物流,打造中国绿色物流新样本

warehouse distribution, and intelligent path planning.

除了发力消费侧,菜鸟还联合商家一同减碳、减塑。得益于多个商家品牌和菜鸟 2021 年联合发起的"双 11 绿色包裹倡议",从 2021 年 10 月 21 日预售开始至 14 日,从菜鸟仓发出的"绿色包裹"(含原箱发货、回收箱利旧发货、无胶带拉链箱以及环保寄件袋)超过 9 000 万个,减少的胶带长度超过 8 400 万米。

In addition to the consumer side, Cainiao also cooperated with merchants to reduce carbon emissions and use of plastics. Thanks to the "Double 11 Green Parcel Initiative" jointly launched by several merchant brands and Cainiao in 2021, from the pre-sale on October 21 until 14 in 2021, more than 90 million "green parcels" (including original package delivery, recyclable carton delivery, adhesive-free zipper cartons and green mailing bags) were delivered from Cainiao warehouses, reducing more than 84 million meters of adhesive tape.

回顾菜鸟 8 年成长历程,基于战略演进视角,或许不难找到一些蛛丝马迹。菜鸟诞生于快递电商转折背景下,阿里开始发力 B2C,成立初期战略是构建"三张网",包括数据信息网络、覆盖全国的仓配基础设施网络以及快递员及消费者服务网络,重点解决的是物流行业效率与质量。2016 年菜鸟再将战略细化至物流全链条,为行业赋能。2018 年菜鸟又提出第二个 5 年战略"一横两纵",即推动快递行业数字化升级("一横"),以及构建围绕新零售的智慧供应链能力和全球化供应链能力("两纵")。

Looking back on the past eight years of Cainiao's growth, it may not be difficult to find some clues from the perspective of strategic evolution. Cainiao was born at the turning point of express e-commerce, when Alibaba began to set foot in B2C. The initial strategy was to build "three networks", including data information network, warehouse distribution infrastructure network covering the entire country, and courier and consumer service network, focusing on the efficiency and quality of the logistics industry. In 2016, Cainiao refined the strategy to the whole logistics chain to empower the industry. In 2018, Cainiao put forward the second five-year strategy of "one horizontal and two verticals", namely promoting the digital upgrade of the express delivery industry ("one horizontal"), and building smart supply chain capacity and global supply chain capacity for the new retail ("two verticals").

不论战略如何更迭，技术和供应链一直是贯穿菜鸟长期发展的两条交织的主线。而在2021年6月的菜鸟全球智慧物流峰会上，CEO万霖重新定义了菜鸟：一家客户价值驱动的全球化产业互联网公司，并提出未来聚焦的三大增量赛道，即物流数智化、消费者供应链向产业供应链升级、全球化。

Despite changes in its strategies, technologies and supply chain have always been two intertwined main lines that run through the long-term development of Cainiao. At the Cainiao's Global Smart Logistics Summit in June, 2021, CEO Wan Lin redefined Cainiao as a globalized industrial Internet company driven by customer value, and proposed three major fields for future development, including digital and intelligent logistics, upgrade of consumer supply chain to industrial supply chain, and globalization.

案例 5.2 菜鸟绿色物流,打造中国绿色物流新样本

点评
Comments

"绿色"是我国经济社会发展中必须坚持的节约资源和保护环境的基本国策。"绿色"作为"创新、协调、绿色、开放、共享"新发展理念之一,是我国经济社会发展中必须坚持的节约资源和保护环境的基本国策。对绿色经济和物流产业融合的研究,比如绿色经济视角下物流产业融合模式、绿色物流产业组织模式及运行机制,为我国物流产业绿色发展提供了理论参考。

"Green" is the basic national policy of resource conservation and environmental protection that must be adhered to in China's economic and social development. "Green", as one of the new development concepts of "innovation, coordination, green, openness and sharing", is a basic national policy of resource conservation and environmental protection that must be adhered to in China's economic and social development. The research on the integration of green economy and logistics industry, such as the integration mode of logistics industry from the perspective of green economy, as well as the organization mode and operation mechanism of green logistics industry, provides theoretical reference for the green development of logistics industry in China.

菜鸟既是电商物流领域的龙头企业,也是绿色快递物流的带头企业。菜鸟在推进绿色物流实践中极具代表性。菜鸟网络"绿色联盟"的"绿动计划",代表了绿色物流对分享经济发展的作用,带给我

们一个重要的启示:首先是其社会环保责任担当,其次是其绿色物流实践效应,均给整个电商、快递领域做出示范;同时也可以看出,电商、快递企业在提高自身绿色物流能力的同时,正亟待寻求新的科技手段,来提高绿色物流运行效率,尤其是需要降低绿色物流运行成本。

Cainiao leads in both e-commerce logistics and green express logistics. Cainiao is a typical example in promoting the practice of green logistics. The "Green Plan" of the Cainiao Network "Green Alliance" represents the role of green logistics in the development of sharing economy, which brings us an important insight. Both its social environmental responsibility and the practical effect of green logistics set a good example for the e-commerce and express delivery sectors. Meanwhile, it can be seen that e-commerce and express delivery enterprises are urgently seeking new scientific and technological means to improve their operating efficiency of green logistics, especially reducing the operating costs of green logistics, while improving their own green logistics capacity.

绿色物流的发展必须通过物流能力来体现。有学者提出了绿色物流能力的概念,即在保证对环境产生的危害控制在最小化程度的基础上,物流系统充分利用资源满足客户需求的能力。进而给出衡量区域或企业物流可持续发展和环保程度的重要准则层指标,包括三个方面:一是资源回收和再利用能力,例如包装材料的回收利用率、再循环利用率等;二是废物排放与废物处理能力,例如绿色包装的使用率、废物的排放达标率、废物的处理率等;三是资源综合利用能力,例如完全报废的商品和包装材料的循环利用率等。

案例 5.2 菜鸟绿色物流,打造中国绿色物流新样本

The development of green logistics must be reflected by logistics capacity. Some scholars put forward the concept of green logistics capacity, which means that on the basis of minimizing environmental hazards, the logistics system can make full use of resources to meet the needs of customers. It gives an important criterion-level index to measure the sustainable development and environmental protection efforts of regional or enterprise logistics, including three aspects. First, it measures the capacity of resource recycling and reuse, such as the recycling rate of packaging materials. Second, it evaluates the capacity of waste discharge and waste treatment, such as the utilization rate of green packaging, the waste discharge compliance rate, the waste treatment rate, etc. Third, it looks into the comprehensive utilization capacity of resources, such as the recycling rate of completely scrapped goods and packaging materials.

讨论题
Discussions

(1)什么是绿色物流? 绿色物流可以体现在什么方面? 菜鸟绿色物流给你带来什么启示?

What is green logistics? From what aspects can we see green logistics? What insights have you gained from green logistics of Cainiao?

(2)描述减量化的含义和意义。

Describe the meaning and significance of reduction.

(3)实现绿色是有成本的。使用生物降解塑料包装袋的成本,可能是现有包装袋的两倍以上,这对快递行业成本控制提出了新挑战。你愿意为未来可能实行的"环保快递"支付更多费用吗?

Green comes at a price. The cost of biodegradable plastic packaging bags may be more than twice that of existing packaging bags, which poses a new challenge to the cost control of express delivery industry. Are you willing to pay more for the possible "environmentally-friendly express" in the future?

资料来源

中国"低碳时刻",菜鸟网络全链路发力,打造中国绿色物流新样本[EB/OL].[2023-03-10]. https://new.qq.com/omn/20211116/20211116A06NFS00.html.

可持续发展[EB/OL].[2023-03-10]. https://www.cainiao.com/green.html.

尤美虹,颜梦铃,何美章.5G应用驱动下绿色物流能力拓展模式探析——以菜鸟、京东为例[J].商业经济研究,2020(19):103-106.

刘春沐阳.电商真的开始变"绿"了吗[EB/OL].[2023-03-10]. http://www.ce.cn/cysc/stwm/gd/202101/29/t20210129_36271099.shtml.

References

China's "low-carbon moment": Cainiao Network makes efforts along the entire link to set a new example of green logistics in China[EB/OL]. [2023-03-10]. https://new.qq.com/omn/20211116/20211116A06NFS00.html.

Sustainable development[EB/OL]. [2023-03-10]. https://www.cainiao.com/green.html.

You Meihong, Yan Mengling, He Meizhang. Analysis of the green logistics capability expansion model driven by 5G applications-taking Cainiao and JD.com as examples[J]. Journal of Commercial Economics, 2020(19):103-106.

案例 5.2　菜鸟绿色物流,打造中国绿色物流新样本

Liuchun Muyang. Has e-commerce truly started to turn "green"[EB/OL].[2023—03—10]. http://www.ce.cn/cysc/stwm/gd/202101/29/t20210129_36271099.shtml.

案例 5.3 顺丰冷运一路领先,靠的是什么?
Case 5.3 What has SF Cold Chain Relied on to Lead All the Way?

教学目标
Teaching Objectives

冷链物流已由起初的新兴需求转变为社会发展的基础设施与刚性需求,冷链产业体系现代化进入了"快车道",面临着全新的机遇与挑战。如何在保证质量的前提下降低成本和碳排放,是冷链企业义不容辞的责任。顺丰冷运蝉联中国冷链物流百强榜首,其冷链运输主要集中在食品、医药两个业务板块。顺丰冷运整合顺丰控股现有门店、网点及末端配送资源,为生鲜食品行业客户提供专业、定制、高效、全程可视化可控的冷链物流服务。本节通过案例分析,帮助学生更好地理解冷链物流的重要意义和内涵、特点,所需的特殊物流技术,提升学生的专业视野、专业自豪感和社会责任感。

Cold chain logistics has changed from the initial emerging demand to the infrastructure and rigid demand of social development.

案例 5.3　顺丰冷运一路领先，靠的是什么？

The modernization of cold chain industrial system has taken the "fast lane", facing brand-new opportunities and challenges. How to reduce costs and carbon emissions while ensuring quality is the incumbent responsibility of cold chain enterprises. SF Cold Chain ranks first among the top 100 cold chain logistics enterprises in China. Its cold chain transportation focuses on two business segments: food and medicine. SF Cold Chain integrates the existing stores, outlets and terminal distribution resources of SF Holdings to provide specialized, customized, efficient, visible and controllable cold chain logistics services for customers in the fresh food industry. Through case analysis, this section helps students better understand the significance, connotations and characteristics of cold chain logistics, and the special logistics technologies needed, so as to broaden their horizon, foster their sense of pride in related disciplines and strengthen their sense of social responsibility.

案例涉及物流与供应链管理中冷链物流、仓储、包装、物流信息技术等相关知识点。

The case involves cold chain logistics, warehousing, packaging and logistics information technology, and other related concepts in Logistics and Supply Chain Management.

案例内容
Contents

随着生活水平的提高，人们对食品质量的要求大幅度提高，对冷链的需求亦迅速增加。冷链物流不仅可以保证人们对生鲜产品质量的要求，还可以减少生鲜产品在物流过程中的损耗。一方面保证食品在物流过程中的质量，提供全程可控可视的冷链物流方案，另一方面尽量降低碳排放，是冷链面临的新要求。"十四五"冷链物流首次被纳入国家层面五年发展规划，地位举足轻重，冷链物流的发展变得更加掷地有声。

The improvement of people's living standards leads to the great improvement in their requirements for food quality and the rapid increase of their demand for cold chain. Cold chain logistics can not only ensure people's requirements for the quality of fresh products, but also reduce the loss of fresh products in the logistics process. On the one hand, it ensures the quality of food in the logistics process and provides a controllable and visible cold chain logistics scheme in the whole process. On the other hand, it can minimize carbon emissions, which is a new requirement to be satisfied. For the first time, cold chain logistics was included in the "14th Five-Year Plan", the national five-year development plan with decisive influence. Since then, the development of cold chain logistics has become even more prominent.

2014年9月，顺丰控股正式推出顺丰冷运，依托顺丰控股强大的空中、地面运输网络，冷链仓储运输实力，专业的温控技术以及先进的系统管理能力，顺丰冷运逐渐发展成为我国供应链型农产品冷链物流龙头企业。据中物联冷链委《中国冷链物流百强企业分析报告》，顺丰冷运业务自2018年起，连续3年蝉联行业第一。

In September 2014, SF Holdings officially launched SF Cold Chain. Relying on SF Holdings' well-developed air and ground transportation networks, cold chain warehousing and transportation strength, specialized temperature control technologies and advanced system management capabilities, SF Cold Chain has gradually developed into a leading enterprise specialized in cold chain logistics of agricultural products in China's supply chain industry. According to the Analysis Report of Top 100 Cold Chain Logistics Enterprises in China issued by the China Federation of Logistics and Purchasing Cold Chain Logistics Committee, SF's cold chain transportation business has been ranking first in the industry for three consecutive years since 2018.

一、顺丰：农产品冷链物流业务的布局历程

Ⅰ. SF: Development course of cold chain logistics layout for agricultural products

2014年9月25日,顺丰速运有限公司成立冷运事业部,推出顺丰冷运,专注为生鲜食品行业客户提供"一站式供应链解决方案"。

On September 25, 2014, SF Express Co., Ltd. established the Cold Chain Division and launched SF Cold Chain, focusing on providing "one-stop supply chain solutions" for customers in the fresh food industry.

2015年1月,顺丰成立包装技术实验室,推进快递包装绿色化进程,健全产业链环保体系。

In January 2015, SF set up a packaging technology laboratory to promote the green process of express packaging and improve the environmental protection system of the industrial chain.

2016年8月,顺丰冷运食品陆运干线网正式发布,成为国内唯一一家覆盖东北、华北、华东、华南、华中、华西等重点核心城市的冷链物流企业。

In August, 2016, SF Cold Chain's trunk network for land transportation of food was officially released, becoming the only cold chain logistics enterprise in China covering key cities in Northeast China, Northern China, East China, Southern China, Central China and West China.

2017年7月,顺丰冷运荣获2016年度中国冷链物流百强企业第三名,业务发展初见成效,向着更高目标前进。

In July 2017, SF Cold Chain took the third place among the top 100 cold chain logistics enterprises in China in 2016, with its business development achieving initial results and moving towards higher goals.

2018年6月,顺丰冷运荣获2017年度中国冷链物流百强企业第二名,夯实基础,整装待发,致力于成为高品质、端到端、全程可控可视的冷链解决方案的领先供应商。

In June 2018, SF Cold Chain won the second place among the top 100 cold chain logistics enterprises in China in 2017. After laying a solid foundation and preparing itself for future development, it was committed to becoming a leading supplier that offers high-quality, end-to-end, controllable and visible cold chain solutions throughout the process.

2019年6月,顺丰冷运荣登2018年度中国冷链物流百强企业榜首,同年12月,成为国内首家获颁ISO 22000食品安全管理体系国际标准认证证书的物流企业。

案例 5.3　顺丰冷运一路领先,靠的是什么?

In June 2019, SF Cold Chain ranked first among the top 100 cold chain logistics enterprises in China in 2018. In December 2019, it became the first logistics enterprise in China to be awarded the ISO 22000 certification for food safety management system.

2022年第十四届全球冷链峰会,顺丰冷运连续4年蝉联"中国冷链物流百强榜"第一,通过科技赋能、智慧物流推动冷链行业转型、升级,2021年实现营业收入78亿元,同比增长20.1%。

At the 14th World Cold Chain Summit in 2022, SF Cold Chain ranked first in the "Top 100 Cold Chain Logistics List of China" for 4 consecutive years, and promoted the transformation and upgrade of the cold chain industry through technology empowerment and intelligent logistics. In 2021, it achieved an operating income of 7.8 billion yuan, with a year-on-year increase of 20.1%.

顺丰地网由中国数以万计的营业网点、自动化中转场、四通八达的运输网络、庞大的仓储面积、人性化的客服呼叫网点和最后一千米网络组成,顺丰的基础设施建设、固定资产规模遥遥领先于其他快递公司。顺丰在直营转运中心数量、自持土地规模以及自动化设备投入均处于行业领先地位。在干线运输环节,顺丰自有车队规模也远超同行。此外。顺丰还积极与国家铁路总局合作,依托高铁、普铁资源开展冷链物流业务。

SF's land transportation network consists of tens of thousands of business outlets across China, automatic transit depots, a transportation network extending in all directions, huge warehousing area, humanized customer service call outlets and the last-kilometer networks. SF's infrastructure construction and scale of fixed assets are far ahead of other express delivery companies. SF maintains in the leading position in the number of directly-operated transshipment centers, the area of self-Owned land and the investment in automation equipment. At the trunk transportation link, SF's own fleet is also far larger than its peers. Besides, SF actively cooperates with the National Railway Administration to develop its cold chain logistics business relying on high-speed rail and general freight resources.

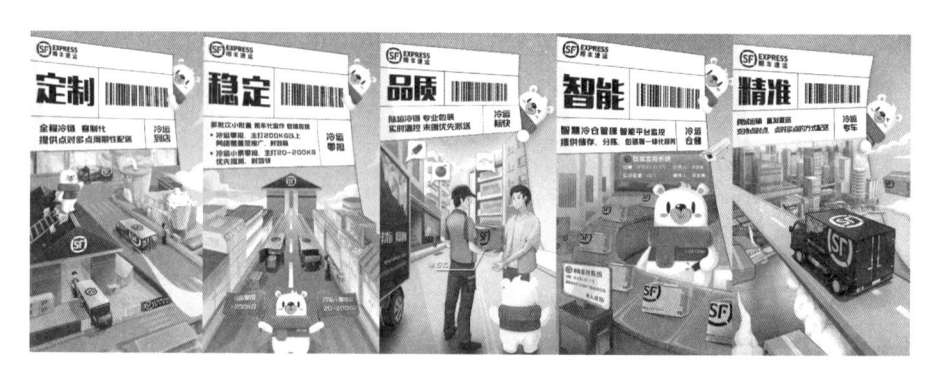

图片来源:顺丰冷运公众号。

Source: Official account of SF Cold Chain.

图 5-3 顺丰冷运特点

Figure 5-3 Characteristics of SF Cold Chain

二、顺丰:冷运物流运营现状

Ⅱ. SF: Status quo of cold chain logistics operation

顺丰的冷链运输主要集中在食品、医药两个业务板块。顺丰冷运整合顺丰控股现有门店、网点及末端配送资源,为生鲜食品行业客户提供专业、定制、高效、全程可视化可控的冷链物流服务(如图 5-3 所示)。

案例 5.3　顺丰冷运一路领先,靠的是什么?

SF's cold chain transportation focuses on two business segments: food and medicine. SF Cold Chain integrates the existing stores, outlets and terminal distribution resources of SF Holdings to provide professional, customized, efficient, visual and controllable cold chain logistics services for customers in the fresh food industry (as shown in Figure 5—3).

目前,顺丰冷运以推出冷运特惠、冷运到店、顺丰冷运零担、冷运仓储、冷运专车以及冷运速配等相关服务。

At present, SF Cold Chain has services including cold chain special offers, cold chain delivery to stores, SF Cold Chain LTL, cold chain warehousing, cold chain specific trucks, cold chain fast delivery and other related services.

医药。2021 年,顺丰医药持续加强医药仓网与服务网络建设,顺丰医药网络覆盖 240 个地级市,2 068 个区县,拥有 12 个医药仓(11 个 GSP 标准验证、1 个定制仓),总面积超 17 万平方米,自有冷藏车 292 辆(GSP 标准验证),医药运输干线 50 条,贯通全国核心城市,顺丰控股已处于第三方医药物流行业的领先地位。

Medicine. In 2021, SF Pharma continued to strengthen the construction of its medical warehouse network and service network. Its network covers 240 prefecture-level cities and 2,068 districts and counties, with 12 medical warehouses (11 GSP-certified warehouses and 1 customized warehouse) covering a total area of more than 170,000 m^2, 292 self-Owned refrigerated trucks (GSP-certified) and 50 medical transportation trunk lines, which run through the core cities in China. Now SF Holdings has been in the leading position in the third-party medical logistics industry.

值得注意的是,顺丰成为疫苗运输保障工作组正式成员单位,自首次服务起至今已累计安全平稳保障 1.8 亿剂新冠疫苗安全运输。在生物样本、IVD 试剂、胰岛素等冷链运输、智慧医药物流方面,可提供行业领先的医药冷链包装、集成物联网 Polar 平台(温湿度、GPS 路由等可视与监控),实现-80℃到 25℃ 范围内各种温区的精准控制,提供 GSP 认证的医药冷仓服务。

It is worth noting that SF used to be a member unit of the vaccine transportation guarantee working group, and since its first service, it had ensured the safe and stable transportation of 180 million doses of COVID-19 vaccines. For the cold chain transportation and intelligent medical logistics of biological samples, IVD reagents and insulin, it can provide industry-leading pharmaceutical cold chain packaging and the Polar platform integrated with the Internet of Things (temperature and humidity, GPS routing and other visualization and monitoring functions) for accurate control of various temperature zones ranging from -80℃ to 25℃, and offer GSP-certified medical cold storage services.

食品冷链。顺丰冷运拥有 35 个食品冷库(不含新夏晖的冷库),合计 20.1 万平方米,涵盖 5 个温区,可供客户个性化选择;159 条食品干线、23 000 多辆可调配冷藏车、200 多套定制化包装解决方案,服务 193 个城市,开通 3 619 条流向,农产品上行服务网络已覆盖全国 2 800 多个县区级城市,拥有先进的车辆 GPS 全球定位及车载温控实时监测系统进行全程控温。

Food cold chain. SF Cold Chain has 35 food cold storage ware-

案例 5.3 顺丰冷运一路领先,靠的是什么?

houses (excluding those of the SF-HAVI joint venture) covering a total area of 201,000 m², with 5 temperature zones available for customers. There are 159 food trunk lines, over 23,000 refrigerated trucks for allocation and more than 200 customized packaging solutions, serving 193 cities with 3,619 routes. The upstream service network of agricultural products has covered more than 2,800 county-level cities in China, with advanced GPS and real-time monitoring system for whole-process vehicle temperature control.

冷运仓储。冷运仓储提供货物冷库存储、分拣、包装、配送、信息流转等一体化冷运服务。冷仓覆盖范围广,仓储能力强,通过每个仓的辐射范围,干、配可覆盖全国;整进零出,可提供小批次多品类操作服务;可提供全国分仓服务。部分城市仓储可提供库内生鲜加工服务。

Cold chain warehousing. The cold chain warehousing solution provides integrated cold chain services such as storage, sorting, packaging, distribution and information circulation of goods in cold storage warehouses. The cold storage warehouse has a wide coverage and strong storage capacity. With the radiation range of each warehouse, the trunk transportation and terminal distribution can cover the entire country. Through wholesale warehouse-in and retail warehouse-out, it can provide small-batch and multi-category operation services in addition to sorting and repacking for delivery services nationwide. Besides, fresh food processing services are available in some urban warehouses.

冷运特惠。基于冷仓,对冷冻食品提供全程陆运冷链运输,末端优先派送的专属快递服务。

Cold chain special offers. Based on the cold storage warehouses, SF Cold Chain provides the whole-process cold chain transportation by land and the exclusive express services with priority terminal delivery.

冷运到店。为有温度要求的食品类货物进行周期性集中配载,提供基于陆运的点到多点的区域型城市配送服务。全程冷链:全程冷链配送,杜绝半冷链和脱温。温度监控:全程冷链监控。专业配送:专业冷藏车、专业团队配送。

Cold chain delivery to stores. SF Cold Chain carries out regular centralized loading arrangements of food goods that have high requirements for temperature, and provides point-to-multipoint regional urban distribution services based on land transportation. It offers whole-process cold chain distribution (no semi-cold chain and loss of temperature control), whole-process cold chain temperature monitoring and specialized distribution with special refrigerated trucks and teams.

冷运零担。为了满足客户货物不足整车运输的需求,根据货物的属性和温、湿度要求,通过集拼或分拨、多温控制、多产品配载等技术和管理手段,为客户提供多批次、小批量的零担物流服务。班车化运作:每天固定时间发车、固定时间到车。时效稳定:固定时间发车,有稳定的整体运输时效。覆盖范围广:覆盖全国大部分一、二线城市。

SF Cold Chain LTL. In order to meet the customers' LTL demand, according to the properties of goods and the requirements on temperature and humidity, it provides customers with multi-batch and

案例 5.3 顺丰冷运一路领先，靠的是什么？

small-lot LTL logistics services through technical and management means such as consolidation or de-consolidation, multi-temperature control and multi-product loading arrangements. It provides shuttle operation, namely trucks run and arrive at a fixed time every day, and keeps a regular schedule with a stable overall transportation time limit. It boasts a wide coverage over most first-and second-tier cities in China.

冷运专车。根据客户线路提供跨区域冷藏车运输，满足客户发运整车货物的运输要求而定制的、符合行业规范的专运产品。它通过点对点、点对多点的方式实现货物完全直达，避免中转环节；同时为客户提供温度全程数据、单价回收、保价等增值服务。

Cold chain specific trucks. According to the customers' routes, it provides trans-regional refrigerated truck transportation to deliver special products that are customized to meet customers' transportation requirements of full-load shipment and conform to industrial norms. It delivers goods in a point-to-point and point-to-multipoint manner, without any transit links. Meanwhile, it provides customers with value-added services such as whole-process temperature data, unit price recovery and value insurance.

①点对点：针对同一寄件客户收件地址只有一个的订单。

Point-to-point: It is designed for orders with only one delivery address from the same customer.

②点对多点：针对同一寄件客户收件地址有多个的订单，按收件地址数生成多个运单，运费仅挂在其中一单上，其他费用按每一单计算。

Point-to-multipoint: It is designed for orders with multiple delivery addresses from the same customer. Multiple shipping orders are generated according to the number of delivery addresses. The freight is paid for only one shipping order, while other expenses are calculated based on the actual quantity of shipping orders.

冷运速配。基于冷仓,对有温度控制要求的食品,通过包装方案满足温控,提供优先配载、优先派送的专属快递服务。

Cold chain fast delivery. Based on the cold storage warehouses, for the food with temperature control requirements, temperature control is achieved through the packaging scheme, and exclusive express delivery services with priorities in loading and delivery are provided.

三、顺丰冷运物流运营模式:"仓配网"和"干线网"

Ⅲ. Logistics operation mode of SF Cold Chain: "warehouse distribution network" and "trunk network"

顺丰冷运整合顺丰控股现有门店、网点及末端配送资源,为生鲜食品行业客户提供专业、定制、高效、全程可视可控的冷链服务。目前顺丰冷运业务已覆盖食品行业生产、电商、经销、零售等多个领域。主要客户有:全家、双汇、大希地等。

SF Cold Chain integrates the existing stores, outlets and terminal distribution resources of SF Holdings to provide professional, customized, efficient and visually controllable cold chain services for customers in the fresh food industry. At present, SF's cold chain business covers numerous fields such as production, e-commerce, distribution and retail of food industry. Its main customers include FamilyMart, Shineway, Hitomorrow and so forth.

案例5.3 顺丰冷运一路领先,靠的是什么?

顺丰冷运始终致力于成为高品质、端到端、全程可视可控的冷链解决方案的领先供应商,围绕着"仓配网"和"干线网"两种模式深耕生鲜食品冷链物流行业。依托已搭建的覆盖全国的自有冷链物流基础设施网络和专业化的服务团队,顺丰冷运已形成国内领先的冷链物流产品体系和服务能力。

SF Cold Chain has always been committed to becoming a leading supplier offering high-quality, end-to-end, controllable and visible cold chain solutions throughout the process, and has been deeply involved in the cold chain logistics industry of fresh food based on two modes of "warehouse distribution network" and "trunk network". Relying on its own cold chain logistics infrastructure network and specialized service team covering the entire country, SF Cold Chain has established a leading cold chain logistics product system and service capacity in China.

仓配网。"仓配网"是顺丰冷运重要的模式之一。整个仓配网以冷库为核心,向供应链前端和后端做服务延伸,即消费地冷仓向前延伸的产地整发服务,向后延伸的对企业和对消费者的城市配送服务。供应链前端的产地整发是通过整车和冷运零担将商品从产地冷库运输至消费地的冷库,中间环节通过冷仓内的存储、分拣包装作业以及冷仓间的商品调拨支撑商品的流通,末端则是通过对企业的冷运到店和对消费者的冷仓速配、冷冻到家实现交付。

Warehouse distribution network. This is one of the important modes of SF Cold Chain. The whole warehouse distribution network, with cold storage warehouses as the core, extends its services to the front end and rear end of the supply chain, namely the cold warehouses at the place of consumption extends forward to transport all goods from the origin, and extends backward to offer urban distribution services to enterprises and consumers. At the front end of the supply chain, all goods are transported from the cold storage warehouses at the origin to those at the place of consumption through the full load mode and cold chain LTL. At the middle link, the circulation of goods is supported by the storage, sorting and packaging operations in the cold storage warehouses and the allocation of goods among the cold warehouses. At the rear end, the goods are delivered through enterprises' cold chain delivery to the store, fast delivery to consumers from the cold storage warehouses and refrigerated delivery to the door.

干线网。顺丰冷运已经开通运营食品干线 143 条，覆盖 117 个城市，727 个区县，共 2 583 条流向，贯通东北、华北、华东、华南、华中、华西等重点地区的核心城市。自有食品冷藏车 256 辆，外包储备冷藏车 1.4 万余辆，皆配备完善的物流信息系统及自主研发的 TCEMS 全程可视化监控平台。

Trunk network. SF Cold Chain has launched 143 food trunk lines, covering 117 cities and 727 districts and counties, with a total of 2,583 routes, running through core cities in key regions such as Northeast China, Northern China, Eastern China, Southern China, Central China and West China. It possesses 256 refrigerated trucks for food and more than 14,000 outsourced backup refrigerated trucks, all of which are equipped with a complete logistics information system and a self-developed TCEMS whole-process visual monitoring platform.

案例 5.3　顺丰冷运一路领先,靠的是什么?

作为冷链行业的领航者,顺丰冷运将依托高质量冷链物流发展要求,以智慧冷链物流及上下游产业为核心驱动,以顺丰集团多元产业资源为动力支撑,打造高标准冷运供应链服务,构建高质量发展新引擎。

As the leader of the cold chain industry, in order to meet the development requirements of high-quality cold chain logistics, SF Cold Chain takes intelligent cold chain logistics and upstream and downstream industries as the major drivers and the diversified industrial resources of SF Group as the support to provide high-standard cold chain services and build a new engine for high-quality development.

四、顺丰运输新冠疫苗全流程:中国速度

Ⅳ. The whole process of SF's transportation of COVID-19 vaccines: Chinese speed

数以亿计的新冠疫苗如何从生产企业运输到各地? 通过什么方式运输? 运输能力能不能达到要求? 安全性有没有保障?

How can hundreds of millions of COVID-19 vaccines be transported from manufacturers to various destinations? By what means? Can the transportation capacity meet the requirements? Is safety guaranteed?

运输疫苗累计超 3 亿剂——以顺丰医药为代表的冷运供应链跑出了"中国速度"。

Transporting more than 300 million of vaccines, the cold transportation supply chain epitomized by SF Pharma shows the "Chinese speed".

289

"不同于一般的生鲜冷链,疫苗冷链门槛较高。新冠疫苗的运输有着更高的要求。"顺丰医药行业解决方案高级经理元航康介绍,疫苗需要全程冷链,储存、运输全过程温度必须恒定在2℃～8℃,并定时监测、记录温度。疫苗冷链要求医药物流公司具备实时追踪位置与温度、高性能包装、多温度控制、多种运输模式等全方位能力。

"Compared with the ordinary fresh cold chain, the vaccine cold chain has a higher threshold. The transportation of COVID-19 vaccines has stricter requirements." Yuan Hangkang, senior manager of SF Pharma Industry Solutions, said that vaccines need the whole-process cold chain, with the temperature during storage and transportation kept constant between 2℃ and 8℃, and monitored and recorded regularly. Vaccine cold chain requires pharmaceutical logistics companies to have all-round capabilities such as real-time tracking of location and temperature, high-performance packaging, multi-temperature control and multiple transportation modes.

"2020年6月,顺丰医药初步接触新冠疫苗运输项目;2021年6月,累计保障新冠疫苗运输突破1亿剂;目前,运输总量超3亿剂。任何一剂疫苗、一个环节、一个时间段均未发生冷链'断链'的情况。"一年多时间里,元航康见证了这项重大项目从无到有、从摸索期到成熟期的成长发展。

"In June 2020, SF Pharma set the foot in the COVID-19 vaccine transportation projects for the first time. By June 2021, the cumulative volume of COVID-19 vaccines transported had exceeded 100 million doses. So far, the total transportation volume has exceeded 300 million doses. There is no 'broken' cold chain for any dose of vac-

案例 5.3 顺丰冷运一路领先，靠的是什么？

cine, link or time period. " For more than a year, Yuan Hangkang had seen the growth and development of this major project from nothing, and from the trial to maturity.

物联网、区块链等科技全面赋能疫苗运输，顺丰医药已形成完整的疫苗全程追溯闭环体系，具备所有疫苗全品种、所有相关冷链设施全覆盖、所有流通环节全过程、24 小时全天候"四全"优势。

The Internet of Things, blockchain and other technologies have fully empowered vaccine transportation. SF Pharma has developed a complete closed-loop system with whole-process traceability for all kinds of vaccines, covering all related cold chain facilities and all circulation links, and available 24/7.

顺丰医药针对疫苗类产品的运输保障，常规提供 4 种不同模式的供应链服务解决方案。一是"一站式"干线运输，从疫苗生产企业直接配送至全国县市疾控机构和接种单位，提供冷运专车、公航联运、水域滚装运输等多种运力解决方案。二是城市配送，从各城市的疾控机构配送至末端接种单位，提供城市配送及包裹类的疫苗运输服务。三是仓配服务，自建医药仓助力分担疾控机构储存压力，提供仓配一体的疫苗服务一体化解决方案。四是原液运输，保障生产药厂之间的原液跨区域运输。

SF Pharma provides four different modes of supply chain service solutions for the transportation of vaccine products. The first is "one-stop" trunk transportation. It refers to direct distribution from vaccine producers to disease control institutions and vaccination units in counties and cities across the country, providing a variety of transport capacity solutions such as cold chain specific vehicles, combined transport by land and air, and rolling transport by water. The second is urban distribution from disease control institutions in cities to terminal vaccination units, providing urban distribution and parcel vaccine transportation services. The third is warehouse allocation service. It adopts self-built medical warehouses to help share the storage pressure of disease control institutions and provides an integrated solution for vaccine services. The fourth is the trans-regional transportation of stock solutions among pharmaceutical factories.

无论是哪种模式,温度全程控制、数据完整可追溯、时效准时稳定都是疫苗运输的核心。而在这个全程可视不断链的背后,是一系列软硬件科技系统或设施的高效赋能。顺丰科技提供了一系列科技能力为药品安全保驾护航,结合顺丰医药网、地网、信息网,构建了端到端的一体化供应链管理系统,覆盖订单、运输、仓储、结算等供应链业务全环节,实现全链路、全场景数字化管理。针对疫苗运输业务,顺丰科技研发的百川供应链底盘系统整合串联起订单周期、温湿度、路由信息等数据,提供全程可视化的预警监控,以保障疫苗运输的质量与安全。

No matter which mode is adopted, the whole-process temperature control, complete and traceable data, and strict and stable schedule are the key factors of vaccine transportation. This continuous visual chain is efficiently empowered by a series of software and hardware systems or facilities. SF Technology has provided a series of scientific and technological capabilities to protect the safety of medicine. Combined with SF Pharma's network, land transportation network and information network, an end-to-end integrated supply chain man-

案例 5.3 顺丰冷运一路领先,靠的是什么？

agement system has been built, covering all aspects of supply chain business such as ordering, transportation, warehousing and settlement, and realizing all-link and all-scenario digital management. The Baichuan supply chain system developed by SF Technology for the vaccine transportation business integrates data such as order cycle, temperature and humidity, routing information and so forth, and provides visual early warning monitoring throughout the process, so as to ensure the quality and safety of vaccine transportation.

在保障疫苗运输安全的全程可追溯链条中,数据安全无疑也成为最重要的一环。据了解,为保障数据的可信与安全,顺丰科技提供私有云、公有云、边缘云、专有云等多种存储方式,可实现多地存储和异地存储。同时,引入区块链技术,确保用户的单一数字身份以安全和可信的方式存储,并可以实时同步最新信息,确保各节点的数据无篡改及可追溯。

In the whole-process traceability chain for ensuring the safety of vaccine transportation, data security is undoubtedly the most important link. It is understood that in order to ensure the credibility and security of data, SF Technology provides various storage methods such as private cloud, public cloud, edge cloud and proprietary cloud, which can realize multi-site storage and off-site storage. Meanwhile, the application of blockchain technology ensures that the digital identity of each user is stored in a safe and credible manner, and the latest information can be synchronized in real time to guarantee that the data of each node is tamper-free and traceable.

"相比普通疫苗,新冠疫苗配送有五大特殊之处:保密措施升级、资格审查加码、质量要求提升、安全意识更高、应急预案全面。"在元航康看来,新冠疫苗运输虽然高投入短回报,但确实是一项值得骄傲、值得继续深耕和为之付出的事业。未来,医疗改革不断深入,药品流通线上化发展,拥有多货主、多种解决方案、定制化药品供应链处理能力的专业第三方企业将获得更多发展机遇。随着全球疫情多点散发,疫苗运输的市场需求和发展空间仍然十分广阔。

"Compared with ordinary vaccines, COVID-19 vaccine distribution has five features: upgraded confidentiality measures, stricter qualification examination, improved quality requirements, stronger safety awareness and comprehensive emergency plan." For Yuan Hangkang, despite its high investment and low return, transportation of COVID-19 vaccines is indeed a cause worthy of pride, continuous cultivation and dedication. In the future, with the deepening of medical reform and the online development of pharmaceutical circulation, specialized third-party enterprises with multi-consignors, multiple solutions and customized pharmaceutical supply chain capacity will gain more development opportunities. As the epidemic outbreaks from time to time in different regions, the vaccine transportation has huge market demand and broad development space.

"真的很自豪!顺丰医药用运送新冠疫苗的方式丈量祖国东西南北的土地,用高效和用心的服务参与十几亿的国民项目。我们不但是在运送疫苗,更是在传递健康。"元航康坦言,2016年山东疫苗事件发生后,顺丰便下定决心要做深做强医药疫苗业务,做让老百姓放心、传递更多健康的良心医药供应链。

"I feel really proud! SF Pharma has travelled across our mother-

案例 5.3 顺丰冷运一路领先，靠的是什么？

land by transporting COVID-19 vaccines, and engaged in a project worth billions for all Chinese people with efficient and dedicated services. We are not only transporting vaccines, but also delivering health." Yuan Hangkang said frankly that after the vaccine scandal in Shandong province in 2016, SF was determined to deepen and strengthen its medical vaccine business, and build a trustable pharmaceutical supply chain that reassures the people for better health.

疫苗运送途中，司机们遇到过大雾、高寒缺氧，也遭受了塌方、泥石流的冲击，然而困难重重却始终不放弃，不辱使命。"得知成功入选，骄傲啊！这么重要的疫苗，能由我一路护送，真的很自豪，同时深感责任重大。"让赵师傅感到骄傲的，是去西藏运输疫苗的任务，8次奔赴西藏，他都圆满地完成了任务。"高原上气候变化快，我们把一年四季的衣服都背上了车，事实证明也派上了大用场。进藏前气温回升，在北京时穿短袖，一旦到了高海拔地区，立马就得换上大棉袄。"10天后，人黑了，瘦了一大圈，嘴唇上有一圈死皮。赵师傅的主管在朋友圈感叹道："这些逆行者，不是没有家人、没有牵挂，但没有他们的负重前行，哪来我们的春暖花开。最美的人，也请保护好自己，愿师傅们平安凯旋！"在疫苗运送中，还有许多像赵师傅一样可爱可敬的人在路上奔波着，"召之即来，来之能战，战则必胜，永不言败"是对他们最真实的写照。

On the way of vaccine delivery, drivers encountered fog, chillness and lack of oxygen, and also suffered the impacts of landslides and debris flow. However, they never gave up and successfully accomplished their mission. "I am proud to learn that I was chosen! I am really proud that such an important task of vaccine transportation will be undertaken by me all the way, and I also feel a heavy burden of responsibility." What makes Mr. Zhao proud is the task of transporting vaccines to Tibet. He has been to Tibet eight times and successfully completed his task each time. "The weather on the Tibetan plateau is highly changeable, so we carry clothes of four seasons aboard, which has been proven to be of great use. Before entering Tibet, the temperature rose. I wore short-sleeve shirts in Beijing and had to immediately dress myself in a big cotton-padded jacket when arriving at the high altitude." Ten days later, they became tanned, lost a lot of weight and had dead skin surrounding their lips. Zhao's supervisor sighed in his WeChat Moments, "These heroes do have families to concern, but they still chose to forge ahead and finally brought us a spring with blooming flowers. You are the most beautiful people, so please protect yourself, and may you return home safely in triumph!" During the vaccine delivery, there are numerous lovely and respectable people like Zhao running around. "Come at the call and make a difference, fight to win and never give up" is the most realistic portrayal for them.

疫苗研制、疫苗传递、疫苗接种,一起汇聚最有力量的"中国速度"。

Vaccine development, vaccine delivery and vaccination together brought us the most powerful "Chinese speed".

五、顺丰冷运,持续改进
V. SF Cold Chain under continuous improvement

2022 年上半年,顺丰冷运及医药业务实现不含税营业收入 40.7

案例 5.3　顺丰冷运一路领先,靠的是什么?

亿元,同比增长 9.3%。在政策端,国家部委围绕农产品冷链、国家骨干冷链物流基地、城乡冷链建设、疫情消杀查验等出台多项政策规划,冷链标准提高、建设发展加速;在市场端,多元化生鲜电商快速发展,线上线下全渠道拓展趋势加强。行业趋势更有利于网络型、高质量、实力强的冷链服务商,顺丰冷运凭借全国领先的网络一体化综合冷链物流能力,有望在竞争中捕捉更多市场机会。

In the first half of 2022, SF's cold chain and pharmaceutical business achieved a taxable revenue of 4.07 billion yuan, with a year-on-year increase of 9.3%. On the policy side, the national ministries and commissions have introduced a number of policies for the cold chain of agricultural products, the national backbone cold chain logistics bases, the construction of urban and rural cold chains, and the epidemic disinfection and inspection, which has improved the cold chain standards and accelerated the construction and development. On the market side, diversified fresh food e-commerce has gone through rapid development, and the trend of omni-channel development integrating both online and offline business has been strengthened. The industry development trend is more beneficial to network-based and high-quality cold chain service providers with competitive edge. SF Cold Chain is expected to capture more market opportunities in the competition with its leading network integration and comprehensive cold chain logistics capabilities in China.

点评

Comments

"十四五"规划、中央一号文（2020年《中共中央国务院关于抓好"三农"领域重点工作确保如期实现全面小康的意见》）等重要文件对冷链物流发展做出了明确指示，冷链物流在国内国际双循环当中的地位越来越重要，成为改善和解决国计民生痛点问题的重要保障手段，许多国家和地方冷链新政策落地在即，冷链产业环境将迎来根本性利好。在"双循环"新发展格局背景下，随着供给侧结构性改革的持续深入推进，"需求牵引供给、供给创造需求"的内生动力将更加强劲，为冷链行业新秩序的确立提供丰沃的土壤和广阔的空间。借助冷链市场需求增加、冷链行业监管规范、冷链产业资源投入力度持续增强等利好，冷链领域全产业链将加快转型升级，快速向数字化、智能化和体系化等纵深方向发展，冷链产业持续向好。

Important documents, such as the "14th Five-Year Plan" and China No. 1 Central Document of 2020 (Opinions of the Central Committee of Communist Party and the State Council of China on Doing a Good Job in the Key Areas of Agriculture, Rural Areas, and Farmers to Ensure the Building of a Moderately Prosperous Society in All Respects), have given clear instructions on the development of cold chain logistics. Cold chain logistics which is playing an increasingly important role in the dual circulation at home and abroad has become an important guarantee for improving and solving the pain spots of the national economy and people's livelihood. As a number of new cold

案例 5.3 顺丰冷运一路领先，靠的是什么？

chain policies at the national and local levels will be introduced soon, the development environment of the cold chain industry will usher in fundamental benefits. Under the "dual circulation" development pattern, with the continuous deepening of supply-side structural reform, the endogenous power of "demand pulls supply and supply creates demand" will become even stronger, providing fertile soil and broad space for establishing a new order in the cold chain industry. Driven by the growth in cold chain market demand, the strict regulation on cold chain industry, and the continuous increase of resources investment in the cold chain industry, the whole industrial chain of the cold chain logistics segment will pick up speed in transformation and upgrade, and become more digital, intelligent and systematic for sustained improvement.

"十四五"规划开局之年，对中国冷链物流企业来说利好不断。新一轮政策红利释放的同时，对冷链物流也提出了更高的要求。无论是国际和国内企业、传统企业还是新入局者，都面临着全新的机遇与挑战。保证产品质量的同时，降低成本和碳排放，为客户提供专业、定制、高效、全程可视化可控的冷链物流服务是冷链物流企业艰巨的任务。未来冷链物流行业中的各类参与者仍将沿着不同的路径前进，各细分领域的商业模式也将在互联网经济、产业发展、技术革新之下持续演进。顺丰冷运作为中国冷链物流百强榜首，应持续以物流的价值推动冷链行业标准的建立与升级，致力于"十四五"高质量冷链物流建设与发展，共享双循环格局新机遇，共谱冷链华章新秩序！

The first year of the "14th Five-Year Plan" period is good for cold chain logistics enterprises in China. The new round of favorable policies put forward higher requirements for cold chain logistics. Both international and domestic enterprises, and veterans and newcomers in the industry are facing new opportunities and challenges. It is an arduous task for cold chain logistics enterprises to reduce costs and carbon emissions while ensuring product quality and providing customers with specialized, customized, efficient, visual and controllable cold chain logistics services throughout the process. In the future, all kinds of players in the cold chain logistics industry will keep moving forward along different paths, and the business models of various segments will continue to evolve under the Internet economy, industrial development and technological innovation. As the No. 1 among the top 100 cold chain logistics enterprises in China, SF Cold Chain should continue to promote the establishment and upgrade of cold chain industry standards by adhering to the value of logistics, and devote itself to the construction and development of high-quality cold chain logistics during the "14th Five-Year Plan" period to share new opportunities under the "dual circulation" development pattern and jointly build a new order for a prosperous cold chain industry!

讨论题
Discussions

(1)讨论冷链物流的特点。
Discuss the characteristics of cold chain logistics.
(2)讨论冷链物流所需的各种物流信息技术。

案例 5.3　顺丰冷运一路领先,靠的是什么?

Discuss various kinds of logistics information technologies necessary for cold chain logistics.

(3)讨论冷链物流碳减排的方法。

Discuss the methods for reducing carbon emissions in cold chain logistics.

资料来源

李天骄.干货!2021 年中国农产品冷链物流行业龙头企业分析——顺丰冷运:我国供应链型农产品冷链物流龙头企业[EB/OL].[2022-12-10]. https://www.qianzhan.com/analyst/detail/220/210917-8898da80.html.

顺丰冷运 一路领鲜[EB/OL].[2022-12-10]. https://p.sf-express.com/#/.

一路领"鲜",靠的是什么[EB/OL].[2022-12-10]. 顺丰冷运 App.

徐翔.顺丰冷链:行业的标杆 未来的希望[J].中国储运,2022(02):49.

苗琳.突破 3 亿剂!顺丰运输新冠疫苗全流程首次曝光![EB/OL].[2022-12-11]. https://m.thepaper.cn/baijiahao_14278923.

赵思宇.干货!2022 年中国医药物流行业龙头企业分析——顺丰控股:加快智慧物流建设[EB/OL].[2022-12-11]. https://www.qianzhan.com/analyst/detail/220/211201-9dc8eadc.html.

顺丰控股:2022 年半年度报告[R/OL].[2022-12-11]. http://news.10jqka.com.cn/20220831/c38134773.shtml.

References

Li Tianjiao. Real stuff! Analysis of leading enterprises in cold chain logistics industry for agricultural products in China in 2021—SF Cold Chain: A leading enterprise in cold chain logistics for agricultural products[EB/OL].[2022-12-10]. https://www.qianzhan.com/analyst/detail/220/210917-8898da80.html.

SF Cold Chain leads all the way[EB/OL].[2022-12-10]. https://p.sf-express.com/#/.

What has SF Cold Chain Relied on to Lead All the Way? [EB/OL]. [2022-12-10]. App of SF Cold Chain.

Xu Xiang. SF Cold Chain: Industry benchmark and hope for the future[J]. China Storage & Transport, 2022(02):49.

Miao Lin. Transporting more than 300 million of vaccines! The whole process of SF Express's transportation of the COVID-19 vaccine is exposed for the first time! [EB/OL]. [2022-12-11]. https://m.thepaper.cn/baijiahao_14278923.

Zhao Siyu. Real Stuff! Analysis of leading enterprises in China's pharmaceutical logistics industry in 2022-SF Holdings: Accelerating the construction of intelligent logistics [EB/OL]. [2022-12-11]. https://www.qianzhan.com/analyst/detail/220/211201-9dc8eadc.html.

SF Holdings: Semi-annual Report 2022[R/OL]. [2022-12-11]. http://news.10jqka.com.cn/20220831/c38134773.shtml.

第六篇　财务管理
PART Ⅵ　FINANCE MANAGEMENT

案例 6.1　瑞幸咖啡财务问题分析
Case 6.1　Analysis of Financial Fraud of Luckin Coffee

教学目标
Teaching Objectives

一度风靡中国的瑞幸咖啡于 2020 年 4 月 2 日发布公告自曝财务造假,承认虚假交易 22 亿元人民币,引发社会各界的广泛关注和讨论。财务造假是一种严重破坏资本市场秩序,侵害投资者利益的行为,通常由公司高层管理者通过各式各样的舞弊行为蒙骗投资者和公众,以达到自身目的。本节通过案例分析,帮助学生理解健全内部控制体系对避免类似财务造假案例的发生具有重要意义,以及启发学生对于诚信与法治在公司财务信息披露过程中的作用进行思考。

On April 2, 2020, Luckin Coffee, once popular in China, made an announcement to expose its financial fraud and admitted false transactions amounted to 2.2 billion yuan, which aroused widespread concern and discussion from all walks of life. Financial fraud is a misconduct that seriously disrupts the order of the capital market and infringes on the interests of investors. In a financial fraud, senior managers of companies usually deceive investors and the public through various fraudulent acts to achieve their goals. Through case analysis, this section helps students understand and improve the internal control system, which is of great significance to avoid similar cases of financial fraud. Besides, it can also inspire students to think about the role of integrity and legal system in the process of corporate financial information disclosure.

案例涉及财务管理中内部控制制度、外部审计等相关知识点。

The case involves the internal control system, external audit and other related concepts in Financial Management.

案例内容

Contents

瑞幸咖啡2017年成立，于2019年5月在美国纳斯达克上市，创造了中国公司在美国上市的最短时间记录及世界最快首次公开募股记录。截至2019年年底，瑞幸直营门店数达到4 507家，交易用户数突破4 000万，App持续霸屏App Store美食佳饮排行榜首超过200天，门店与用户拓展速度远高于其他同类品牌，是中国最大的连锁咖啡品牌，在中国市场的门店数超过了星巴克。2020年1月，瑞幸完成增发并发行可转债，融资规模超过11亿美元，迎来市值巅峰，总市值高达126亿美元。瑞幸快速扩张的同时，也产生了一系列问题，因连

案例 6.1 瑞幸咖啡财务问题分析

年亏损、对融资的需求等原因,瑞幸粉饰公开披露的财务数据,进行财务造假。财务造假事件被揭露后,瑞幸在美股退市,引发了投资者对上市公司内部控制与治理的广泛关注与讨论。

Luckin Coffee was established in 2017 and listed on NASDAQ in the US in May 2019, setting a record for the quickest listing of a Chinese company in the US and the fastest initial public offering in the world. By the end of 2019, Luckin Coffee had owned 4,507 directly-operated stores, with more than 40 million consumers. It kept the first place on the APP Store food and drink list for more than 200 days, and its expansion in opening stores and gaining consumers was much faster than that of other similar brands. It was the largest chain coffee brand in China, with the number of stores in the Chinese market exceeding that of Starbucks. In January 2020, Luckin Coffee completed the issuance of additional shares and convertible bonds, with a financing scale over 1.1 billion US dollars. After that, it ushered in the peak of its market value totaling 12.6 billion US dollars. Along with its rapid expansion, Luckin Coffee also found itself stuck in a series of problems. Due to years of losses, the demand for financing and other reasons, Luckin Coffee committed financial fraud by whitewashing its publicly disclosed financial data. After the financial fraud was exposed, Luckin Coffee withdrew from the US stock market, which aroused extensive concern and discussion among investors on the internal control and governance of listed companies.

一、瑞幸咖啡财务造假事件
Ⅰ. Financial fraud of Luckin Coffee

2020年1月31日,美国知名做空机构浑水声称,收到了一份厚达89页的匿名做空报告,直指瑞幸数据造假。当时的报告称,调查动用了92名全职和1 418名兼职人员在现场进行实时监控,记录了981个经营日的客流量,覆盖了620家店铺100%的营业时间,总时长为11 260小时,还收集了25 843张小票。报告称,瑞幸2019年第三和第四季度每店每日商品数量分别夸大了至少69%和88%。其中第四季度受监控门店的日销量仅为263件商品,但是瑞幸给出的销售预计为483~506件。与此同时,调查者还发现瑞幸的门店大量使用"跳单"——取餐码数字不再按照序号递增,而是随机数字递增。根据在151家随机选取门店的尽调记录,同一家商店在同一天的在线订单数量膨胀范围从34个到232个,平均每天多106个订单。报告认为,这是瑞幸的管理层为了防止投资者追踪订单故意为之。瑞幸还将每件商品的净售价至少提高了12.3%,在实际情况中,实体店面的损失高达24.7%~28%。

On January 31, 2020, Muddy Waters Research, a well-known short-selling institution in the US, claimed that it had received an 89-page anonymous short-selling report, pointing to the data fraud of Luckin Coffee. According to the report, 92 full-time and 1,418 part-time employees were hired for the survey to conduct real-time monitoring on the spot, and recorded the passenger flow of 981 business days, covering 100% of the business hours of 620 outlets, with a total duration of 11,260 hours and 25,843 receipts collected. The report said that in Q3 and Q4 of 2019,

案例 6.1 瑞幸咖啡财务问题分析

Luckin Coffee exaggerated the quantity of items sold per outlet per day by at least 69% and 88% respectively. In Q4, the monitored outlets only sold 263 items per day, which was far less than the sales forecast given by Luckin Coffee of 483～506 items. Meanwhile, the investigators also found that Luckin Coffee's outlets generated a lot of "discontinuous orders", where the pick-up number was no longer increased by serial number, but by random number. According to the records of 151 randomly selected outlets, the number of online orders of an outlet on the same day increased from 34 to 232, with an average of 106 fake orders per day. According to the report, this was done deliberately by the executives of Luckin Coffee to prevent investors from tracking orders. Luckin Coffee also increased the net selling price of each item by at least 12.3%. In fact, the loss rates of outlets were up to 24.7%～28%.

2020年2月3日,瑞幸否认所有指控,并回应称报告毫无依据,论证方式存在缺陷,属于恶意指控。2020年4月2日晚间,瑞幸审计机构安永表示,在对公司2019年年度财务报告进行审计工作的过程中,发现公司部分管理人员在2019年第二季度至第四季度通过虚假交易虚增了公司相关期间的收入、成本及费用。2020年4月5日下午,瑞幸发布道歉声明表示,涉事高管及员工已被停职调查,瑞幸咖啡董事会已委托独立董事组成的特别委员会及委任的第三方独立机构,进行全面彻底调查,公司会第一时间向公众披露调查结果,并采取一切必要的补救措施,不回避此事带来的一切问题。最终2020年6月29日,瑞幸咖啡宣布在美股退市。

On February 3, 2020, Luckin Coffee denied all the allegations and called them malicious accusation. They said that the report was groundless and the way of argumentation was flawed. On the evening of April 2,2020, Ernst & Young, the audit agency of Luckin Coffee, said that during the audit of Luckin Coffee's annual financial report in 2019, it found some executives inflated the company's income, costs and expenses during the relevant period through false transactions from Q2 to Q4 of 2019. On the afternoon of April 5,2020, Luckin Coffee issued an apology statement saying that the executives and employees involved had been suspended for investigation. It also stated that its Board of Directors had entrusted a special committee composed of independent directors and an appointed third-party independent agency to conduct a comprehensive and thorough investigation, and that the company would disclose the investigation results to the public as soon as possible, and take all necessary remedial measures to avoid any problems brought about by the fraud. Finally, on June 29,2020, Luckin Coffee announced its delisting from the US stock market.

二、瑞幸咖啡财务造假事件动因

Ⅱ. Causes of financial fraud of Luckin Coffee

(一)连年亏损

(1) Suffer losses for years

首先,在中国市场,茶文化源远流长,相较于茶,咖啡占市场份额的比重较低,消费市场规模较小,大众对茶依赖程度相对更高,因此从传统文化方面,折射出咖啡消费内动力不足、缺乏用户粘性等问题。根据相关调查,全球咖啡市场总额约12万亿元,中国咖啡市场占比仅

案例6.1 瑞幸咖啡财务问题分析

为全球市场总额的不足6%,人均年咖啡消费中国仅为5～6杯,为世界人均年咖啡消费的2%～2.5%。其次,极具影响力的咖啡品牌星巴克在中国市场的地位不容小觑,除咖啡品质高之外,星巴克的营销优势、门店环境因素等都给同业品牌带来了巨大的压力,且其在中国市场发展时间较长,瑞幸与其竞争抢占市场具有一定难度。作为初创公司,瑞幸在商业模式等诸多方面都存在不足。再次,瑞幸采取的销售策略具有局限性。利用薄利多销甚至亏本销售的手段,以免费、高折扣等营销方式吸引消费者,虽然取得了一定收益,获得了更多注册用户,但这种方法仅短期有效,这部分消费者往往受价格因素影响较大,当价格回归初始水平或免单活动次数用完,就会失去消费粘性,进而流失,不再消费咖啡,无法形成品牌效应,缺失长期效益。但是瑞幸如果停止采用此类营销手段,便无法维持销量,导致其财务数据不符合股东预期,增大财务风险,因此陷入两难的境地。

First of all, in the Chinese market, tea culture has a long history and occupies a larger share and consumer base than coffee due to people's greater dependency on tea. Therefore, under the influence of the traditional culture, there are problems like insufficient motivation and lack of consumer stickiness in coffee consumption. According to relevant surveys, the size of global coffee market is about 12 trillion yuan, while China's coffee market only accounts for less than 0.6% of the global total. The average annual coffee consumption in China is only five to six cups, which is about 2%～2.5% of the global average. Second, Starbucks, an influential coffee brand, plays an important role in the Chinese market. In addition to its high quality of coffee, Starbucks' advantages in marketing and dining environment, etc. have brought huge pressure on its peers. Moreover, as Starbucks has been operating in China for a long time, it is difficult for Luckin Coffee to compete and grab its market share. As a start-up, Luckin Coffee has shortcomings in many aspects such as business model. Third, the sales strategy adopted by Luckin Coffee has limitations. By resorting to small profits but quick turnover or even selling at a loss to attract consumers with free offers and large discounts, it did make some profits and obtain more registered customers, but this approach is only effective in the short term, as these customers are often greatly influenced by the price. When the price returns to normal or free offers are used up, the consumers will lose their stickiness and no longer consume coffee, thus Luckin Coffee fails to develop a brand effect and lacks long-term benefits. However, if Luckin Coffee stops utilizing these marketing tools, it will not be able to maintain its sales volume and its financial data will not meet the expectations of shareholders, which leads to increased financial risks and eventually a dilemma.

根据公开的财务报表数据，瑞幸成立后一直未能取得盈利。通过分析其现金流量表，可以得出其在经营活动、投资活动与融资活动方面具有不同表现，其经营活动、投资活动现金流量在连续季度财务报表中基本为负，但是融资活动现金流量基本为正。这进一步印证了瑞幸未能取得业务增长与盈利预期，无法满足投资者期望，未实现可持续性发展，而快速扩张门店主要依靠对外大量融资，于是最终导致财务造假。

According to the data of disclosed financial statements, Luckin Coffee has not been able to make profits since its founding. By analyzing its cash flow statement, it can be concluded that Luckin Coffee's performance varies in business, investment and financing activities. The cash flow of business and investment activities is basically negative in the financial statements for consecutive quarters, though that of financing activities is basically positive. This further proves that Luckin Coffee failed to reach expectations on business growth and profitability to meet investors' expectations and achieve sustainable development. The rapid expansion of its stores mainly relied on a large amount of external financing, which eventually led to the financial fraud.

(二)对融资的需求

(2) Demand for financing

2018年第一季度,瑞幸在微信朋友圈广告的投放金额超过了800万元,广告曝光次数超过1亿次,广告总曝光人数超过4 500万。而根据央视市场研究公司(CTR)2018年前三季度广告市场回顾报告,瑞幸在2018年前三季度主要选择了电视、电梯电视、电梯海报和影院视频作为宣传渠道。瑞幸在电梯电视媒体的广告花费占其投放总体的73%。"买2赠1"及"买5赠5"的优惠仍是瑞幸咖啡吸引新客流的主要方式。大量广告投放、发放优惠券及补贴的营销手段都需要足够的现金流支撑。在股票市场中,主营业务收入规模越大,公司估值就会越高。因此,为了提升公司估值,方便后续融资进程,瑞幸咖啡铤而走险,选择了财务数据造假的不归之路。为了维持更大的融资需求,包括股权融资、债权融资或者股票质押融资等,瑞幸粉饰财务报表,捏造虚假的门店营业收入同时隐藏巨额亏损,人为制造信息不对称,以保证能够吸引更多的股票投资者。

In Q1 of 2018, by spending more than 8 million yuan advertising in WeChat Moments, Luckin Coffee obtained over 100 million view counts and 45 million viewers in total. According to the advertising market review report of CVSC-TNS RESEARCH (CTR) for the first three quarters of 2018, Luckin Coffee mainly chose TV, elevator TV, elevator poster and cinema video as its publicity channels. Its advertising expenses in elevator TV media accounted for 73% of its total. "Buy two, get one free" and "buy five, get five free" were still the major promotion campaigns adopted by Luckin Coffee to attract new consumers. A large number of commercials, coupons and subsidies need to be supported by sufficient cash flow. In the stock market, the larger the income from the main business, the higher its valuation will be. Therefore, in order to improve its valuation and push forward the follow-up financing processes, Luckin Coffee took risks and chose the unreturnable path of falsifying financial data. In order to maintain greater financing demand from equity financing, debt financing or stock pledge financing, etc., Luckin Coffee whitewashed financial statements, fabricated false operating income and hid huge losses, creating information asymmetry deliberately to attract more stock investors.

（三）内部治理机制不够完善

(3) Inadequate internal governance mechanism

瑞幸上市之后，原股份持有者尽可能地高价减持，股价越高，利益相关者才能够尽可能高价交易套现。在所有粉饰报表的财务舞弊动机中，维持股价是最直观的原因。给投资者们编织华美的泡沫，维持

案例 6.1　瑞幸咖啡财务问题分析

令人满意的股价水平,使企业持股的高管、员工提前减持获取巨额利益。同时,瑞幸股权结构高度集中,在瑞幸内部公司治理结构中股东与管理层存在着密切关联。而且瑞幸运用互联网技术通过修改订单编码顺序允许跳号情况存在,这对只专注于纸质传统审计人员来说无疑是时代带来的新挑战,从而为销售部门通过"互联网+"技术利用审计盲区舞弊创造了契机,内部审计监管部门的督查审核难度大大提升,因此内部监管的缺失也是此次事件的重要因素。

After going public, the original shareholders of Luckin Coffee reduced their shares at prices as high as possible, as the higher the share price is, the more likely the stakeholders could trade and cash out. Among all the motives of financial fraud in whitewashing statements, maintaining the stock price is the most obvious reason. By blowing a gorgeous bubble for investors, they manage to maintain a satisfactory stock price, so that the executives and employees of enterprises can reduce their holdings in advance and gain huge benefits. Meanwhile, the ownership structure of Luckin Coffee is highly concentrated, and shareholders and executives are closely correlated in its internal corporate governance structure. Moreover, Luckin Coffee generated discontinuous orders by modifying the order coding sequence with Internet technologies, which was undoubtedly a new challenge for the traditional auditors only focusing on paper documents, thus creating an opportunity for the sales department to utilize the "Internet+" technology to engage in fraud in the blind spots of auditing. This greatly increases the difficulty of supervision and examination by the internal audit and supervision department, so inadequate internal supervision is also a significant factor to be considered in this case.

三、经历造假事件风波后的瑞幸咖啡
Ⅲ. Luckin Coffee after the financial fraud

2020年4月3日,中国证监会高度关注瑞幸咖啡财务造假事件,对该公司财务造假行为表示强烈的谴责。不管在何地上市,上市公司都应当严格遵守相关市场的法律和规则,真实准确完整地履行信息披露义务。中国证监会声明将按照国际证券监管合作的有关安排,依法对相关情况进行核查,坚决打击证券欺诈行为,切实保护投资者权益。2020年6月27日,瑞幸发布声明称,公司将于6月29日在纳斯达克停牌,并进行退市备案。同时,瑞幸咖啡中国4 000多家门店将正常运营。2020年7月31日,财政部表示,已经完成对瑞幸咖啡公司境内运营主体会计信息质量检查。在检查中发现,自2019年4月起至2019年年末,瑞幸咖啡公司通过虚构商品券业务增加交易额22.46亿元,虚增收入21.19亿元(占对外披露收入51.5亿元的41.16%),虚增成本费用12.11亿元,虚增利润9.08亿元。2020年9月18日,市场监管总局及上海、北京市场监管部门,对瑞幸咖啡(中国)有限公司、瑞幸咖啡(北京)有限公司等公司做出行政处罚决定。

On April 3, 2020, China Securities Regulatory Commission paid close attention to Luckin Coffee's financial fraud and strongly condemned its misconduct. No matter where they are listed, listed companies should strictly abide by the laws and rules of relevant markets and fulfill their information disclosure obligations truthfully, accurately and completely. China Securities Regulatory Commission stated that it would look into the case in accordance with the relevant ar-

案例 6.1 瑞幸咖啡财务问题分析

rangements of international cooperation on securities regulation, resolutely crack down on securities fraud and effectively protect the rights and interests of investors. On June 27, 2020, Luckin Coffee issued a statement saying that it would suspend trading on NASDAQ on June 29 and file for delisting. Meanwhile, more than 4,000 stores of Luckin Coffee in China would operate as usual. On July 31, 2020, the Ministry of Finance indicated that it had completed the quality inspection on accounting information of operating entities of Luckin Coffee in China. During the inspection, it found that from April 2019 to the end of 2019, Luckin Coffee increased its transaction volume by 2.246 billion yuan through made-up merchandise coupon business, and inflated its income by 2.119 billion yuan (accounting for 41.16% of its publicly disclosed income of 5.15 billion yuan), its cost by 1.211 billion yuan and its profit by 908 million yuan. On September 18, 2020, the State Administration for Market Regulation and the market regulators in Shanghai and Beijing imposed administrative penalties on Luckin Coffee (China) Co. , Ltd. and Luckin Coffee (Beijing) Co. , Ltd.

2021年9月，瑞幸咖啡发布公告，内容涵盖与美国集体诉讼的原告代表签署了1.875亿美元的和解意向书，金额则普遍被认为小于预期。对于瑞幸咖啡而言，这无疑再次释放了"减负"的信号。上述三则公告发布后，资本市场报以正向回应，截至2021年9月底，瑞幸咖啡股价上涨了近10倍。

In September, 2021, Luckin Coffee announced that it had signed a letter of intent for settlement of 187.5 million US dollars with the plaintiff's representative of the class action lawsuit in the US, and the amount was generally considered to be less than expected. For Luckin Coffee, this undoubtedly released a signal of "reducing the burden" again. After the above three announcements were issued, the capital market responded positively. By the end of September 2021, Luckin Coffee's share price had risen nearly tenfold.

图片来源：https://www.socialmarketings.com/articldetails/20914,2022-12-08。
Source: https://www.socialmarketings.com/articldetails/20914,2022-12-08.

图 6-1 冬奥会自由式滑雪世界冠军谷爱凌为瑞幸咖啡代言

Figure 6-1 Winter Olympics Freestyle Skiing World Champion Eileen Gu endorses Luckin Coffee

2022年，瑞幸咖啡在冬奥会之际与谷爱凌合作，对其本人进行了深度了解，自律、自控、自信、高效……这些谷爱凌身上具备也是年轻人渴望培养和锻炼自己达成的优秀品质，又恰好与瑞幸的品牌宣言"专业、年轻、健康、时尚"不谋而合，"谷爱凌×瑞幸"（Luckin，中文意

案例 6.1 瑞幸咖啡财务问题分析

为"幸运")强强联名的效益远高于单纯的名人代言(如图 6-1 所示)。瑞幸咖啡将年轻人作为自己的主要消费群体,把握当下年轻人的消费点,在提升咖啡口感和品质的同时,洞见年轻人的精神需求,寻找合适的品牌代言人,将人物的精神气质与自身的品牌气质融为一体,加上冬季奥运赛事的热度助力,实现了销量提升和品牌推广的双赢。

In 2022, Luckin Coffee cooperated with Eileen Gu on the occasion of the Winter Olympics after getting a deep understanding of Gu, such as her self-discipline, self-control, self-confidence and efficiency… These excellent qualities that are just what the young people eagerly pursue through self-cultivation and exercise are consistent with Luckin Coffee's brand manifesto of "Professionalism, Youth, Wellness and Fashion". The co-branding benefits of "Eileen Gu × Luckin" (Luckin means "lucky" in Chinese) are much more than those brought by celebrity endorsements(as shown in Figure 6-1). Regarding the young people as its major target group and looking into the consumption hotspots of younger generations nowadays, Luckin Coffee improves the taste and quality of coffee, strives to understand the spiritual needs of the young adults, and then seeks an appropriate brand spokesperson to integrate the spiritual temperament of celebrity with its own brand characteristics. Thanks to the popularity of the Winter Olympic Games, it achieved win-win results between sales and brand promotion.

点评

Comments

在社会主义核心价值观中,"自由、平等、公正、法制"是整个社会的道德规范和行为准则。"诚信"即诚实守信,是人类社会千百年传承下来的道德传统,也是社会主义道德建设的重点内容。瑞幸咖啡财务造假造成了巨大的损失和不良的国际影响,这其中的原因包含舞弊者的道德与价值观的缺失,和世界最大的会计师事务所安达信因为安然公司造假而荣誉尽毁的案例相似。诚信为本、操守为重、实事求是、依法执业是各行业从业者所应该具备的基本品德,诚信是企业生存的基础,也是商业活动的基本准则。任何企业蓄意的造假和欺骗行为都会引发资本市场的不信任。很多新创企业不注重脚踏实地,而是急于"赚快钱",忙着"赶风口",小信诚则大信立,信誉需要点滴积累,任何企业,只有重信守诺,方能行稳致远。

Among the core socialist values, "freedom, equality, justice and rule of law" are the moral norms and codes of conduct of the Chinese society. "Integrity" means honesty and trustworthiness, which is an ethical tradition passed down by human society for thousands of years and also the key to the construction of socialist ethics. Luckin Coffee has suffered huge losses and obtained a negative image globally due to the financial fraud caused by the lack of morality and values of fraudsters. This is similar to the case of Andersen, once the world's largest accounting firm, whose reputation was completely destroyed by Enron's fraud. Integrity-oriented, ethics-based, seeking truth from facts

案例 6.1 瑞幸咖啡财务问题分析

and practicing according to law are the basic qualities that practitioners in various industries should possess. Integrity is the basis for the survival of enterprises and the basic criterion for business activities. Any enterprise's deliberate fraud and deception will lead to distrust in the capital market. Many start-ups fail to be down-to-earth, but eagerly pursue "making quick money" and "catching up with the latest development trend". Building a great reputation starts with little things. Enterprises can only maintain sustainable growth by keeping its promises.

瑞幸咖啡的财务造假事件暴露出有些上市公司存在的内部控制缺陷。例如,关联交易相关的内部控制缺失,导致供应商及客户的引入未受到有效评估和控制;内部监督机制缺失致使监管不力,未能使内部控制体系形成闭环。因此在审计过程中,企业应该在财务方面加强内部控制,手段主要包括:完善财务管理内控制度,构建完善的内部控制体系,加大内部控制监督力度,加强企业财务信息化建设等。在经历财务造假事件后,瑞幸咖啡通过调整董事会和高级管理层、解决债务重组问题等方式,积极求变、努力自救,并通过提升产品能力、助力冬奥会、降本增效、数字化运营等蛰伏两年,重获新生。

The financial fraud of Luckin Coffee exposed many internal control defects of listed companies. For example, the lack of internal control associated with related party transactions leads to ineffective evaluation and control of suppliers and customers. The lack of internal supervision mechanism results in ineffective supervision and failing to develop a closed loop of internal control system. Therefore, in the auditing process, enterprises should strengthen internal control in finance mainly by improving the internal control system of financial management, building a well-developed internal control system, increasing their efforts to supervise internal control, and pushing forward the construction of an information-based corporate financial system. After the financial fraud, Luckin Coffee actively sought changes and strove to help itself by adjusting the board of directors and senior management and handling the debt restructuring. Then, it gained a new life by improving product capabilities, supporting the Winter Olympics, reducing costs and increasing efficiency, and practicing digital operation for two years.

讨论题
Discussions

(1)从一名"会计人"的角度如何看待瑞幸咖啡暴雷事件？

What do you think of the financial fraud of Luckin Coffee from the perspective of an accountant?

(2)瑞幸咖啡事件对于完善公司内部控制方面有哪些启示？

What insights can we gain from the financial fraud of Luckin Coffee for improving the internal control of an enterprise?

(3)你如何看待诚信与法制在财务信息披露过程中的作用？

What do you think of the roles played by integrity and rule of law in the process of financial information disclosure?

资料来源

张新民,陈德球. 移动互联网时代企业商业模式、价值共创与治理风险——基于瑞幸

案例 6.1　瑞幸咖啡财务问题分析

咖啡财务造假的案例分析[J].管理世界,2020(36):11,74—86.

贾佳.瑞幸咖啡财务造假案例分析[J].现代商贸工业,2021,42(16):133—134.

石金.瑞幸咖啡财务造假案例分析[J].中国管理信息化,2021,24(09):25—26.

王素娟.瑞幸咖啡财务造假案例分析[J].山西农经,2020(13):157,159.

张梓萱.瑞幸咖啡财务造假案例分析[J].中国管理信息化,2021,24(11):32—33.

Achieving 鹿.瑞幸咖啡案例分析[EB/OL].[2022－12－08].https://baijiahao.baidu.com/s? id＝17257127764715182158&wfr＝spider&for＝pc.

References

Zhang Xinmin,Chen Deqiu. Enterprise business model,value co-creation and governance risks in the mobile Internet era-a case analysis based on Luckin Coffee's financial fraud[J]. Management World,2020(36):11,74—86.

Jia Jia. Analysis on the case of Luckin Coffee's financial fraud[J]. Modern Business Trade Industry,2021,42(16):133—134.

Shi Jin. Analysis on the case of Luckin Coffee's financial fraud[J]. China Management Informatization,2021,24(09):25—26.

Wang Sujuan. Analysis on the case of Luckin Coffee's financial fraud[J]. Shanxi Agricultural Economy,2020(13):157,159.

Zhang Zixuan. Analysis on the case of Luckin Coffee's financial fraud[J]. China Management Informatization,2021,24(11):32—33.

Achieving Deer. Analysis on the case of Luckin Coffee[EB/OL]. [2022－12－08]. https://baijiahao.baidu.com/s? id＝17257127764715182158&wfr＝spider&for＝pc.

案例 6.2　中集车辆从收购整合 Vanguard 到全球运营
Case 6.2　CIMC Vehicles: From Acquisition and Integration of Vanguard to Global Operation

教学目标
Teaching Objectives

"走出去"战略是指中国企业充分利用国内和国外"两个市场、两种资源",通过对外直接投资、对外工程承包、对外劳务合作等形式积极参与国际竞争与合作,实现经济可持续发展的现代化强国战略。实施"走出去"战略对于鼓励企业参与海外竞争与合作,拓展国际市场至关重要,也是对外开放的重要举措。本节通过案例分析,帮助学生理解对外直接投资、兼并与收购等知识,在世界经济高度国际化和一体化背景下,启发学生对于企业如何运用财务管理手段更好地实现"走出去"进行思考。

"Going global" strategy refers to the strategy where Chinese en-

案例 6.2　中集车辆从收购整合 Vanguard 到全球运营

terprises make full use of "two markets and two resources" at home and abroad to achieve sustainable economic development by actively participating in international competition and cooperation through foreign direct investment, international engineering contracting and international labor service cooperation. This strategy, as a significant move for opening up, is very important for encouraging enterprises to participate in overseas competition and cooperation and expanding the international market. Through case analysis, this section helps students understand the knowledge about foreign direct investment, mergers and acquisitions, and inspires students to think about how enterprises can better realize "going out" using financial management tools when the world economy is highly internationalized and integrated.

案例涉及财务管理中对外直接投资、兼并与收购等相关知识点。

The case involves foreign direct investment, merger and acquisitions and other related concepts in Finance Management.

案例内容

Contents

中集车辆(集团)股份有限公司是全球领先的半挂车与专用车高端制造企业,公司于 2002 年进入行业以来,围绕"专注、创新"形成了经营优势、技术优势。根据 *Global Trailer* 公布 2022 年全球前 50 名半挂车制造商按产量排名数据,公司连续 10 年蝉联全球第一。回顾中集车辆的发展历程,2009 年 12 月具有里程碑式意义,彼时中集车辆面临进一步实现国际化经营的重大机遇,其通过境外收购,建立了先锋国家拖车公司（Vanguard National Trailer Corporation），先锋（Vanguard）在2020年通过一系列新实施的优化治理措施，实现扭亏为盈，助力中集车辆国际运营战略部署，使其"走出去"计划取得了重大成果。同时，也为其他企业如何通过海外收购进入全球市场，如何进行资产管理与整合实现快速发展提供了思路。中集车辆的实践可供"走出去"的中国企业借鉴。

CIMC Vehicles (Group) Co., Ltd. is the world's leading high-end manufacturer of semi-trailers and special vehicles. Since the company entered the industry in 2002, it has developed its advantages in business and technology based on "concentration and innovation". According to the ranking data of the top 50 semi-trailer manufacturers in the world in 2022 published by the Global Trailer, it had been No. 1 globally for 10 consecutive years. Looking back on the development of CIMC Vehicles, December 2009 was a milestone. At that time, CIMC Vehicles was faced with a great opportunity to further develop its international operation. Vanguard National Trailer Corporation was established through overseas acquisition. Vanguard turned losses into profits through a series of newly-adopted optimized governance measures in 2020, which helped CIMC Vehicles to deploy its international operation strategy and achieved great results for its "going global" plan Meanwhile, it also serves as an example for other enterprises on how to enter the global market through overseas acquisitions and how to manage and integrate assets to achieve rapid development. The practice of CIMC Vehicles can serve as a reference for Chinese enterprises that "going global".

案例 6.2　中集车辆从收购整合 Vanguard 到全球运营

一、破产到重生:从收购 HPA Monon 起步

Ⅰ. From bankruptcy to rebirth:Starting with the acquisition of HPA Monon

在美国的道路上现在经常可以看到带有中集或 Vanguard 标志的车辆,它们看起来非常漂亮,质量也很好,与其他同行相比丝毫不逊色。中集车辆推出的产品主要为半挂车系列,美国拥有半挂车行业中世界最大的市场,也是监管最严格的市场之一。这里的大型半挂车公司是世界上最具竞争力的对手,世界十大半挂车公司中有五家来自美国,而且这些公司都已经营了几十年甚至一百多年。自 2003 年正式进入美国市场,收购濒临破产的美国第八大拖车公司万格勒(HPA Monon)以来,中集作为一家美国市场的新公司,经过多年努力,进入美国拖车行业前五强,成为销量全球第一的公司,中集及其美国品牌 Vanguard 是北美半挂车行业首屈一指的品牌,甚至在某些类别中位居北美第一。在美国本土市场,其性能和产品质量都得到了认可,然而这一成就的取得并不容易。

Vehicles with CIMC or Vanguard Logo can often be seen on the highways in the US. They boast attractive appearance and good quality, not inferior to its competitors. The products launched by CIMC Vehicles are mainly semi-trailer series. The US has the largest semi-trailer market in the world and is also one of the most strictly regulated markets, thus the large semi-trailer manufacturers here are the strongest competitors in the world. Five of the top 10 semi-trailer manufacturers in the world are from the US, which have been operating for decades or even more than a century. CIMC officially entered

327

the US market in 2003 and acquired HPA Monon, the eighth largest trailer manufacturer in the US, which was on the verge of bankruptcy. After years of efforts, CIMC, a newcomer, has become one of the top five trailer manufacturers in the US, with the largest sales volume in the world. CIMC and its American subsidiary Vanguard are the leading brands in the semi-trailer industry in North America, even ranking first in some categories. In the American market, its performance and product quality are well received, which is not an easy achievement.

改革开放以来,中国进一步融入全球制造产业链。中集从一开始就专注于国际市场,1999年实现营业额已超50亿元,成为中国500强企业之一。中集当时已连续3年在集装箱生产方面处于世界领先地位,集装箱销售收入占总收入的96%,公司希望横向拓展业务板块争取未来长足的发展,拓展后推出的第一个产品是厢式半挂车,后来逐渐发展包括平板车、仓栅车、自卸车、冷藏车等多种产品,形成了中集车辆板块,这也是中集集团下属的一家上市公司。

Since the reform and opening up, China has further integrated into the global manufacturing industry chain. CIMC has been concentrating on the international market from the very beginning. In 1999, it achieved a turnover of over 5 billion yuan and became one of the top 500 enterprises in China. At that time, CIMC had been the leader in container manufacturing for three consecutive years, with its sales revenue of containers accounting for 96% of the total. It hoped to expand its business segment horizontally for rapid development in the future. Its first product launched after expansion was the van semi-

案例 6.2　中集车辆从收购整合 Vanguard 到全球运营

trailer. Later, it gradually developed a variety of products including flatbed trucks, stake trucks, dump trucks, refrigerated trucks and so forth. Then, the CIMC Vehicles was founded, which now has become a listed company under CIMC Group.

整车产品的开发过程和集装箱关系密切。回溯到1999年2月25日,在澳大利亚调研的中集管理层麦伯良等人看到一辆在公路上行驶的厢式半挂车,觉得和中集的箱体非常相似,似乎是有四个轮子的箱子(如图6-2所示)。经过详细了解后,发现厢式半挂车不仅承担货物运输任务,而且很好地解决了超重、乱洒堆土破坏环境、压塌路面破坏公共设施等问题。由于当时中国国内公路建设蓬勃发展,而运输和物流系统较为落后。中集认为这是一个很好的商机,具有商业机遇和社会意义,从此便开启了车辆领域的发展。

The development process of vehicle products is closely related to containers. On February 25, 1999, Mai Boliang and other executives of CIMC, during their visit in Australia, saw a van-semi-trailer running on the highway, and found that it was highly similar to the containers of CIMC, as it looked like a container with four wheels (as shown in Figure 6-2). After further looking into it, they found that in addition to transporting cargoes, the van semi-trailer can solve many problems such as overweight, dirt littering and destroying the environment, and crushing the road surface to damage public facilities. At that time, China's highway construction was booming, but its transportation and logistics systems were relatively backward. CIMC thought it was a good business opportunity with social significance, so it started to enter the vehicle manufacturing industry.

图片来源：http://tech.sina.com.cn/csj/2021-07-08/doc-ikqciyzk4312288.shtml，2022-12-28。

Source: http://tech.sina.com.cn/csj/2021-07-08/doc-ikqciyzk4312288.shtml, 2022-12-28.

图 6—2　中集半挂车

Figure 6—2　CIMC's semi-trailer

然而，实际进入这个领域并不像给集装箱装上轮子那么简单。中集不仅向美国和澳大利亚等处于行业领先地位的专家请教，还在 2001 年聘请麦肯锡进行深入的战略发展咨询。当时的研究结果显示，半挂车的全球年营业额为 140 亿美元，是集装箱市场的 3.8 倍，有很大的市场潜力与发展空间。事实上，这一原则也是中集进入每个细分市场的前提条件，这些细分市场都受到了充分的调研与评估。

However, stepping into this field is not as simple as installing wheels on containers. CIMC not only consulted the leading experts in the industry from the US and Australia, but also hired McKinsey for

案例 6.2 中集车辆从收购整合 Vanguard 到全球运营

in-depth strategic development consulting in 2001. The research results showed that the global annual turnover of semi-trailers then was 14 billion US dollars, 3.8 times that of the container market, thus there was huge market potential and development space. In fact, this principle is also a prerequisite for CIMC to enter every market segment, which has been fully investigated and evaluated.

中集集团为了减少进入北美市场的时间和员工培训成本等,决定使用收购整合手段。2003 年 6 月,中集车辆实施"走出去"战略,收购了美国正处于破产程序的第 8 大拖车制造商 HPA Monon 公司,正式开启了进入海外市场的序幕。

In order to reduce the time to enter the North American market and the cost of staff training, CIMC decided to resort to acquisition and integration. In June, 2003, CIMC Vehicles implemented the strategy of "going global" and acquired HPA Monon, the eighth largest trailer manufacturer in the US, which officially unveiled its entry into overseas markets.

二、整合扩张海外业务

Ⅱ. Integrate and expand overseas business

中集 2003 年 6 月收购 HPA Monon 后,在汽车行业的全球化之路并非一帆风顺。在完成收购后,为了更好地整合 HPA Monon 的资产,在北美建立高端汽车品牌,中集的北美子公司——中集北美有限公司(CIMC USA, INC.)于 2003 年 4 月出资成立了 Vanguard。正式成立后,Vanguard 经历了一个快速增长期,半挂车产量快速增长,但公司始终处于亏损状态,2008 年爆发的金融危机也对 Vanguard 发展

331

带来了不利影响。这时,李贵平被任命为中集美国公司的总经理。

After CIMC acquired HPA Monon in June 2003, its globalization in the automobile industry was not smooth. After the acquisition, CIMC established a high-end automobile brand in North America in order to better integrate HPA Monon's assets. In April 2003, CIMC USA,INC., a North American subsidiary of CIMC, invested and established Vanguard. Then, Vanguard experienced a period of rapid growth, with its production of semi-trailers increasing significantly. However, Vanguard was always at a loss and even adversely affected by the financial crisis in 2008 when Li Guiping was appointed as the General Manager of CIMC US.

李贵平开始了对 Vanguard 的第二次重组。2004 年中集第一次重组的重点是减少复杂的产品线和对过时的生产流程进行现代化改造,而这一次重点是管理和效率。李贵平同意关闭中集的美国办公室,以减少支出,并且 Vanguard 的管理层则在管理和效率方面进行了大胆改革。Vanguard 管理层制定了具体的改进计划,具体目标包括提高生产力、缩短库存周期、降低采购成本和提高产品毛利率等。李贵平把这个计划称为"出海计划",其目的是在集团范围内采取一些关于采购和产品的举措,提高生产效率,降低运营和生产成本,提高产品利润。

Li Guiping started the second restructuring of Vanguard. The first restructuring by CIMC in 2004 focused on reducing complex product lines and transforming outdated production processes, while this time it concentrated on management and efficiency. Li Guiping agreed to close the US Office of CIMC to reduce expenses. Vanguard's

案例 6.2　中集车辆从收购整合 Vanguard 到全球运营

executives made bold reforms to improve its management and efficiency, and formulated specific improvement plans, with clear objectives including improving productivity, shortening inventory cycle, reducing procurement costs and increasing gross profit margin of products. Li Guiping named this a "going overseas plan", which was designed to take measures on purchasing and products within the group to improve production efficiency, reduce operation and production costs, and enhance profitability.

为有效降低采购成本,李贵平组织会议并邀约 Vanguard 核心零部件的供应商管理层与采购部门协商,这是 Vanguard 被收购后采购部门第一次与供应商最高层谈判。采购部门提出以原有价格为基点降价 100 美元,但是经过长期协商,对方未能接受此项条件,并提出只能接受降价 50 美元,但是在中集车辆提出全球市场产业链的集采业务全部与供应商接洽后,对方不仅接受了谈判条件,还额外降价 200 美元,双方以 2 150 美元采购价格达成一致。此后 Vanguard 不仅成为中集车辆全球采购系统的一员,而且双方就集采业务开展了长久且深入的合作,有效减少采购成本,与被收购前相比,具有与供应商议价更为有利的条件。

To effectively reduce procurement cost, Li Guiping organized a meeting between Vanguard's Procurement Department and the executives of Vanguard's supplier of core components for negotiation. It was the first negotiation between the Procurement Department and the top leadership of the supplier after Vanguard was acquired. The Procurement Department proposed to reduce the original price by 100 US dollars, but after long-term negotiation, the other party only accepted a price reduction of 50 US dollars. However, after CIMC Vehicles put forward that the supplier could engage in all its centralized purchasing business in the industrial chain of global market, the other party not only accepted the terms, but also reduced the price by an additional 200 US dollars, and both parties reached an agreement on the purchase price of 2,150 US dollars. Since then, Vanguard became a member of the global procurement system of CIMC Vehicles, and the two sides carried out long-term and in-depth cooperation on centralized procurement business, effectively reducing procurement costs. It has gained more favorable conditions for bargaining with suppliers than before being acquired.

财务数据显示,出海计划取得了显著收益。计划实施的第一年,Vanguard 的亏损总额即降至 100 万美元以下。在中集全球采购体系的助力下,Vanguard 产品的销售价与采购成本间的差额比计划实施前扩大了 1/3,达到了行业中较好的管理与盈利水平。随着经济形势的好转,业务量实现了大规模增长。2022 年,Vanguard 的年营运收入为 3.337 亿美元。

According to the financial data, the "going overseas plan" has achieved remarkable benefits. In the first year of its implementation, Vanguard's total loss fell below 1 million US dollars. Thanks to CIMC's global procurement system, the difference between the sales price and procurement cost of Vanguard products increased by one third compared with that before the implementation, reaching a better management and profitability level in the industry. With the improvement of the economic situation, its business volume achieved a large-

案例 6.2 中集车辆从收购整合 Vanguard 到全球运营

scale growth. In 2022, Vanguard's annual operating income reached 333.7 million US dollars.

从2011年中集车辆加快国际化进程到2012年更新国际化战略，中集车辆在"全球运营，地方智慧"的理念下加快实施国际化战略，收购了美国的荷兰博格、LAG和瑞特朗等公司，并在西澳大利亚、沙特阿拉伯、马来西亚、南非、波兰、美国弗吉尼亚州和佐治亚州等地开设了海外工厂。与其他并购交易不同，中集车辆专注于扩大其销售和营销渠道，而非单方面地扩大规模。中集车辆公司利用海外公司的技术和渠道来提高其市场份额，并注重整合海内外工厂的资源，实现优势互补。不仅产品，管理和采购也在进行整合。例如，中集车辆下属的欧洲公司LAG与国内公司扬州通华密切合作，新型铝合金油罐车打开了中东沙特阿拉伯市场的大门，获得了50%以上的市场份额，成为该地区的主要设备供应商。

From speeding up its internationalization process in 2011 to updating its internationalization strategy in 2012, CIMC Vehicles accelerated the implementation of its internationalization strategy adhering to the philosophy of "global operation with local wisdom", and acquired companies such as Dutch Borg, LAG and Ritron in the US, and opened overseas factories in Western Australia, Saudi Arabia, Malaysia, South Africa, Poland, Virginia and Georgia in the US. Unlike other M&A transactions, CIMC Vehicles prioritizes the expansion of its sales and marketing channels over mere scale expansion. It uses the technology and channels of overseas companies to increase its market share, and pays attention to integrating the resources of factories at home and abroad to complement each other's advantages. In addition to products, management and procurement are also being integrated. For example, LAG, a European company affiliated to CIMC Vehicles, worked closely with Yangzhou Tonghua, a Chinese company, to successfully enter the market of Saudi Arabia in the Middle East with the newly-developed aluminum alloy tanker, gaining more than 50% of the market share and becoming the leading equipment supplier in the region.

点评
Comments

"走出去"是中国发展外向型经济的必由之路,是中国参与经济全球化的重要条件,是中国企业参与国际市场竞争的重要条件,也是中国企业发展壮大后国际扩张的必然选择。"走出去"是以中国的公司为主导,服务于中国公司战略的一种跨国整合模式。贴近全球市场,贴近创新趋势,这是中国企业坚定"走出去"的最大动力,"走出去"让这些企业有了更强生命力。"走出去"可获取的优势十分显著,如拓展市场规模,获取技术支持,完善产业链布局,破除贸易保护限制等。培育中国具有国际竞争力的大型跨国公司,"走出去"是一种必然选择,这不仅标志着中国的对外开放水平,也体现了中国企业的全球影响力。

For China, "going global" is the only way to develop an export-oriented economy and a significant condition to engage in economic globalization. For Chinese enterprises, it is an essential condition to participate in international market competition and an inevitable choice to expand globally after it became strong. "Going global" is a transna-

案例 6.2 中集车辆从收购整合 Vanguard 到全球运营

tional integration mode which is led by Chinese enterprises and serves the strategy of Chinese enterprises. Being close to the global market and the innovation trend is the biggest motivation for Chinese enterprises to firmly "go global", which will give them stronger vitality. The advantages of "going global" are quite obvious, such as expanding market scale, obtaining technical support, improving the layout of industrial chain, and breaking trade protection restrictions. It is an inevitable choice to cultivate large multinational companies with international competitiveness in China, which not only shows China's opening to the outside world, but also reflects the global influence of Chinese enterprises.

中集车辆通过对外直接投资范畴中跨国收购与整合 Vanguard 的方法，实现了利润增值效应。通过跨国收购的投资方式，企业可以剥离脱离其核心竞争力的资产，并购买能够提高其竞争力的重要资产，来保护、巩固和提高其全球竞争地位。中集车辆在收购 Vanguard 后，不仅缩短了进入海外市场的时间，实现了海外市场经营部署，而且利用海外技术资源进一步优化产品，与国内市场形成优势互补、互利共赢。通过出海计划，中集车辆进一步完善了产业链，集中优势力量，并且凭借雄厚的品牌优势、管理优势和资源整合能力，着力于集中采购，降低了采购成本，进而减少生产成本，扩大营业收入，提高了毛利率，并且扩大了市场份额，从而进一步"走出去"，更好地实现国际化运营。

CIMC Vehicles has realized the profit appreciation effect by means of transnational acquisition and integration of Vanguard in the field of foreign direct investment. Through cross-border acquisition, enterprises can protect, consolidate and improve their global competitive edge by divesting assets unrelated to their core competitiveness and buying important assets that can improve their competitiveness. After acquiring Vanguard, CIMC Vehicles not only shortened the time to enter the overseas market, but also realized the operation and deployment in the overseas market. Besides, it further improved its products by using overseas technical resources, and complemented each other's advantages and achieved win-win results with the domestic market. Through the plan of going overseas, CIMC Vehicles has further enhanced the industrial chain. By pooling its strengths, it focused on centralized procurement with its strong advantages in brand and management and resource integration capacity, so as to reduce procurement and production costs, improve operating income, increase gross profit margin and grab a larger market share. In this way, it realized further "going global" and better international operation.

讨论题
Discussions

(1)什么是出海计划？中集车辆如何通过该计划降低采购成本？

What is the "going overseas plan"? How did CIMC Vehicles reduce its procurement cost with this plan?

(2)你认为企业在进行兼并与收购时需要注意哪些问题？

What are the problems that enterprises need to pay attention to in mergers and acquisitions?

案例 6.2　中集车辆从收购整合 Vanguard 到全球运营

（3）中集车辆收购整合 Vanguard 对其"走出去"进行国际化运营有何积极意义？

What is the positive influence of CIMC Vehicles' acquisition and integration of Vanguard on its "going global" international operation?

资料来源

"VANGUARD NATIONAL TRAILER"公司收入[EB/OL].[2023－01－08]. https://www.zippia.com/vanguard-national-trailer-careers-419437/revenue/.

项兵,杨谷川,周一,等.从整合 Vanguard 到全球运营[J].中国外汇,2013(22):16－19.

曲佳音.从中集集团收购荷兰博格看中国企业的海外并购[J].黑龙江对外经贸,2007(10):59－61.

纪鹏飞.全球化运营 助推"新中集"[EB/OL].[2023－01－08]. https://www.fx361.com/page/2016/0211/12624380.shtml.

改变世界的集装箱 中集集团 24 个产品全球产销量世界第一[EB/OL].[2023－01－08]. http://www.hg-news.cn/chuangxin/202209/999951440.html.

References

VANGUARD NATIONAL TRAILER REVENUE[EB/OL].[2023－01－08]. https://www.zippia.com/vanguard-national-trailer-careers-419437/revenue/.

Xiang Bing, Yang Guchuan, Zhou Yi, et al. From integrating Vanguard to global operation[J]. China Forex, 2013(22):16－19.

Qu Jiayin. Exploring the overseas mergers and acquisitions of Chinese enterprises through CIMC Group's acquisition of Dutch Borg[J]. HLJ Foreign Economic Relations & Trade, 2007 (10):59－61.

Ji Pengfei. Global operations build a "new CIMC"[EB/OL].[2023－01－08]. https://www.fx361.com/page/2016/0211/12624380.shtml.

Containers that have changed the world: CIMC Group ranks top in global output and sales of its 24 products[EB/OL]. [2023-01-08]. http://www.hg-news.cn/chuangxin/202209/999951440.html.

案例6.3　小米智能家居财务战略
Case 6.3　Financial Strategy of Xiaomi Smart Home

教学目标
Teaching Objectives

"AI+IoT+5G"构成了如今令人振奋的"智能新时代",在现代社会中,智能家居的概念被提起时,已不再局限于个体,更多的则是关注整体的智能联接。2019年科技部将小米AIoT平台列为面向智能家居的新一代人工智能开放创新平台,小米公司在智能家居、AIoT领域的布局得到了国家的认可。2020年,小米公司董事长雷军将"手机×AIoT"作为长期的核心发展战略。小米公司通过加快财务战略布局、完善商业生态的重要方式,构建生态链,降低成本,放大了经济效益。本节通过案例分析,帮助学生理解财务战略、投资战略等知识,启发学生对于企业如何利用财务战略发展重点业务进行思考。

"AI + IoT + 5G" comprises an exciting "intelligent new era".

In modern society, the concept of smart home is no longer about individuals only, but is more correlated with the overall intelligent connections. In 2019, the Ministry of Science and Technology rated Xiaomi AIoT platform as a new-generation AI open innovation platform for smart homes, which means that the layout of Xiaomi in smart homes and AIoT fields was recognized by the state. In 2020, Lei Jun, Chairman of Xiaomi, took "mobile phone × AIoT" as a long-term core development strategy. Xiaomi has built an ecological chain by accelerating its financial strategic layout and improving its business ecology, so as to reduce costs and increase economic benefits. Through case analysis, this section helps students understand the knowledge about financial strategy and investment strategy, and inspires them to think about how enterprises use the financial strategies to develop key businesses.

案例涉及财务管理中财务战略、投资战略等相关知识点。

The case involves financial strategy, investment strategy and other related concepts in the Finance Management.

案例内容

Contents

近年来，随着5G、人工智能、物联网的快速发展与应用，人们越来越关注家居生活的智能化、便捷性等多方面体验。智能电视、健身镜、扫地机等智能家居产品也逐渐进入大多数家庭。根据奥维云网数据显示，2016—2020年中国智能家居市场规模保持在20%左右的年复

案例 6.3　小米智能家居财务战略

合增长率。智能家居领域市场需求的快速增长引发了多家资本雄厚的企业关注,竞争愈发激烈,产品多种多样,投资所需资金量大、周期较长、风险较大,其发展趋势备受关注。

In recent years, with the rapid development and application of 5G, artificial intelligence and Internet of Things, people are increasingly concerned about the intelligent and convenient experiences of home life. Smart home products such as smart TV, fitness mirror and robot vacuum have gradually been adopted by most families. According to the data of Aowei Cloud, the smart home market in China maintained a compound annual growth rate of around 20% from 2016 to 2020. The rapid growth of market demand in the field of smart home has attracted the attention of so many capital-rich enterprises that the competition is getting increasingly fierce. As the investment in this field with a large variety of products features large amounts of money, a prolonged period of time and high risks, the development trend of smart home industry has aroused much attention.

小米公司很早便进入了智能家居领域,小米的 IoT 战略定义为"1+4+X",即围绕一部手机为核心,电视、智能音箱、路由器和笔记本 4 项智能产品为支点,X 则由生态链企业和合作企业提供。小米除以手机为主营业务外,智能家居生态也已变为其不可或缺且具有竞争力的优势业务。

Xiaomi entered the field of smart home a long time ago. Its IoT strategy is defined as "1+4+X", which means that a mobile phone is taken as the core device, and four smart products, including TV, smart speaker, router and notebook, as the supporting devices, and X

is provided by ecological chain enterprises and partners. Apart from its main business of mobile phones, smart home ecology has also become an indispensable and competitive part of Xiaomi.

一、小米智能家居发展历程

Ⅰ. Development course of Xiaomi Smart Home

当清晨还在熟睡时,轻柔的音乐缓缓响起,卧室窗帘自动拉开,温暖的阳光轻洒入室,呼唤开启全新的一天。当起床洗漱时,营养早餐已经自动做好,餐毕,音响自动关机。在上班回家的路上,智能家居已经开始忙碌,保证回家时便是舒服的室温,并放好洗澡水保温。到家开门的瞬间,已亮起温馨的灯光,香薰机已发出淡淡的鸢尾草香。智能家居在带来便利的同时可以提升生活的品质,增添幸福感,因此备受关注。许多公司都已布局了自己的智能家居业务,小米也不例外。

When you are still asleep in the morning, soft music is played, then the curtains in the bedroom are automatically opened, allowing the warm sunshine into the bedroom to usher in a brand-new day. When you are brushing your teeth after getting up, the nutritious breakfast has been made automatically, and the music will be automatically off after you finish your meal. On your way home from work, the smart home has been busy with ensuring a comfortable room temperature and keeping the bath water warm. When you get home and open the door, the warm light will be on, and the aromatherapy diffuser is giving off a faint scent of iris. Smart home can improve the quality of life and increase happiness while bringing convenience, which is why it has attracted much attention. Numerous companies have launched their own smart home products, and Xiaomi is no exception.

小米公司从 2010 年开始到 2013 年发布了智能手机、智能电视、路由器、定制操作系统 MIUI 等具有关键战略意义的产品。首先,智能手机是小米的主营业务,也是操控智能家居的工具之一,可以做到远程操控。2013 年 11 月 20 日,小米路由器正式发布,路由器与智能家居布局密切相关,从路由器第一次公测时标榜的"顶配路由器"到第三次公测时成为"玩转智能家居的控制中心",彰显了小米路由器最初的产品定义:"第一是最好的路由器,第二是家庭数据中心,第三是智能家庭中心,第四是开放平台。"截至 2015 年 1 月,小米路由器销量已突破百万,在国内智能路由器市场遥遥领先。截至 2022 年 3 月,小米在全球范围内的 AIoT 连接设备数达 4.78 亿,拥有 5 件以上 IoT 设备的用户数超过 950 万。

From 2010 to 2013, Xiaomi released products with key strategic significance, such as smart phones, smart TVs, routers and the customized operating system MIUI. First of all, as Xiaomi's main business, smart phones are utilized as one of the tools to remotely control smart homes. On November 20, 2013, Xiaomi Router was officially released, which is closely related to the layout of smart home. From the "top router", as it is called, in its first public beta to the "control center for smart home" in its third public beta, the evolution process reflects its original product descriptions of Xiaomi Router: best router, home data center, smart home center, and open platform. " As of January 2015, the sales volume of Xiaomi Router had exceeded one million, which is far ahead other competitors in the domestic intelligent router market. By March 2022, Xiaomi had possessed 478 million AIoT connected devices worldwide, and the number of its users with more than five IoT devices had been over 9.5 million.

小米智能家居主要是围绕小米手机、小米电视、小米路由器这三大核心产品以及其他衍生品,一起组成一条小米生态链。三大战略产品相互补充、相互配合,诠释了物联网的便利之处。手机中的信息例如照片、视频等能够通过智能电视显示,路由器利用高速的网络实现设备之间的互联,三大产品既可以各自发挥功效,又可以实现互联互通,构建完整的智能家居生态链。

Xiaomi Smart Home is mainly based on its three core products, including Xiaomi mobile phone, Xiaomi TV, Xiaomi Router, which constitute the Xiaomi ecological chain together with other derivatives. These three strategic products complement and work with each other, fully reflecting the convenience of the Internet of Things. Information on mobile phones, such as photos and videos, can be displayed by smart TV and routers interconnect devices via the high-speed network. The three products can play their respective roles while achieving interconnectivity to jointly build a complete smart home ecological chain.

小米首届 IoT 开发者大会于 2017 年在北京召开,通过这次大会,小米带来了更完善的 IoT 软硬一体化解决方案,更丰富的 AI 开放生态,以及更贴近生活的全球合作伙伴。大会之后,小米全力打造"云计算+AI+大数据"三位一体的技术支持体系,米家 App 和 IoT 开放平台成为小米物联网战略的重要基石。米家 App 是智能硬件管理平台,不仅连接小米及生态链公司的智能产品,同时也开放接入第三方

案例 6.3 小米智能家居财务战略

智能硬件,为用户提供智能生活整体解决方案,能够简单便捷地通过手机与智能硬件交互,实现智能硬件之间的互联互通。米家 App 进一步优化了智能家居生态,利用手机可以便捷控制所有产品设备,还提供定制化、个性化服务,丰富了用户的物联网体验,实现了产业链产品的联动与管理(如图 6—3 所示)。

Xiaomi's first IoT Developer Conference was held in Beijing in 2017. Through this conference, Xiaomi launched an improved IoT software and hardware integrated solution, built a richer AI open ecosystem, and became a global partner closer to life. After the conference, Xiaomi made every effort to build a three-in-one technical support system featuring "cloud computing ＋ AI ＋ big data", and the open platform of Mi Home and IoT became a crucial cornerstone of Xiaomi's Internet of Things strategy. Mi Home, as an intelligent hardware management platform, not only connects the intelligent products of Xiaomi and its ecological chain enterprises, but also offers access to third-party intelligent hardware, providing users with an overall solution of intelligent life. By interacting with the intelligent hardware through the mobile phone in an easy and convenient manner, it realizes interconnectivity of the intelligent hardware. Mi Home further improves the smart home ecology, making it easy to control all products and equipment by mobile phones. It also provides customized and personalized services to enrich users' IoT experience and realize linkage and management of industrial chain products(as shown in Figure 6—3).

小米 IoT 平台秉承开放共赢的合作理念,在探索和推动 IoT 技术

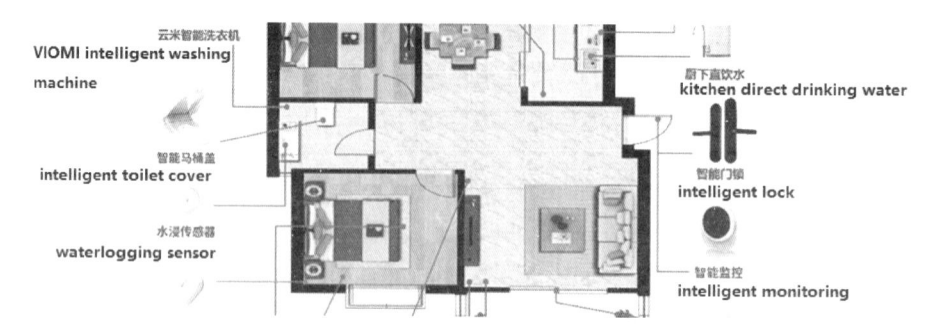

图片来源：https://post.smzdm.com/p/ar08g0vz/,2022－12－08。
Source:https://post.smzdm.com/p/ar08g0vz/,2022－12－08.

图 6－3　小米智能家居联动示例

Figure 6－3　Interconnectivity of Xiaomi Smart Home

和生态发展的同时，全面开放小米 IoT 的资源和能力，支持开发者开发出在不同场景下，用户对智能家居生态链的产品多种体验。

Adhering to the concept of open and win-win cooperation, Xiaomi IoT platform offers full access to the resources and capabilities of Xiaomi IoT while exploring and promoting IoT technology and ecological development, and supports developers to develop a large variety of product experiences on the smart home ecological chain for users in different scenarios.

凭借 IoT 平台积累的大量活跃用户以及海量的使用体验与反馈，小米智能家居业务进入了发展的快车道。2021 年第二季度财报显示，小米当前投资生态链企业超 330 家，账面价值 579 亿元，同比增长 57.3%。2021 年小米正式进入第二个 10 年，从一家用互联网思维做超高性价比手机的终端公司向物联网这艘"航空母舰"转身，先后打造了供应链和场景链。第一，供应链，也是小米初期所谓的"生态链企

案例 6.3　小米智能家居财务战略

业",2014年天津金米成立,开始围绕手机周边进行投资,被投资企业为小米提供智能家居、生活用品、可穿戴设备和出行等多个领域的产品,在小米之家以及有品商城等渠道销售。当时的小米主要通过供应链上下游关系构建生态圈。第二,场景链,小米在个人物联网、家庭物联网、车联网、卫星互联网这四大物联网场景的布局初步成型。家庭互联场景中连接规模为王,小米通过低价硬件策略,快速布局智能家居,这为小米集团的 IoT 生态链布局提供了广泛的基础。

With a large number of active users and massive experience and feedback accumulated by IoT platform, Xiaomi's smart home business started its rapid development. The financial report for Q2 of 2021 showed that Xiaomi had invested in more than 330 eco-chain enterprises with a book value of 57.9 billion yuan, up 57.3% year on year. In 2021, Xiaomi officially entered its second decade. It was transforming from a manufacturer that utilized Internet thinking to make ultra-cost-effective mobile phones to a company engaged in the Internet of Things, a new sector with broad prospects, and successively built a supply chain and a scenario chain. First, it built the supply chain, the so-called "eco-chain enterprises" in the early days of Xiaomi's development. Tianjin Jinmi was established in 2014 and began to invest in mobile phone peripherals. The invested enterprises provided Xiaomi with products covering smart homes, daily necessities, wearable devices, travel and other fields, which were sold in Xiaomi Fans Club and Xiaomi Youpin. At that time, Xiaomi built an ecosystem mainly through cooperation with upstream and downstream enterprises of the supply chain. Second, it created the scenario chain. Xiaomi's layout in the four IoT scenarios of Consumer IoT, IoT-based Smart Home, Internet of Vehicles (IoV) and satellite Internet has taken shape. In the home interconnectivity scenario, the scale is foremost. Xiaomi quickly entered the smart home industry through its low-cost hardware strategy, which laid a broad foundation for the layout of its IoT ecological chain.

二、财务战略与智能家居业务发展

II. Financial strategy and development of smart home business

（一）低成本财务战略

(1) Low cost strategy

在刚步入智能家居领域阶段，小米还不具备充足的资本支持，不足以创建自己的制造厂房，因此采用了外包生产的方式以降低生产成本，减少资金花费。通过外包的生产模式，小米不仅可以利用产业链上游公司的优质技术提高生产效率，同时C2B模式下互联网销售渠道可以直接与顾客对接供给产品，从而降低运输成本，减少整体营运成本，提高利润率。

When it initially entered the field of smart home, Xiaomi did not have sufficient capital support to create its own factory, so it adopted outsourcing production to reduce production costs and expenditure. Through the outsourcing production mode, the high-quality technology of upstream enterprises in the industrial chain can be used to improve production efficiency, and the online sales channel can also directly connect with customers to supply products under C2B mode, thus reducing transportation costs, overall operating costs and impro-

案例6.3 小米智能家居财务战略

ving profit margins.

小米集团财报数据显示,2019 年,IoT 与生活消费产品毛利率是11.2%,2020 年,IoT 与生活消费产品毛利率为 12.8%,这主要是由物联网产品的强劲增长以及更高的毛利率导致的。

According to the financial report data of Xiaomi Group, its gross profit margin of IoT and consumer goods was 11.2% in 2019 and 12.8% in 2020, mainly attributable to the strong growth of IoT products and higher gross profit margin.

(二)低库存财务战略

(2) Low inventory strategy

小米在构建智能家居生态链早期,运用的关键财务战略是稳定用户群体,提高营运能力,小米的资产周转率较同行相对较高,具有较强的运营能力。小米采取低库存的管理方式,致力于提高智能家居的品牌辨识度,增强市场的认可度,形成自身的品牌风格与品牌优势,从而提高销量,降低库存,增强资产的利用效率,提高产品在市场中的竞争力。

In the early stage of building smart home ecological chain, Xiaomi adopted the key financial strategy of stabilizing user groups and improving operational capacity. With strong operational capacity, it had a relatively higher asset turnover rate than that its competitors. By adopting the management mode of low inventory, Xiaomi was committed to improving the brand recognition of smart homes, enhancing market recognition, and forming its own brand style and brand advantage, thereby increasing sales, reducing inventory, raising the utilization efficiency of assets and improving the competitiveness of its products in the market.

小米的智能家居产品外观统一为白色系列,也使消费群体印象深刻,白色象征着简洁、规整,独特的家居面貌得到了市场的一致认可,产品之间的一致性、协调性也体现得淋漓尽致,增加了曝光度,也为推广节能环保的品牌印象增加了市场认知度,吸引了更多消费者的关注。

All of Xiaomi's smart home products are in white, which impresses the consumer groups. The color of white symbolizes simplicity and regularity, and this unique home characteristic has been unanimously recognized by the market. The consistency and harmony among products are also vividly reflected. It enhances the exposure and market awareness of products for promoting Xiaomi's brand impression of energy conservation and environmental protection to attract the attention of more consumers.

(三)投资孵化财务战略

(3) Investment incubation strategy

小米利用投资孵化的方式于2013年开始高速扩张,并创设了智能硬件生态链事业部,为了发展智能家居业务、优化相关产品,在横向与纵向两个维度采用针对性财务战略。

Xiaomi began to expand rapidly in 2013 by means of investment incubation, and created the Intelligent Hardware Ecological Chain Business Division. In order to develop smart home business and optimize related products, it adopted targeted financial strategies in both horizontal and vertical dimensions.

在横向维度,为了拓展市场,小米专门与企业文化和公司相适应且可以为完善物联网产业链带来价值的初创企业合作,采用投资不控

案例6.3 小米智能家居财务战略

股的方式,保持合作企业本身的创造性与独立性,同时"投资＋孵化"的"平台＋"模式优化了业务的整体战略布局。得益于这一战略的实施,小米智能硬件取得了巨大进步,推出了丰富的智能硬件产品,如手环、空气净化器、监控摄像头等,并发展成为全球最大智能硬件IoT平台。小米公司创始人、前董事长兼CEO雷军表示:"小米IoT平台日活设备超过1 000万台的数据更加值得欣喜,在日活跃用户这一表现用户粘性的指标方面,小米IoT平台在业界遥遥领先。这也证明了小米IoT确实通过智能硬件产品改变了用户的生活习惯,真正提升了用户体验。"小米快速建立了初期市场智能家居业务的优势地位,是全球最早布局物联网智能家居硬件的企业。

In the horizontal dimension, in order to expand the market, Xiaomi cooperated with the start-ups that could adapt to its corporate culture, work smoothly with it, and bring value to the improvement of the IoT industrial chain. Xiaomi managed to maintain the creativity and independence of the cooperative enterprises by means of non-controlling investment. Meanwhile, the "platform ＋" model based on "investment ＋ incubation" optimized the overall strategic layout of the business. With the implementation of this strategy, Xiaomi's intelligent hardware made great progress, launching a large variety of intelligent hardware products, such as bracelets, air purifiers, surveillance cameras, etc., and became the world's largest intelligent hardware IoT platform. According to Lei Jun, founder, former Chairman and CEO of Xiaomi, "The data of more than 10 million daily active devices on Xiaomi IoT platform is even more gratifying. In terms of daily active users, which show user stickiness, Xiaomi IoT platform is far ahead in the industry. This also proves that Xiaomi IoT has indeed changed the living habits of users through intelligent hardware products, and truly improved the user experience. " As the first enterprise in the world to launch IoT smart home hardware, Xiaomi quickly secured a dominant position in the smart home business market at the initial stage.

在产业链纵向维度,小米采用并购策略,扩展产业链上游。2019年,小米共有6笔对外战略投资,其中3家被投企业是芯片生产商,分别是智多晶、VeriSilicon、恒玄科技。这一系列投资活动反映出小米已经清晰意识到对芯片这一重要原材料控制的重要性。小米之前的芯片供应商为美国高通公司,而高通公司对华为的急刹车必定对其他手机制造商造成很大的威慑,小米遂加大了对芯片的研发力度。如果能在芯片领域研发成功,就能在一定程度上确保终端产品的价格稳定。

In the vertical dimension of industrial chain, Xiaomi adopted M&A strategy to expand the upstream of industrial chain. In 2019, Xiaomi made six strategic investments, among which three invested companies were chip manufacturers, including Intelligence? Silicon, VeriSilicon and Bestechnic. From these investment activities, it could be clearly seen that Xiaomi realized the importance of controlling chips, an important raw material. Xiaomi's previous chip supplier was Qualcomm, an American manufacturer. Qualcomm's sudden supply cut-off on Huawei had greatly influenced other mobile phone manufacturers, so Xiaomi increased its research and development efforts on chips. If it could achieve something in this field, Xiaomi would ensure the price stability of its end products to some extent.

案例 6.3　小米智能家居财务战略

截至 2022 年 6 月 30 日，小米共投资了超过 400 家物联网的相关公司，为用户提供了多场景、多需求的智能化服务，家居物联网体验实现了大幅度提升。随着上百款智能硬件产品的推出，小米 AI 也进入了快速发展阶段，小米 AI 音箱、小米金服"米小贝"等产品展现威力，赢得业内广泛好评。在未来的 5 至 10 年，智能手机仍将是人工智能技术的最大平台，"智能手机＋IoT"会成为人工智能的无限生态。基于强大的产品能力，小米与生态链企业形成了和谐共生、相辅相成的互联生态系统。小米通过投资孵化战略将企业的核心资源部署到核心型产品上，在智能家居生态系统中发挥强有力的作用，奠定了其整个物联网的基石，并快速抢占了市场。

As of June 30, 2022, Xiaomi had invested in more than 400 companies related to the Internet of Things, providing users with multi-scenario and multi-demand intelligent services, with its home IoT experience greatly improved. The launch of hundreds of intelligent hardware products enabled Xiaomi AI to start its rapid development. Xiaomi Mi AI speakers, Xiaomi Jinfu "Mi Xiaobei" and other products showed their muscle and won wide acclaim in the industry. In the next 5 to 10 years, smart phones will remain the largest platform for artificial intelligence technology, and "smart phones＋IoT" will become the boundless ecology of artificial intelligence. Based on strong product capabilities, Xiaomi and eco-chain enterprises have formed an interconnected ecosystem that is harmonious and complementary. Xiaomi allocated its core resources to the core products through the investment incubation strategy, which allowed it to play a significant role in the smart home ecosystem, lay the cornerstone of its entire

IoT ecology, and quickly seize the market.

点评
Comments

抓重点,就是抓住主要矛盾,这能推动事物发展。推动事物发展的过程,就是正确认识矛盾、有效化解矛盾的过程。在复杂的事物发展过程中,有许多矛盾存在,其中必有一种是主要的矛盾,它的存在和发展规定或影响着其他矛盾的存在和发展。由于矛盾有主次之分,在想问题办事情的方法论上也应当有重点与非重点之分,要善于抓重点、集中力量解决主要矛盾。善于抓住重点,是获得发展的宝贵历史经验。小米重点发展关键产品,并将资金注入价值量高的环节,对价值量低的业务采用外包等方式,减少资金消耗,打通产业链上下游,优化业务发展方式,并在投资孵化财务战略的指导下,赢得了智能家居业务市场的先机,快速布局生态系统,利用关键产品(智能手机+IoT平台)形成先导优势,进一步推进小米智能家居业务的发展。小米公司制定了针对性财务战略,重点发展核心产品,在物联网生态布局方面,主要采用了运营管理(低成本、低库存)及投资管理的财务战略,采用部分生产业务外包、产品外观设计等手段,达到了降低产品生产成本、节约营运资金、增加利润率的目的,并利用投资孵化策略进一步扩展了智能家居业务生态链。

Focusing on priorities means focusing on the principal contradictions and promoting the development of things. The process of promoting development is the process of correctly understanding contradictions and effectively resolving them. In the development of com-

案例 6.3 小米智能家居财务战略

plex things, there are many contradictions, including the principal contradiction, whose existence and development stipulates or affects the existence and development of other contradictions. As there are principal and secondary contradictions, there should also be key and non-key points in the methodology of thinking about problems and doing things. We should be good at grasping key points and concentrating our efforts on solving major contradictions, which is valuable experience for development. Xiaomi focuses on the development of key products, and puts in funds into high-value links, and outsources low-value businesses to reduce capital consumption, connect the upstream and downstream of the industrial chain, and optimize the business development mode. Under the guidance of the financial strategy of investment incubation, Xiaomi took the opportunity, quickly built up its ecosystem, and utilized key products (smart phone + IoT platform) to form a leading advantage to further advance the development of its smart home business. It formulated targeted financial strategies, focusing on the development of core products. In terms of the ecological layout of IoT, Xiaomi mainly adopted the financial strategies of operation management (low cost and low inventory) and investment management, and utilized production outsourcing and industrial design to reduce production costs, save working capital and increase profit margin. It also further expanded the ecological chain of its smart home business by means of the investment incubation strategy.

讨论题

Discussions

(1) 小米公司发展智能家居业务采用了哪些财务战略重点发展智能家居业务？

What financial strategies did Xiaomi adopt to develop smart home business?

(2) 小米公司采用的财务战略效果如何？

What were the effects of the financial strategies adopted by Xiaomi?

(3) 你认为案例中提及的财务战略有哪些风险及应对措施。

What do you think are the risks and countermeasures of the financial strategy mentioned in the case?

资料来源

王国弘,宋彦锟. 物联网商业生态系统演化路径与策略——小米物联网生态案例分析[J]. 创新科技,2020,20(10):24—33.

翟楷文. 智能家居行业的财务战略分析——以 S 公司为例[J]. 商业 2.0(经济管理),2021(11):59—61.

黄鑫璨,刘君宜. 小米公司价值链分析与应用[J]. 合作经济与科技,2022(04):138—140.

郭飞,向乐静,于畅. 公司创业投资如何影响价值创造？——基于小米生态链构建的研究[J]. 财务管理研究,2022(02):1—14.

References

Wang Guohong, Song Yankun. Evolution path and strategy of IoT business ecosystem-case analysis of Xiaomi's IoT ecosystem[J]. Innovation Science And Technology,2020,20(10):24

案例 6.3 小米智能家居财务战略

—33.

Zhai Kaiwen. Analysis of financial strategy in smart home industry taking company S as an example[J]. Business 2.0 (Economic Management),2021(11):59—61.

Huang Xincan,Liu Junyi. Analysis and application of Xiaomi's value chain[J]. Co-operative Economy & Science,2022(04):138—140.

Guo Fei,Xiang Lejing,Yu Chang. How does corporate venture capital affect value creation?—Research based on the construction of Xiaomi's ecological chain[J]. Financial Management Research,2022(02):1—14.

第七篇 国际结算
PART Ⅶ INTERNATIONAL SETTLEMENT

案例 7.1 人民币被越来越多国家作为国际结算货币
Case 7.1 RMB-A Key Currency for International Settlement by an Increasing Number of Countries

教学目标
Teaching Objectives

当前世界范围内国际结算货币呈现多元化的趋势,美元、欧元、英镑、日元等一直是国际结算的主要货币选择。长期以来,中国一直在推动人民币国际化,希望通过人民币在国际范围内的广泛使用来增强中国在国际经济领域的影响力,为发展中国家在国际经济领域的发展贡献更大的力量,为人类命运共同体的实现起到推动作用。当前世界上越来越多的国家开始使用人民币作为国际结算货币,这意味着中国在经济上获得了这些国家的信任,中国的国际影响力正在逐渐增强。这一案例的选择,正是要通过国际结算货币的发展变迁和人民币在国际结算中的地位提升来反映中国在国际经济领域里的地位提升。

At present, there are diversified currencies for international settlement in the world. The US Dollar, Euro, British Pound and Japanese Yen have long been the major currencies for international settlement. For a long time, China has been promoting the internationalization of RMB, hoping to enhance its influence in the international economy through the extensive use of RMB globally, make greater contributions to the economic development of developing countries, and advance building a community of shared future for mankind. At present, an increasing number of countries in the world start to adopt RMB for international settlement, which means that China has gained the trust of these countries economically, and China's international influence is gradually increasing. This case reflects the promotion of China's position in international economy through the development and changes of currencies for international settlement and the rise in status of RMB in international settlement.

本案例涉及课程包括国际贸易理论与实务、国际金融、国际结算等，涉及专业知识点主要包括国际货币体系、国际结算货币选择、人民币国际化等。

The courses involved in this case include international trade theory and practice, international finance, international settlement, etc., and the concepts involved mainly consist of international monetary system, choice of international settlement currencies, internationalization of RMB, etc.

案例 7.1 人民币被越来越多国家作为国际结算货币

案例内容
Contents

"我知道柬埔寨当地货币面值高,携带大量外币比较麻烦,如今可以使用人民币,真的太方便了。"2023 年 2 月 8 日,南宁市民蒋女士从柬埔寨东盟通讯社的报道中获知柬埔寨政府宣布允许全国所有旅游业者直接接受人民币的消息后,计划今年夏天和家人一起去向往已久的柬埔寨吴哥窟旅游。柬埔寨东盟通讯社报道称,柬埔寨政府 2 月 7 日在首都金边国际机场对抵达柬埔寨的中国游客举行隆重欢迎仪式,柬埔寨旅游部部长唐坤在仪式上表示,为更好地接待中国游客和方便中国游客入境游玩,柬埔寨政府允许全国所有旅游业者直接接受人民币,包括酒店、餐厅等。

"I know that Cambodia's local currency features a high face value, and it is troublesome to carry a large amount of local currency. Therefore, it is really convenient that we can use RMB now." On February 8, 2023, Ms. Jiang, a citizen of Nanning, learned from the report of ASEAN News Agency in Cambodia that the Cambodian government had announced its decision to allow all the tourism practitioners across the country to accept RMB directly. Jiang has been longing to visit Angkor Wat in Cambodia, which will be realized with his family this summer. The ASEAN News Agency in Cambodia reported that the Cambodian government held a grand welcoming ceremony for Chinese tourists who arrived in Cambodia at the Phnom Penh International Airport on February 7. At the ceremony, Cambodian Tourism Minister H. E. Dr. Thong Khon said that in order to better receive and make it convenient for Chinese tourists to visit Cambodia, the Cambodian government allowed the tourism practitioners across the country to accept RMB directly, including hotels and restaurants.

人民币国际化是指人民币能够跨越国界，在境外流通，成为国际上普遍认可的计价、结算及储备货币的过程。人民币国际化的初级阶段就是人民币在境外流通的数量不断增加，随着其被各国逐渐地认可和接受，在国际经济活动中的影响力和重要性越来越大，最终达到"国际货币"的地位。我们可以从以下几个指标来衡量人民币国际化的进程：一是人民币现金在境外的流通度指标；二是以人民币计价的金融产品成为国际各主要金融机构，包括中央银行的投资工具的金融市场规模指标；三是国际贸易中以人民币结算的交易规模。

The internationalization of RMB refers to the process that RMB can cross boundaries, circulate abroad and become an internationally recognized currency for pricing, settlement and reserve. The initial stage of RMB internationalization is epitomized by the increasing amount of RMB circulating abroad. As it is gradually recognized and accepted by other countries, its influence and importance in international economic activities will increase, and it will finally become an "international currency". We can measure the process of RMB internationalization with the following indicators, such as the indicator for circulation of RMB banknotes abroad, the financial market scale indicator showing that financial products denominated in RMB have become the investment instruments of major international financial in-

案例 7.1 人民币被越来越多国家作为国际结算货币

stitutions (including central banks), as well as the scale of transactions settled in RMB in international trade.

美国是当前世界上经济实力强大的经济体之一,其在经济领域的发展优势很多得益于其在第二次世界大战后建立的以美元为中心的国际货币体系,让其在国际经济发展中占据了先天优势。美元作为国际结算的主要货币,在世界经济的发展中具有重要的影响力。虽然美元目前还是全球各国结算时主要采用的国际货币,但随着中国经济实力不断提高,人民币国际化的进程也逐步加快,除了与中国经济关系较为紧密的亚洲国家已经广泛使用人民币作为结算货币外,中东的石油大国伊朗开始使用人民币进行石油交易,南美的委内瑞拉也用人民币代替美元计价。沙特、俄罗斯、阿联酋、巴基斯坦、土耳其等 28 个国家和地区已经可以使用人民币作为结算货币。

At present, the US is one of the most powerful economies in the world, and its developing advantages in the economic field benefit from its dollar-centered international monetary system established after World War II, which gives it an innate advantage in international economic development. As the main currency for international settlement, the US dollar has a significant influence on the development of the world economy. Although the US dollar is still the major international currency for settlement in the world, with the improvement of China's economic strength, the process of RMB internationalization has gradually accelerated. In Asian countries with close economic ties with China, RMB has been widely used as the settlement currency. In addition, other major oil producers, like Iran in the Middle East and Venezuela in South America, have also turned to RMB for oil transactions instead of US dollar. Now, twenty-eight countries and regions such as Saudi Arabia, Russia, United Arab Emirates, Pakistan, Turkey can use RMB as the settlement currency.

人民币国际化带来的结果远大于这个过程的付出,所以进行人民币国际化是我国必然要走的一条道路。未来人民币要在国际结算领域发挥更加重要的作用,受到更多国家的认可和信任,还需要国家不断加强金融市场的监管体系建设、完善货币汇率市场等。人民币国际化不是我国的最终目的,最终目的在于获得在国际结算领域属于自己的话语权,从而助力提高国家的经济实力,为世界经济的发展贡献更大的力量(如图7-1所示)。

The gains of RMB internationalization will be far greater than the efforts made throughout this process, thus RMB internationalization is an inevitable path for China. In the future, RMB will play an even more prominent role in international settlement, and it will win recognition and trust of more countries. Meanwhile, China also needs to continuously strengthen the construction of its financial market supervision system and improve its currency exchange rate market. The internationalization of RMB is not our ultimate goal, instead we will strive to make our voice heard in the field of international settlement, so as to enhance our economic strength and contribute more to the development of the world economy(as shown in Figure 7-1).

案例 7.1　人民币被越来越多国家作为国际结算货币

图片来源：https://baijiahao.baidu.com/s?id=1679900320845732226&wfr=spider&for=pc,2023—03—08。

Source：https://baijiahao.baidu.com/s?id=1679900320845732226&wfr=spider&for=pc,2023—03—08.

图 7—1　人民币国际化

Figure 7—1　Internationalization of RMB

点评

Comments

结算货币在国际上的使用标志着一国综合实力的提升,越来越多的国家使用人民币作为国际结算货币,其背后反映的事实是中国的综合国力越来越强大,在国际经济活动中的影响力和公信力越来越强。但是我们也必须清醒地认识到,目前人民币国际化的道路才刚刚起步,美元在国际结算领域的统治地位还很明显,对内我们需要不断地稳定发展经济水平,提升经济发展质量,获得国际范围内更大的认可和信任,对外我们需要扩大交流,逐步推行创新尝试,在更多的国家和更广泛的领域里采用人民币作为国际结算货币。相信随着国家经济的稳步发展,未来人民币在国际结算货币中的地位会逐步提升。

The use of its currency for international settlement indicates stronger comprehensive strength of a country. An increasing number of countries have adopted RMB as their international settlement currency, reflecting the fact that China's comprehensive national strength and its influence and credibility in international economic activities are getting stronger. However, we must also be clearly aware that the internationalization of RMB has just started, and the US dollar still takes a dominant position in international settlement. We need to continuously develop our economy, improve the quality of economic development, and gain greater recognition and trust in the international community. We also need to expand exchanges, gradually implement innovative attempts, and promote RMB to be adopted as the international settlement currency in more countries and wider fields. It is believed that with the steady development of the national economy, the status of RMB as an international currency for trade settlement will be gradually enhanced in the future.

讨论题
Discussions

(1)使用人民币结算有什么重要意义?
What is the significance of using RMB for settlement?

案例 7.1　人民币被越来越多国家作为国际结算货币

（2）人民币国际化还需要做哪些推进工作？

Is there anything else that should be done to promote the internationalization of RMB?

（3）人民币作为国际结算货币还需要哪些支持条件？

What other supporting conditions does RMB need as a currency for international settlement?

资料来源

黄静.最新消息！中国游客在柬埔寨旅游可直接使用人民币[EB/OL].[2023－03－08].http://www.gxnews.com.cn/staticpages/20230209/newgx63e45be1-21056814.shtml.

百度百科.人民币国际化[DB/OL].[2023－03－08].https://baike.baidu.com/item/%E4%BA%BA%E6%B0%91%E5%B8%81%E5%9B%BD%E9%99%85%E5%8C%96/8983091?fr=aladdin.

Akie木鱼.世界上已有28国使用人民币结算，这对中国来说意味着什么？[EB/OL].[2023－03－08].https://www.bilibili.com/read/cv5464612.

刘梦珂,徐如一.浅谈人民币国际化进程对我国经济的影响[J].商展经济,2022(04)：21－23.

References

Huang Jing. Latest news! Chinese tourists are allowed to use RMB directly when traveling in Cambodia[EB/OL].[2023－03－08]. http://www.gxnews.com.cn/staticpages/20230209/newgx63e45be1-21056814.shtml.

Baidu Baike. Internationalization of RMB[DB/OL].[2023－03－08]. https://baike.baidu.com/item/%E4%BA%BA%E6%B0%91%E5%B8%81%E5%9B%BD%E9%99%85%E5%8C%96/8983091?fr=aladdin.

Akie Wooden Fish. 28 countries in the world are using RMB for settlement. What does this mean for China? [EB/OL].[2023－03－08]. https://www.bilibili.com/read/

cv5464612.

Liu Mengke,Xu Ruyi. A brief discussion about the impact of RMB internationalization on the economic development of China[J]. Trade Fair Economy,2022(04):21-23.

案例7.2 新冠疫情防控背景下出口信用保险护航外贸企业"走出去"
Case 7.2 Export Credit Insurance (ECI) Supports Foreign Trade Enterprises to "Go Global" During COVID-19

教学目标
Teaching Objectives

通过分析出口信用保险等政策及其实施,来介绍国家如何支持本国出口企业的发展,在国际贸易中政府如何协助企业克服经营困难,在国际市场竞争中立于不败之地。对出口企业的支持不仅在风险防范、资金压力方面,还有政策指导方面的措施。本节通过案例讲解,使同学们更加理解在世界范围内新冠疫情爆发的背景下,中国出口企业在国际竞争中的压力所在,同时看到政府在缓解企业压力和支持企业发展上的积极行动。国家通过市场化的手段来支持和保护本国企业在国际市场上的竞争是一种合理合规的政策,也是国际范围内各国通用的做法,企业必须在经营过程中善于合理地利用好国家相关的政策,让自己在激烈的国际竞争中立于不败之地。

By analyzing the export credit insurance policies and their implementation, we aim to introduce how the state supported the development of Chinese export enterprises and how the government helped them overcome operational difficulties in international trade and remain invincible in the international competition. In addition to helping them deal with risk prevention and financial pressure, the government supported export enterprises through policy guidance. Through case study, this section enables students to better understand the pressure facing China's export enterprises in international competition under worldwide outbreaks of COVID-19, and see the positive actions taken by the government to ease the heavy burden on enterprises and support their development. It is a reasonable and compliant for a country to support and protect its own enterprises in international competition with market-oriented means, which is also a common practice across the world. Enterprises must make reasonable use of relevant national policies in their operation to make themselves stand out in the fierce international competition.

本案例涉及的课程主要包括国际结算和国际贸易实务等。

The case mainly involves international settlement, international trade practice and other courses.

案例 7.2　新冠疫情防控背景下出口信用保险护航外贸企业"走出去"

案例内容
Contents

在国际结算问题上,出口企业很容易遭遇进口企业的违约,难以顺利收回货款而造成经济损失。山东威海的一家服装出口企业在向韩国客户出运了多票货物后迟迟没有收到货款,调查后发现对方企业已经因疫情影响而破产。但由于企业负责人曾在政府的引导下投保了出口信用保险,在提交理赔申请后,不到 10 天时间,企业就顺利拿到了 15 万美元的赔款。

In terms of international settlement, export enterprises are vulnerable to defaults by import enterprises, making it difficult to recover the payments and thus leading to economic losses. A clothing export enterprise in Weihai, Shandong Province, failed to receive the payment after several shipments to a Korean client. After investigation, it was found that the other enterprise had gone bankrupt due to the epidemic. However, as the head of the enterprise had covered export credit insurance under the guidance of the government, the enterprise successfully got the insurance indemnity of 150,000 US dollars within less than 10 days after submitting the claim.

出口信用保险是承保出口商在经营出口业务的过程中因进口商的商业风险或进口国的政治风险等而遭受损失的一种结算信用保险,是国家为了推动本国的出口贸易,保障出口企业的收汇安全而制定的一项由国家财政提供保险准备金的非营利性的政策性保险业务。出口信用保险相对于其他险种而言,保险人承担了较大的风险,因此一般各国都由政府来主导进行,帮助本国企业分散国际结算风险。

Export credit insurance is a kind of settlement credit insurance that covers exporters' losses due to the commercial risks of importers or the political risks of importing countries in the process of operating export business. It is a non-profit policy-based insurance business developed by a country to promote its own export trade and ensure the security of export enterprises' foreign exchange collection, for which the insurance reserve is provided by the government. Compared with other types of insurance, export credit insurance bearing greater risks is usually guided by the government to help domestic enterprises spread their risks in international settlement.

随着新冠疫情在全球的蔓延,各国的经济发展都受到前所未有的影响,中国作为一个外贸大国,出口业务也受到巨大的冲击和压力,出口企业的生产效率、交易成本与风险管控都面临着前所未有的挑战,国家为了缓解由于疫情对外贸企业带来的影响,积极从多方面采取应对措施。

With the spread of COVID-19 around the world, the economic development of all countries was affected as never before. As a major foreign trader, China's export business was also under huge impacts and pressure, and the productivity, transaction costs and risks of Chinese export enterprises encountered unprecedented challenges. In order to alleviate the impacts of the epidemic on foreign trade enterprises, the government took active countermeasures in various aspects.

中国出口信用保险在疫情爆发后,开辟了定损核赔的绿色通道,并且在合规的基础上放宽理赔条件,加大支持外贸企业复工复产力

案例 7.2　新冠疫情防控背景下出口信用保险护航外贸企业"走出去"

度,提高了对外贸企业投保出口信用保险的支持比例,对小微外贸企业投保短期出口信用保险保费给予全额支持。作为一家政策性信用保险企业,其在疫情防控期间,主动分担了对外贸企业的国际结算风险,对国家稳定经济起到了重要的作用(如图 7—2 所示)。

After the outbreak of COVID-19, China Export & Credit Insurance Corporation opened up a green channel for loss and compensation assessment, and lowered the threshold for claims on the basis of compliance, so as to strengthen the support for foreign trade enterprises to resume work and production and increase the supported proportion of export credit insurance premiums for foreign trade enterprises. What's more, the short-term export credit insurance premiums of small and micro foreign trade enterprises were fully supported. As a government-backed credit insurance company, it played a crucial role in stabilizing the national economy by actively sharing the international settlement risks facing foreign trade enterprises during the epidemic(as shown in Figure 7—2).

点评

Comments

出口信用保险是为了保障出口结算安全而采取的一种金融风险分担手段,目前在实践中已经很好地保障了国际结算的安全。疫情防控期间,国际贸易和结算的风险增加较为明显,如何克服这个国际贸易的障碍,保障国际贸易的稳定和发展,需要从结算的风险控制角度多下功夫,出口信用保险正是基于这一目标而存在的,在疫情防控期

图片来源:https://supplier.alibaba.com/content/detail/PXC21ATL.htm,2023－03－05。

Source:https://supplier.alibaba.com/content/detail/PXC21ATL.htm,2023－03－05.

图 7－2　出口信用保险"护航"外贸企业

Figure 7－2　Export Credit Insurance (ECI) supports foreign trade enterprises

间发挥出很好的作用。在我国,出口信用保险的发展相对于国际贸易的发展起步较晚,但到此次疫情防控期间,发展已经相对成熟,真正发挥出了结算保障功能,贸易的稳定需要政策从各方面进行支持,这也标志着我国在国际贸易和结算领域形成了良好的风险分担体系。

Export credit insurance is adopted to share financial risks so as to ensure the security of export settlement, which has well guaranteed the security of international settlement in practice. During the epidemic, the risks of international trade and settlement increased sharply. How to overcome this obstacle and ensure the stability and development of international trade needed more efforts in the risk control

案例 7.2　新冠疫情防控背景下出口信用保险护航外贸企业"走出去"

of settlement. Export credit insurance which was designed to achieve this goal played a prominent role during the epidemic. In China, the development of export credit insurance started relatively late compared with the development of international trade. However, by the time of the epidemic outbreak, it had been relatively mature and did serve as the settlement guarantee. The stability of trade requires policy support from all sides, which indicates that China has established an effective risk sharing system in international trade and settlement.

讨论题
Discussions

(1)什么是出口信用保险？

What is export credit insurance?

(2)疫情防控背景下出口企业在出口时一般面临哪些风险？

What risks do export enterprises usually face in exports during COVID-19?

(3)出口信用保险对国际结算有什么支持作用？

What support does export credit insurance have for international settlement?

资料来源

政策"组合拳"稳住外贸基本盘[EB/OL].[2023－03－05]. http://news.cnr.cn/native/gd/20200318/t20200318_525021535.shtml.

百度百科. 出口信用保险[DB/OL]. [2023－03－05]. https://baike.baidu.com/item/%E5%87%BA%E5%8F%A3%E4%BF%A1%E7%94%A8%E4%BF%9D%E9%

99%A9/4372437? fr=aladdin.

疫情期间外贸出口影响及应对措施有哪些? [EB/OL]. [2023-03-05]. https://www.hishop.com.cn/kuajing/show_111251.html.

References

A combination of polices stabilize the overall performance of foreign trade[EB/OL]. [2023-03-05]. http://news.cnr.cn/native/gd/20200318/t20200318_525021535.shtm.

Baidu Baike. Export Credit Insurance[DB/OL]. [2023-03-05]. https://baike.baidu.com/item/%E5%87%BA%E5%8F%A3%E4%BF%A1%E7%94%A8%E4%BF%9D%E9%99%A9/4372437? fr=aladdin.

What are the impacts and countermeasures taken to improve foreign trade exports during the epidemic? [EB/OL]. [2023-03-05]. https://www.hishop.com.cn/kuajing/show_111251.html.

案例 7.3 美英等国禁止俄罗斯使用 SWIFT 国际结算系统
Case 7.3 Western Countries Like the US and UK Prohibit Russia from Using the SWIFT System for International Settlement

教学目标
Teaching Objectives

通过讲授 SWIFT 系统的由来和内容,介绍其在国际结算中的重要作用。此次欧美对俄罗斯禁止使用 SWIFT 系统,反映了国际结算系统对一国在对外经济往来中的作用。当前世界各国在经济领域相互联系,资金往来越发频繁,稳定的国际结算系统起到了重要的作用。本节通过案例介绍,帮助学生理解这次制裁措施为什么会对俄罗斯经济产生深远的影响,以及引导学生思考俄罗斯应该如何应对,最后,启发学生从全球经济联系的角度来思考结算系统的巨大影响力,从这种"无形的"系统为结算提供的作用方面思考国家如何应对来自结算领域的潜在问题。

By introducing the origin and content of SWIFT system, the case presents its crucial role in international settlement. The ban on Russia's use of SWIFT system by western countries reflects the role of the international settlement system in the foreign economic exchanges of any country. Nowadays, countries all over the world are interconnected in the economic field, with exchanges of funds getting increasingly frequent. Thus, a stable international settlement system is very important. Through case introduction, this section enables students to understand why the sanctions have far-reaching impacts on the Russian economy, and guides students to think about how Russia should respond. Finally, it allows students to think about the huge influence of the settlement system in global economic ties, and how a country should deal with potential settlement problems in terms of the role played by this "invisible" system in the settlement.

本案例涉及课程包括商业银行经营与管理、国际结算等课程。

The case involves commercial bank operation and management, international settlement and other courses.

案例内容
Contents

北京时间 2022 年 2 月 27 日清晨，美国和欧盟、英国及加拿大等发表联合声明，宣布对俄罗斯最新制裁：禁止俄罗斯几家主要银行使用"环球银行金融电信协会"支付系统（SWIFT）并对俄罗斯央行实施

案例7.3 美英等国禁止俄罗斯使用SWIFT国际结算系统

"限制性措施"。随着这些制裁措施开始实施,媒体称此举为"向俄罗斯丢下'金融核弹'",可见其对俄罗斯经济带来的影响之大。目前"环球银行金融电信协会"系统拥有约1.1万个成员,其中包括近300家俄罗斯银行。如果这些俄罗斯银行被移除出这一系统,占俄罗斯财政总收入40%以上的石油和天然气出口收益将被切断,其经济会立即受到重大影响,包括本国货币大幅波动,以及大量资本的外逃。

On the morning of February 27, 2022 (Beijing time), the US, the EU, the UK and Canada issued a joint statement announcing the latest sanctions against Russia, including prohibiting several major Russian banks from using the SWIFT payment system and imposing "restrictive measures" on the Russian central bank. With the implementation of these sanctions, relevant media reported that this move was like "dropping a financial nuclear bomb on Russia", showing its huge impacts on the Russian economy. So far, the SWIFT system has had about 11,000 members, including nearly 300 Russian banks. If these Russian banks are removed from this system, Russia's export income of oil and natural gas, which accounts for more than 40% of its total fiscal revenue, will be cut off, and its economy will suffer immediate losses, such as the sharp fluctuation of its currency and the flight of a large amount of capital.

SWIFT是一种用于传输结算信息的通信系统,全称为"环球银行金融电信协会",总部在比利时,是国际银行间的国际合作组织。SWIFT运营着世界级的金融电文网络,银行和其他金融机构通过SWIFT与同业者交换电文来完成金融交易。SWIFT本质上就是一款全球银行间专门用于传输结算信息的通信软件,所有的银行及其他金融机构都是结算信息终端的使用者,银行间进行结算时,通过系统相互传输信息,同时由其结算中心来处理结算信息(如图7—3所示)。

As a telecommunication system for transmitting settlement information, SWIFT stands for the "Society for Worldwide Interbank Financial Telecommunication". Headquartered in Belgium, it is an international cooperation organization among international banks. SWIFT operates a worldwide financial message network. Banks and other financial institutions exchange messages with other financial institutions through SWIFT to complete financial transactions. SWIFT is essentially a communication software specially used for transmitting settlement information among banks around the world. All banks and other financial institutions are users of settlement information terminals. When banks make settlement, they transmit information to each other through the system, and the settlement information is processed by their settlement centers(as shown in Figure 7—3).

为了应对国际结算领域的这一重大制约,俄罗斯央行早在2014年开始便开发一套本土结算系统,在2019年已经投入使用,不过目前只有8家外国银行参与其中,这也意味着俄罗斯银行依然高度依赖"环球银行金融电信协会"系统。虽然制裁不会导致俄罗斯对外结算系统的整体瘫痪,但是大多数结算交易都将受到影响。

In order to cope with this severe constraint in the field of international settlement, the Central Bank of Russian Federation began to develop a local settlement system as early as 2014 and put it into use in 2019. However, only eight foreign banks are currently involved, which means that Russian banks are still highly dependent on the

案例 7.3 美英等国禁止俄罗斯使用 SWIFT 国际结算系统

SWIFT system. Although the sanctions will not lead to the collapse of Russia's foreign settlement system, most settlement transactions will be affected.

图片来源：https://baijiahao.baidu.com/s? id＝1725881357489485322&wfr＝spider&for＝pc,2023－01－05。

Source：https://baijiahao.baidu.com/s? id＝1725881357489485322&wfr＝spider&for＝pc,2023－01－05.

图 7－3 SWIFT 国际结算系统

Figure 7－3 SWIFT international settlement system

点评

Comments

SWIFT 系统作为当前世界上最重要、被使用最广泛的国际结算系统，业务几乎遍及全球各国和地区，结算效率高、安全性高、结算成本低等优势使其成为最受欢迎的国际结算系统。国家对外的经济交往中，一个重要的方面就是资金的往来，稳定可靠的结算系统是国际资金转移的保证。此次俄罗斯被排除在 SWIFT 系统之外,对其经济影响是深远的,很显然俄罗斯已经为此做了准备。经济全球化的发展依赖稳定的国际结算系统,和平互利的国际环境是先决条件。

As the most important and most widely adopted international settlement system in the world, SWIFT system covers almost all countries and regions around the world. Its advantages such as high settlement efficiency, high security and low settlement cost have made it the most popular international settlement system. In a country's economic exchanges with other countries, the exchange of funds plays a crucial role, thus a stable and reliable settlement system is the guarantee of international capital transfer. Russia's exclusion from the SWIFT system this time has a far-reaching impact on its economy. Obviously, Russia has made preparations for this. The development of economic globalization depends on a stable international settlement system, for which a peaceful and mutually beneficial international environment is a prerequisite.

讨论题

Discussions

(1)什么是 SWIFT 系统?

What is the SWIFT system?

(2)禁止俄罗斯使用 SWIFT 系统会产生什么影响?

What will be the implications of prohibiting Russia from using the SWIFT system?

案例 7.3　美英等国禁止俄罗斯使用 SWIFT 国际结算系统

(3)世界上还有哪些重要的结算系统？

Are there any other important settlement systems in the world?

资料来源

施薇.美欧英对俄实施 SWIFT 禁令有多严重？为何此举被称为向俄罗斯丢下"金融核弹"？[EB/OL].[2023－01－05].https://baijiahao.baidu.com/s? id=1725881357489485322&wfr=spider&for=pc.

什么是 SWIFT 国际结算系统？我国的 CIPS 系统是什么[EB/OL].[2023－01－05].https://baijiahao.baidu.com/s? id=1725880007020920367.

References

Shi Wei. How serious is the SWIFT ban imposed by the US, Europe and the UK on Russia? Why is it called dropping a "financial nuclear bomb" on Russia? [EB/OL].[2023－01－05]. https://baijiahao.baidu.com/s? id=1725881357489485322&wfr=spider&for=pc.

What is the SWIFT international settlement system? What is the CIPS system in China [EB/OL].[2023－01－05].https://baijiahao.baidu.com/s? id=1725880007020920367.

附表 1 案例涵盖的专业知识与跨文化教育元素概览

Exhibit Ⅰ Overview of key concepts and cross-cultural education elements covered by the case

学科 Disciplines	案例应用 Case Application	专业知识 Key Concepts	跨文化教育 Cross-Cultural Education
宏观经济学 Macro-economics	改革开放 40 年中国经济增长的国际比较 China's economic growth over the past 40 years of reform and opening up compared to foreign countries	国民生产总值 GNP	中国经济增长奇迹 China's economic miracle
	中国应对金融危机的一揽子计划 China's package plan for handling the financial crisis	凯恩斯的需求管理理论 Keynes's demand management theory	政府在经济中的作用 Role of government in economy
	中等收入陷阱对于中国是不是一个伪命题 Is the middle-income trap a false proposition for China	经济增长理论 Economic growth theory	经济增长规律 Law of economic growth

附表1 案例涵盖的专业知识与跨文化教育元素概览

续表

学科 Disciplines	案例应用 Case Application	专业知识 Key Concepts	跨文化教育 Cross-Cultural Education
管理学原理 Principles of Management	"一带一路"倡议推动构建人类命运共同体 The "Belt and Road Initiative" (BRI) promotes the construction of a community of shared future for mankind	发展规划 地区贸易联盟 Development planning Regional trade alliances	知华友华 开放开明 Fully understand China and be friendly to China Open and enlightened
	国家电网:"碳达峰""碳中和"行动派的国企担当 State Grid: A state-Owned enterprise undertaking the responsibilities for practicing "peak carbon dioxide emissions and carbon neutrality"	企业社会责任 Corporate social responsibility (CSR)	责任担当 Commitment and responsibility
	文化的力量:百度人工智能革命透视 The Power of Culture: Insights into Baidu's AI revolution	组织文化 Organizational culture	文化同理 Cultural empathy
战略管理 Strategic Management	华为的品牌扩展战略 Brand expansion strategy of Huawei	企业增长战略 Corporate growth strategy	社会责任 Social responsibility
	小米公司的颠覆性创新战略 Disruptive innovation strategy of Xiaomi	战略创新 Strategic innovation	创新精神 Innovative spirit
	上海迪士尼乐园的本土化营销策略 Localization marketing strategy of Shanghai Disney Resort	国际本土化战略 International localization strategy	文化包容 Cultural inclusiveness

续表

学科 Disciplines	案例应用 Case Application	专业知识 Key Concepts	跨文化教育 Cross-Cultural Education
市场营销 Marketing	"人民需要什么，五菱就造什么"——五菱汽车营销案例 "Wuling makes whatever people need"—marketing case of Wuling Motors	品牌营销 用户需求 Brand marketing Demand of users	企业发展目标与企业社会责任 Development goals and social responsibilities of enterprises
	做有温度的品牌：民宿鼻祖 Airbnb（爱彼迎）与中国民宿 A brand with warmth: Airbnb, the originator of B&B, and Chinese B&B	品牌发展 产品服务质量 Brand development Quality of products and services	品牌经营与文化结合，改变消费者生活方式 Brand management and culture work together to change consumers' lifestyle
	2022年上海新冠疫情期间的团购与物流配送 Group purchase and its logistics & distribution during the COVID-19 in Shanghai in 2022	营销渠道 物流配送 社区团购 Marketing channel Logistics and distribution Community group purchase	社会事件（如新冠疫情）改变用户消费习惯 Social events (such as the COVID-19) change users' consumption habits
物流管理 Logistics Management	爱回收：小回收做成大生意 Aihuishou: Small recycling business makes big difference	回收物流 Recycling logistics	资源环境保护 Resources conservation and environmental protection
	菜鸟绿色物流，打造中国绿色物流新样本 Cainiao green logistics sets a new example of green logistics in China	绿色物流 Green logistics	可持续发展 Sustainable development

附表1 案例涵盖的专业知识与跨文化教育元素概览

续表

学科 Disciplines	案例应用 Case Application	专业知识 Key Concepts	跨文化教育 Cross-Cultural Education
物流管理 Logistics Management	顺丰冷运，一路领先，靠的是什么 What has SF Cold Chain relied on to lead all the way	冷链物流 Cold chain logistics	责任担当 创新 Responsibilities Innovation
财务管理 Finance Management	瑞幸咖啡财务问题分析 Analysis of financial fraud of Luckin Coffee	内部控制体系 Internal control system	诚信经营 Integrity-based operation
	中集车辆从收购整合Vanguard到全球运营 CIMC Vehicles: From acquisition and integration of Vanguard to global operation	公司兼并与收购 M&A	全球化 Globalization
	小米智能家居财务战略 Financial strategy of Xiaomi Smart Home	财务战略 Financial strategy	抓重点、盯关键 Focus on priorities
国际结算 International Settlement	人民币被越来越多国家作为国际结算货币 RMB-a key currency for international settlement by an increasing number of countries	人民币国际化 RMB internationalization	国家使命 National mission

续表

学科 Disciplines	案例应用 Case Application	专业知识 Key Concepts	跨文化教育 Cross-Cultural Education
国际结算 International Settlement	新冠疫情背景下出口信用保险护航外贸企业"走出去" Export credit insurance (ECI) supports foreign trade enterprises to "go global" during the COVID-19	出口政策支持 Support from export policies	责任担当 Responsibilities
	美英等国禁止俄罗斯使用SWIFT国际结算系统 Western countries like the US and UK prohibit Russia from using the SWIFT system for international settlement	结算系统 Settlement system	可持续发展 Sustainable development

附表2 术语表
Exhibit Ⅱ　Glossary

（注：按在书中出现的顺序排列）

第一篇

1. 国内生产总值：一个国家和地区在一定时期内所生产的所有最终产品和劳务的市场价值。
Gross Domestic Product (GDP): The market value of all final products and services produced within a country or region during a certain period.

2. 购买力平价：经济学中一种根据各国不同的价格水平计算出来的货币之间的等值系数，以对各国的国内生产总值进行合理比较。
Purchasing Power Parity (PPP): An equivalence factor in economics calculated based on varying price levels in different countries, used for a reasonable comparison of Gross Domestic Product (GDP) across nations.

3. 社会主义市场经济：市场在社会主义国家宏观调控下对资源配置起决定性作用的经济体制。
Socialist Market Economy: An economic system in socialist countries where the market plays a decisive role in resource allocation under the framework of macroeconomic regulation.

续表

4. 金砖国家：最初是指巴西、俄罗斯、印度和中国这四个成长前景看好的新兴市场国家。2010年南非正式加入后，这一合作机制由"金砖四国"变为"金砖五国"。 BRICS: Originally referring to four promising emerging market countries—Brazil, Russia, India, and China. After South Africa joined in 2010, this cooperation mechanism transformed from the "BRIC" to the "BRICS".
5. 经济增长率：末期国民生产总值与基期国民生产总值的比较，可以反映一定时期经济发展水平变化程度和一个国家的经济活力。 Economic Growth Rate: A comparison between the final Gross National Product (GNP) and the base GNP for a specific period. It can reflect the degree of economic development and the economic vitality of a country during a certain period.
6. 通货膨胀：在纸币流通条件下，因货币供给大于货币实际需求，也即现实购买力大于产出供给，导致货币贬值，而引起的一段时间内物价持续而普遍上涨现象。 Inflation: A phenomenon occurring under paper currency circulation, where the supply of money exceeds the actual demand, meaning that the real purchasing power exceeds the output supply, leading to the devaluation of currency and resulting in a sustained and widespread increase in prices over a period of time.
7. 通货膨胀率：一般物价总水平在一定时期（通常为一年）内的上涨率，用以反映通货膨胀的程度。 Inflation Rate: The rate of increase in the general price level over a certain period (usually one year), used to reflect the degree of inflation.
8. 中国梦：中华民族近代以来最伟大的梦想——实现中华民族伟大复兴，其基本内涵是实现国家富强、民族振兴、人民幸福。 Chinese Dream: The greatest dream of the Chinese nation in modern times—achieving the great rejuvenation of the Chinese nation, with its fundamental essence being the realization of national prosperity, ethnic rejuvenation, and the well-being of the people.
9. 需求管理理论：由凯恩斯提出，指的是要确保经济稳定，政府要审时度势，主动采取一些财政政策，即变动支出水平或税率以稳定总需求水平，使之接近物价稳定的充分就业水平。 Demand Management Theory: Introduced by Keynes, it refers to ensuring economic stability by timely and actively adopting fiscal policies. This involves adjusting expenditure levels or tax rates to stabilize total demand, aiming to achieve full employment levels near price stability.

续表

10. IS-LM 模型:反映产品市场和货币市场同时均衡条件下,国民收入和利率关系的模型。其中,"IS"代表"投资"和"储蓄","LM"代表"流动性"和"货币供应"。
IS-LM Model: A model that reflects the relationship between national income and interest rates under simultaneous equilibrium conditions in the product market and the money market. In this context, "IS" represents "Investment" and "Savings", while "LM" stands for "Liquidity" and "Money Supply".

11. "西气东输"工程:将中国西部新疆等地区生产的天然气输往长江三角洲、珠江三角洲等地区的天然气管道工程。
West-East Gas Pipeline Project: A gas pipeline project that transports natural gas produced in western China, including Xinjiang, to eastern regions such as the Yangtze River Delta and the Pearl River Delta.

12. "三驾马车":经济学中用于比喻拉动经济增长的三种动力,即投资、消费和出口。
"Three Engines": A metaphor used in economics to describe the three driving forces that propel economic growth, namely investment, consumption, and exports.

13. 出口退税率:出口产品应退税额与计税依据之间的比例。
Export Rebate Rate: The ratio between the amount of tax refundable on exported products and the taxable basis.

14. 挤出效应:指增加政府投资对私人投资产生的挤占效应,从而导致增加政府投资所增加的国民收入可能因为私人投资减少而被全部或部分地抵消。
Crowding-Out Effect: The displacement effect on private investment caused by an increase in government investment, due to which the increase in national income resulting from increased government investment may be partially or entirely offset by a reduction in private investment.

15. 中等收入陷阱:指当一个国家的人均收入达到中等水平后,由于不能顺利实现经济发展方式的转变,导致经济增长动力不足,最终出现经济停滞的一种状态。
Middle-income Trap: A state of economic stagnation where a country's per capita income reaches a medium level, and its failure to realize the smooth transformation between two economic development modes results in insufficient economic growth momentum.

16. 国民总收入:一个国家或地区所有常住单位在一定时期内收入初次分配的最终结果,等于国内生产总值加上来自国外的初次收入分配净额。
Gross National Income (GNI): The final result of the initial distribution of income among all resident units in a country or region during a certain period, equal to Gross Domestic Product (GDP) plus the net amount of initial income distribution from abroad.

续表

第二篇
1."一带一路"倡议:"丝绸之路经济带"和"21世纪海上丝绸之路"的简称,是中国向世界提供的国际合作平台和公共产品,是一项开放包容的经济合作倡议。 The Belt and Road Initiative (BRI): short for the "Silk Road Economic Belt" and the "21st Century Maritime Silk Road", is an international cooperation platform and public offering provided by China to the world. It is an open and inclusive economic cooperation initiative.
2. 人类命运共同体:一种价值观,也是中国把握世界潮流、人类命运走向上的智慧体现,是每个民族、每个国家的前途命运都紧紧联系在一起,风雨同舟,荣辱与共,努力把我们生于斯、长于斯的这个星球建成一个和睦的大家庭,把世界各国人民对美好生活的向往变成现实。 Community with a Shared Future for Mankind: A set of values and a wisdom reflected in China's understanding of global trends and the direction of human destiny. It signifies that the future of each and every nation and country is interlocked. We are in the same boat, and we should stick together, share weal and woe, endeavor to build this planet of ours into a single harmonious family, and turn people's longing for a better life into reality.
3. "碳达峰":指温室气体排放总量要在2030年前达到顶点,此后便要开始下降。 Peak Carbon Dioxide Emissions: The total amount of greenhouse gas emissions will reach its peak before 2030, and then decline.
4. 碳中和:指温室气体净排放为零,即通过植树造林和碳捕捉等方式抵消全部的温室气体排放。 Carbon Neutrality: The net greenhouse gas emissions are zero, namely all greenhouse gas emissions are offset by afforestation and carbon capture.
5. "双碳"目标:指中国力争2030年前二氧化碳排放达到峰值,2060年前实现"碳中和"这两个目标。 "Dual Carbon" Goals: China's aims to peak its carbon dioxide emissions before 2030 and achieve carbon neutrality by 2060.
6. 社会责任:是指企业在创造利润、对股东和员工承担法律责任的同时,还要承担对消费者、社区和环境的责任。 Social Responsibility: A business's intention, beyond its legal and economic obligation, to do the right things and act in ways that are good for society.

7.可持续发展:既能满足当代人的需要,又不对后代人满足其需要的能力构成危害的发展。
Sustainable Development: Development that meets the needs of the present generation without compromising the ability of future generations to meet their own needs.

8.组织文化:共同的价值观、原则、传统和做事方式,影响组织成员的行为方式,并将组织与其他组织区分开来。
Organizational Culture: The shared values, principles, traditions, and ways of doing things that influence the way organizational members act and that distinguish the organization from other organizations.

第三篇

1.颠覆性创新:指携全新技术(商业模式)的新进入者,起初定位于潜在的高端新市场或低端市场,随着其产品或服务性能的提高,最终吸引主流消费者,并且彻底改变原有技术范式以及市场竞争格局的创新过程。
Disruptive Innovation: The innovation process where new entrants with entirely new technologies (or business models) initially target potential high-end or low-end markets. As their products or services improve in performance, they eventually attract mainstream consumers, fundamentally altering the existing technological paradigms and market competition landscape.

2.关键绩效指标:一种通过对组织内部流程的输入端、输出端的关键参数进行设置、取样、计算、分析,衡量流程绩效的目标式量化管理指标,是企业绩效管理的基础。
Key Performance Indicator (KPIs): Goal-oriented quantitative management indicators that measure process performance by setting, sampling, calculating, and analyzing key parameters at the input and output of organizational processes, serving as the foundation of performance management in businesses.

3.物联网:把所有物品通过频射识别等信息传感设备与互联网连接起来,实现智能化识别与管理。
Internet of Things (IoT): The connection of all objects to the Internet through information sensing devices such as RFID for intelligent identification and management.

4.本土化策略:企业力图融入目标市场,努力成为目标市场中的一员所采取的策略。它要求企业把自己当作目标市场中固有的一员融入当地文化,适应环境来获得更大的发展空间。
Localization Strategy: A strategy adopted by companies aiming to integrate themselves into a target market and become a part of it. It requires companies to position themselves as an inherent part of the target market, assimilate into the local culture, and adapt to the environment to gain more growth opportunities.

第四篇

1. 品牌营销：通过市场营销使客户形成对企业品牌和产品的认知过程。
Brand marketing: The process of creating awareness among customers about a company's brand and products through marketing efforts.

2. 同工同酬：指用人单位对于技术和劳动熟练程度相同的劳动者在从事同种工作时，不分性别、年龄、民族、区域等差别，只要提供相同的劳动量，就获得相同的劳动报酬。
Equal Pay for Equal Work: The principle where an employer provides the same compensation to workers who perform the same job and have the same level of technical expertise and skill, regardless of their gender, age, ethnicity, region, or other differences, as long as they provide an equivalent amount of labor.

3. 4Ps营销理论：四个基本营销策略的组合，即产品、价格、推广、渠道。
4Ps Marketing Theory: The combination of four fundamental marketing strategies, namely Product, Price, Promotion, and Place.

4. 社区团购：指一定数量的消费者通过社区或社会中的一些提供社区团购的组织机构，以低折扣购买同一种商品。
Community Group Purchase: A certain number of consumers purchasing the same product at a discounted price through community or social organizations that offer community group purchase.

第五篇

1. 长尾：指那些原来不受重视的销量小但种类多的产品或服务由于总量巨大，累积起来的总收益超过主流产品的现象。
Long Tail: The phenomenon where products or services that are originally not emphasized, with low sales volume but a wide variety, accumulate significant total revenue due to their large quantity, surpassing that of mainstream products.

2. 回收物流：退货、返修物品和周转使用的包装容器等从需方返回供方所引发的物流活动。
Recycling Logistics: The logistics activities initiated by the return of goods, repaired items, and reusable packaging containers from the demand side to the supply side.

3. 逆向物流：为恢复物品价值、循环利用或合理处置，对原材料、零部件、在制品及产成品从供应链下游节点向上游节点反向流动，或按特定的渠道或方式归集到指定地点所进行的物流活动。
Reverse Logistics: The logistics activities of reversely moving raw materials, components, work-in-process items, and finished products from downstream nodes of the supply chain to upstream nodes, or collecting these items to designated locations through specific channels or methods, so as to recover the value, recycle, or properly dispose of goods.

附表 2　术语表

4. 外包：指企业将非核心业务下放给专门营运该项业务的外部第三者。
Outsourcing: Delegating non-core business of the enterprise to specialized external third parties for operation.

5. 众包：一个公司或机构把过去由员工执行的工作任务，以自由自愿的形式外包给非特定的（而且通常是大型的）大众志愿者的做法。
Crowdsourcing: A company or organization outsources tasks that are traditionally performed by employees to a loosely organized and often large group of volunteers from the general public on a voluntary basis.

6. 3C 行业：指计算机、通信、消费电子一体化的信息家电产业。
3C industry: The information household appliances industry integrating computer, communication and consumer electronics.

7. 商品总销量：公司在指定时间段内的销售总额，常用于电子商务平台。
Gross Merchandise Volume (GMV): Total value of merchandise sold over a given period of time and is commonly used in e-commerce platforms.

8. 循环经济：一种再生系统，借由减缓、封闭与缩小物质与能量循环，使得资源的投入与废弃、排放达成减量化的目标。
Circular Economy: A regenerative system that aims to minimize resource input and waste, as well as reduce emissions by slowing, closing, and narrowing material and energy cycles.

9. 绿色物流：指以降低对环境的污染、减少资源消耗、提高运行效率为目的，利用先进物流技术规划和实施的运输、储存、装卸、流通加工等物流活动。
Green Logistics: Logistics activities such as transportation, storage, loading and unloading, and distribution processing, which are planned and implemented with advanced logistics technology for the purpose of reducing environmental pollution, minimizing resource consumption, and improving operating efficiency.

10. 冷链物流：利用温控、保鲜等技术工艺和冷库、冷藏车、冷藏箱等设施设备，确保冷链产品在初加工、储存、运输、流通加工、销售、配送等全过程始终处于规定温度环境下的专业物流。
Cold Chain Logistics: A specialized logistics process that utilizes temperature control and preservation technologies, along with facilities such as cold storage warehouses, refrigerated vehicles, and refrigerated containers, to ensure that cold chain products remain within specified temperature conditions throughout the entire process, including initial processing, storage, transportation, distribution, processing during circulation, sales, and delivery.

11. 零担货物：指一张货物运单（一批）托运的货物重量或容积不够整车运输条件。
Less-than-Truckload (LTL) Freight: Shipments of goods on a single waybill or consignment that do not meet the requirements for full truckload transportation, either due to their weight or volume.

399

12. 区块链：本质上是一个去中心化的数据库，是指通过去中心化和去信任的方式集体维护一个可靠数据库的技术方案。
Blockchain: Essentially a decentralized database; it refers to a technology solution where a reliable database is collectively maintained through decentralization and trustlessness.

13. "双循环"新发展格局：以国内大循环为主体、国内国际双循环相互促进的新发展格局。
"Dual Circulation" Development Pattern: A new development pattern in which domestic economic cycle plays a leading role while international economic cycle remains its extension and supplement.

第六篇

1. 外部审计：由审计机关派去的审计人员或社会审计机构对被审计单位的经济业务活动的合理性、合法性、准确性、真实性和效益性所进行的审查，并对审查结果做出客观公正的评价。
External Audit: An examination conducted by auditors from an audit agency or an independent auditing organization to assess the rationality, legality, accuracy, authenticity, and effectiveness of the financial and business activities of the audited entity, followed by an objective and impartial evaluation of the audit findings.

2. 债务重组：指在不改变交易对手方的情况下，经债权人和债务人协定或法院裁定，就清偿债务的时间、金额或方式等重新达成协议的交易。
Debt Restructuring: A transaction in which, without changing the counterparty, an agreement is re-reached between the creditor and debtor, or is ruled by the court, to negotiate the time, amount, or method of debt repayment.

3. "走出去"战略：中国企业充分利用国内和国外"两个市场、两种资源"，通过对外直接投资、对外工程承包、对外劳务合作等形式积极参与国际竞争与合作，实现经济可持续发展的现代化强国战略。
"Going Global" Strategy: The strategy where Chinese enterprises make full use of "two markets and two resources" at home and abroad to achieve sustainable economic development by actively participating in international competition and cooperation through foreign direct investment, international engineering contracting and international labor service cooperation.

4. 智能家居：是以住宅为平台，兼备建筑、网络通信、信息家电、设备自动化，集系统、结构、服务、管理为一体的高效、舒适、安全、便利、环保的家居环境。
Smart Home: A residential environment that involves building infrastructure, network communication, information appliances, and equipment automation, and integrates systems, structures, services, and management on a housing platform, aiming to create an efficient, comfortable, safe, convenient, and environmental-friendly living space.

第七篇

1. 人民币国际化：指人民币能够跨越国界，在境外流通，成为国际上普遍认可的计价、结算及储备货币的过程。
Internationalization of RMB: The process that RMB can cross boundaries, circulate abroad and become an internationally recognized currency for pricing, settlement and reserve.

2. 国际货币体系：各国政府为适应国际贸易与国际结算的需要，对货币的兑换、国际收支的调节等所做的安排或确定的原则，以及为此而建立的组织形式等的总称。
International Monetary System: A collective term for the arrangements, principles, and organizational structures established by governments to facilitate international trade and balance of payments. These arrangements encompass aspects such as currency exchange, regulation of international payments, and the institutions created to support these objectives.

3. 出口信用保险：是承保出口商在经营出口业务的过程中因进口商的商业风险或进口国的政治风险等而遭受损失的一种结算信用保险，是国家为了推动本国的出口贸易，保障出口企业的收汇安全而制定的一项由国家财政提供保险准备金的非营利性的政策性保险业务。
Export Credit Insurance: A kind of trade credit insurance that covers exporters' losses incurred during the process of conducting export business, typically due to the commercial risks of importers or the political risks of importing countries. It is a non-profit policy-based insurance, provided by the national government to promote the country's export trade and ensure the security of foreign exchange earnings for export enterprises.

4. "环球银行金融电信协会"支付系统:一种用于传输结算信息的通信系统,全称为"环球银行金融电信协会",总部在比利时,是国际银行间的国际合作组织。

SWIFT Payment System: A telecommunication system for transmitting settlement information, with the full name as "Society for Worldwide Interbank Financial Telecommunication". Headquartered in Belgium, it is an international cooperation organization among international banks.